Contents

Who is Jillion R. Rising?

I am a husband, father, and grandfather from the western suburbs of Chicago, Illinois. My career began in the working trenches of America. What I mean by trenches is, I was willing and, in many cases, did, any job available within the construction industry. Over the last 30 years, my brother/business-partner and I have successfully owned and operated a mid-sized construction company in the Midwest.

Starting my career when and where I did, along with working my way up the ladder provided me with firsthand knowledge as to how the American people live and how they communicate. Although I do hope what I have to say will impact all Americans, including the upper echelon of America's most wealthy, the truth is this book was written specifically for working-class America. The elites will most-likely reject the information I provide, and the government will do all they can to silence the content.

Some of you may know of the epic novel *Atlas Shrugged* by author Ayn Rand. It is a riveting story that depicts what happens when a government grows too big, ultimately burdening and restricting its people and their businesses to a point of suffocation from too much regulation. At the beginning of this tale, the hopeless, downtrodden people use a common phrase: "Who is John Galt?" Throughout the story, each time a citizen becomes overwhelmed by or frustrated with the paralyzing effect of the government bureaucracy that is crushing their spirit, the citizen puts their hands in the air and asks, "Who is John Galt?"—and this person is never to be seen again.

Who was John Galt? He was a fictional character who brilliantly led the charge by convincing those who sought a life of prosperity that they must be willing to leave everything behind. He taught that power-hungry demagogues with an insatiable appetite for control will eventually consume everything that was once prosperous. As the story goes, eventually John Galt was able to convince those who produced the most to leave behind those who produced the least.

Who is Jillion R. Rising, and what is my goal? First and foremost, I am not a fictional character, and I am not asking you to pick up and leave. In fact, I'm asking you to stay and be prepared to fight against deception, corruption, and greed! The truth is we face the same problems today in America as Rand's characters did in her novel yet our story is one that is true.

What follows is a complete breakdown of a great deception being perpetrated against our citizenry. What you're about to discover will change the way you think forever. This is not a tale of conspiracy theories or a promotion of untruths. It is a careful review of events that changed our country in a way none of us could have foreseen. It is a compelling examination of complex issues delivered from a layperson's viewpoint.

Who is Jillion R. Rising? I am the deliverer of truth about the things that you already feel in your heart are real. Yes, our government has gone bad; yes, our monetary system will collapse; yes, Wall Street, the Federal Reserve, and the US government have collectively diminished our wealth and our opportunity to achieve prosperity. Yet the most dangerous truth of all is Washington, DC's attempt to divide our nation's people into political tribes, fueling us to be at war with one another. Why? Because the deception they have participated in shall soon be revealed. They understand that a divided, weakened population will culminate their strength.

The good news is that instead of offering more doom and gloom, I will present a plan to change the way we are governed; eliminate Wall Street's power to manipulate Washington, DC; rebuild our communities; and, most importantly, provide compelling ideas on how to spur innovation within our citizenry, ultimately delivering a game plan that can be used as a guide to a prosperous future.

Introduction

The story of America began with its early settlers joining hands in revolution, demanding their independence and self-worth from the mother country, Great Britain. If we review our nation's history since the American Revolution, one might conclude it has remained in a state of revolution ever since. It seems the current revolution is the American people at war with one another, having lost the concept of working together to build a better future for our children.

It is my belief this division of our nation's people is being manipulated by corrupt politicians who understand their corruptive behavior and bad policies will soon be exposed. The solution to this revolution will not be decided with guns; it will be decided through political and monitorial reform. The question is who will win the battle of what these reforms shall be, the corrupted politicians or a unified citizenship?

As the United States enters a new era of global exchange and technological advancements, we must consider the impact that globalism might have on a nation built on the concept of freedom and independence. If we take a moment to analyze what it means to be free people, on the surface, it sounds easy. But if we dig deeper, we begin to understand that sustaining freedom requires a lot of voluntary work from all the nation's inhabitants.

As a nation, we have, without question, had our share of growing pains. If we review the Civil War, we begin to realize that the battle between the North and the South was essentially a second revolution over which ideology would define the concept of what it means to be free. The idea of referring to the United States as a free country while some of its inhabitants were held captive as slaves had to be settled in order for us to move forward as one nation. The final outcome derived from the conflict was a collective understanding that for one person to be free, we must be willing to fight for the right of all people to be free.

There have been many tragic events and societal battles throughout the years, each making its own distinction in our nation's history. There was the assassination of President Abraham Lincoln; the Industrial Revolution; Prohibition; the fight for women's suffrage; the Great Depression; the labor movement; the civil rights movement; the assassinations of President John F. Kennedy, Robert Kennedy, and Martin Luther King Jr.; the Vietnam War protests; Watergate and the resignation of President Richard M. Nixon; the savings and loan crisis; the technological revolution; the 9/11 terror attacks; and the Great Recession.

How have the American people preserved their independence while struggling through these events? Although the American Revolution defined our nation's collective "Don't tread on me" spirit, I believe the foundation of freedom for all that was derived from the Civil War is at the core of our citizenry's ability to unite during times of turmoil. Each time we've faced life-altering hardships, the common denominator to successfully navigating them has been our ability to band together as *one people* collectively facing the challenge.

This book's concept is simple: for every action, there is a reaction or an outcome. This process applies to everything we do. Whether it's a reaction to what we say or something we did, each of our actions ultimately creates consequences. What I've witnessed over the years is that there are powerful organizations as well as governments that understand how to use this action-reaction process to achieve favorable outcomes for self-gain or, in the governments' case, to slowly whittle away the rights of their citizenry.

There are many people throughout the world who believe the societal and financial problems we have today are manipulated by a select group of wealthy families. We're going to analyze whether or not this is true by analyzing the before and after regarding recent events. The conclusion to my research will define the players in this supposed conspiracy, but more importantly, it will identify the people, as well as the organizations, that have become the driving force to purposely divide our nation. We're going to shine a light on who it is and the reasons behind their destructive policies. Through the use of logic, I will identify the stepping-stones used to turn a free-spirited, independent citizenry into one that is trapped in a life of dependency. After exposing the perpetrators of destruction, I will present compelling ideas that alter the authority of our nation's government, realign our monetary system, and permanently eliminate Washington, DC's ability to deceive its citizens.

The division of our citizens has never been greater. I am aware that finding a common cause to unify a fractured citizenry is without question a daunting task. Yet I believe that once you understand the truth of what our future will be if we don't change Washington, DC's path to destruction, we again will put aside our differences and unite to guarantee our children a better future!

—Jillion R. Rising

The Revolution Continues

The battle between the North and the South taught us that, regardless of your skin color, gender, or religion, the concept of freedom means everyone should have the opportunity to pursue their individual dreams. Yet another lesson learned from the Civil War was the danger when a nation's people become deeply divided and no longer have the ability to reach a peaceful resolution to their differences.

There is at present a preplanned rift being perpetrated by power-hungry politicians, and that is why I decided to write this book. Although there is a plethora of societal issues, such as race, religion, and gender, being debated, what seems to be getting the most attention in the run-up to the 2020 presidential election is whether America should maintain the economic structure of capitalism or change to the redistribution method of socialism. My greatest concern is that this debate about what method will provide economic prosperity for our nation is being purposely coupled with societal issues, not for the purpose of solving those problems, but as a means to distract our attention from the truth.

This argument between the two political parties is nothing more than greed, money, and power for them at the cost of our independence. This battle has been divided into two opposing forces: rebellion and fascism. The question is which one presents the greatest danger to the destruction and takeover of our citizenry's individual rights? In other words, because left-wing and right-wing politics have become so polarized, it seems our choices are either to join a rebellion to preserve independence from a government takeover or to join a fascist movement that forces all people to adhere to the same ideology or be destroyed for thinking differently.

What seems to have happened is this fight for ultimate power has caused the left and right elements of each party to have the loudest voices. Our media portrays the Republicans' far-right faction as religious zealots and antiabortion, racist, and selfish capitalists who care about no one and whose main objective is to profit off the backs of the less fortunate. The media portrays the Democratic far left as people who are willing to kill babies regardless of their stage of development in the womb, who care more about immigrants than they do their fellow citizens, and who believe that anyone who is successful is evil and should ultimately have their wealth confiscated to be redistributed to the disadvantaged.

What is sad is that, although what I described does exist within both parties, these extremes are a relatively small percentage in comparison to the majority of people who identify as centrist. What is fueling the flames of this fire is that the long-held journalistic standard of not covering radical behavior in order to discourage it has changed to finding radical behavior, highlighting it, and even going as far as sensationalizing it.

The brilliance of our political system is that it was designed to create checks and balances in order to maintain a center-based country. This is achieved by electing representatives from individual states and districts throughout America. When envisioning today's two-party political system, we should think of each party as an entity that's applying force to each side of a pendulum. Taking this thought one step further, let's envision our Republican and Democratic representatives battling one another as they attempt to represent the views of their constituents about how a new law or policy should be constructed. It is the pressure of these opposing forces or arguments that, in general, maintains equal left and right pressure on the political pendulum.

When the pendulum remains close to the center, it generally means most citizens feel they are being properly represented in whatever the current issues may be. If there's a sense among the centrists that America is on the precipice of political change within a larger segment of the population, that is when we begin to see heightened activity from the left or right extremes of each party. But what always has prevailed in the past and helped us remain free of radicalization within our politics has been our ability to respect and accept our fellow citizens' opinions and concerns, whether we agree with them or not.

What has changed and seems to be having a much greater influence on our politics is a much more partisan approach to journalism, fueled by a twenty-four-hour news cycle that reports current events. Few could argue that most of our cable networks seem to have become more sources of the minute-by-minute promotion of sensational or polarizing propaganda than providers of unbiased news. Additionally, it seems journalism has become partisan, and some of its practitioners—though not all—may be guilty of reporting on newsworthy events not for the purpose of providing accurate information, but more for promoting a left or right ideological viewpoint.

Has Our Media Become the Judge, Jury, and Executioner?

The question we may be forced to answer is whether or not we should demand integrity and accurate reporting from journalism to ensure the news we receive is real and without bias.

Due to the emergence of social media and the consolidation (or monopolization) of independent news agencies, many of us are unaware of the effect this is having on our culture. It is important to understand the ramifications when our news media and many other industries are allowed to monopolize. The importance of maintaining independence within our news and our businesses, as well as our personal lives, cannot be understated. The only way consumers can pressure the companies that provide us goods and services is to have other options to choose from.

What should concern every citizen is our elected government's attempt to use technological advancements (twenty-four-hour news, social media) as tools to divide or to stir up dissention among us as a method to maintain an energized voting base. This becomes even more dangerous when our news/information no longer remains neutral and, as we've seen in recent elections, becomes more of a propaganda machine for the political party or candidate of their choice.

What this twenty-four-hour news cycle and the advancements in technology have done to our politics has far exceeded what I believe the American people were prepared for. We must consider the ramifications that these changes are having on our free-spirited culture and consider the potential damage it can have on our elections in the future. I mention the latter because of the concern about the media's power to influence candidates of their choice. Additionally, will the media's pursuit of America becoming a more politically correct society have a negative impact on the willingness of the best people to run for public office? As we've witnessed in recent events, the information that the media obtains has been used as a tool to bludgeon candidates, judges, and sports figures, in many cases causing our citizens to socially prejudge or convict them before the accused has been represented by counsel. In a nutshell, the power of the media has put into question whether or not we will remain a nation that believes in the adage of being innocent until proven guilty.

Will You Comply . . . or Will You Revolt?

Will people in powerful positions use technology to instill fear and obedience because they possess the power to destroy? Will technology be used for the purpose of modern-day stoning, condemning the accused before their day in court?

We must realize that if our future candidates' qualifications are based on how little damaging information we can find in their past, it's pretty safe to say we will end up with candidates who've been extremely careful to ensure they have no blemishes. Will we end up with people who, throughout their lives, carefully craft answers to any and all questions for the purpose of protecting their images? Are candidates with lives that seem to be free of mistakes really the type of candidates we need?

We must understand the consequences of an overly restricted society, where our citizenry becomes fearful to say or do anything wrong in order to protect against being judged. We must realize a society that is bound by the fear of making a mistake is a society that will end up producing little gain for its people. One must ponder the question: If we take away the opportunity for the courageous to take risks due to the fear of being judged, how can our nation continue a path to prosperity?

We must understand that the bold sometimes get things accomplished regardless of what others think or say. They see others' opinions as meaning little as they push to pursue a passion that may one day benefit us all. Some of these people may say or do things we don't like, but we must allow them to say them! There will be others who will be just as bold and will challenge or put them in their place, so we must be cautious as a society not to discourage or bind the trailblazers by restricting their ability to innovate.

What Will Cause the Revolution?

One of the immediate challenges facing America is that the baby boomers have started the process of retirement. Investopedia and numerous other data providers list on their public websites that 10,000 boomers will be retiring per day for the next twenty years! I understand this looks like a misprint, but I assure you it is not. The impact this will have on our financial markets, health-care institutions, and entitlement benefits, as well as our nation's state-by-state electoral college, cannot be overstated.

America really has been in a state of revolution since its inception. As the boomers age, it's natural to become less involved and less knowledgeable about current political issues, a highly charged millennial generation will become fully engaged. As this transformation begins, we are seeing that just as the generation preceding the boomers degraded them for their propensity to protest against the things they didn't like, the boomers have become dissenters of the millennials for their complaints. What neither group understands is how much their past and future has aligned them to fight similar battles from our nation's history. The good news is that the millennials' educational system did a far better job of addressing racial discrimination and equality than those of past generations.

The turmoil headed our way will not be driven by the differences between the two mentioned generations. This turmoil will occur because the truth will be revealed about what our government has done to the economic state of our nation. As the boomers enter their retirement and our nation's shrinking prosperity is no longer able to pay for programs such as Social Security and Medicare/Medicaid, this will prompt the political battle that will be waged to save our economic sustainability. Ironically, where I believe the revolution must begin is the governmental system, and the people in power who are responsible for our economic hardship want us to believe they are the people who should fix it.

What follows are the complex moving parts of what I believe is an orchestrated political attack on the American people. The tools they use for this attack are the fiat monetary system, comingled entitlement surplus dollars held in the US Department of the Treasury, consolidation and monopolization of our industries, growth of centralized government, immigration policy, Wall Street, the Federal Reserve/central banks, commercial banking, private equity, and, last but not least, the integrated system that allows lobbying of our elected government.

Another revolution is unquestionably coming to America. The outcome will either leave our citizenry bound to the power of a monopolist controlling our goods and services, along with a centralized government deciding our fate through taxation/wealth redistribution and measures of austerity, or create a citizenry that unites as their founders did, demanding strategic change to the government's authority to manipulate our monetary fiat system and overburden our nation with debt and putting an end to backroom lobbying deals that empower a few to ultimately entrap the many.

Action

In this chapter, I've mentioned several factors that have contributed to a groundswell of extremism from both the Republican and Democratic parties. In a quest for ratings, the media and journalism have, in many cases, fueled or even embraced extremism, which seems to be altering the center-based politics that once governed our nation.

I've named this chapter The Revolution Continues because, once again, our nation must reshape its future. As the boomers move into retirement, the following issues will be front and center: immigration, Social Security, health care, race relations, a growing class of elites versus a shrinking middle class, and socialism versus capitalism.

I will prove through analysis that the leadership in Washington, DC, knows their past policies have severely damaged our economic future. Additionally, I believe these bad policies forced the Federal Reserve to join hands with our government and Wall Street because they, too, realize the clear and present danger of an all-out economic collapse in our near future.

It is my contention that the issues I've mentioned are the reason both the Republican and Democratic parties are collectively dividing and distracting our citizenry. They both know that their kicking the can down the road has reached its end, and their intent is to reduce our input and begin the process of citizens becoming much more dependent on a government that is built on tax redistribution programs.

Reaction

At present, the reaction to these issues seems to be paralyzing normalcy, as well as challenging whether or not we can remain a civil nation. As we watched the confirmation process of the latest Supreme Court judge, what we saw was a willingness of our nation's leaders to abandon the idea of innocent until proven guilty. Additionally, we are beginning to see a willingness to accept the silencing of voices through what has been identified as "political correctness."

We must step back and analyze who is the driving force behind sensationalized politics and the stilling of our voices. We must put a stop to the media being used as a tool to elevate those whom they like and destroy the lives of people they don't.

A revolution is coming. The question is will it be a cultural change guided by a suggestive media? Or will there be another civil war that ultimately results in our states operating under two different economical systems: one using fiat currency and socialism and the other using capitalism based on the monetary system of the gold standard? Or can we find common ground, realizing a fractured America is not something that can be sustained? Will we allow our government to dictate our lives through a constant creation of new laws and regulatory procedures, or will we limit their power to assure government remains a partner helping us succeed?

The next chapter will prove that Washington, DC, the Federal Reserve, and Wall Street joined hands, and the outcome was the Great Recession. Will we continue to allow Washington, DC, to formulate backroom deals with Wall Street, or will *we* join hands and create revolutionary changes to their power?

Connecting the Dots

Connecting the dots is an old phrase used in detective work. In order to solve a crime, you must identify or connect the people involved in committing the crime.

If the last chapter left you with the impression that I am antigovernment or anticorporation, stuck on age-old talking points of less government and corporate trust-busting, I hope this one will make my position clear. I believe this country should have inviting policies such as low taxes and fair regulations to entice wealthy people to continue investing in the innovative spirit of the American people. Additionally, I believe those who invest in individuals should be rewarded for the risk they take when supporting our ideas. What I am not in favor of is allowing them to use their money to (through coercion) persuade politicians to pass laws that work for them in order to gain an unfair advantage over us.

I use the saying, "To not know history is to repeat the same mistakes of the past." Rather than delve into the history of who or what was responsible for the Great Depression in the 1920s or the savings and loan crisis in the 1980s, I decided to use the 2008 mortgage crisis to do our detective work. What we learn from these events is that although the cause of each economic tragedy may vary, the common denominator causing those catastrophes was corruption and greed, and the fix was the American taxpayer bailing out government and corporate corruptive behavior. The mortgage crisis is considered by many historians to be the largest theft in American history of the private citizens' wealth.

As we begin to dissect what happened, it clearly displays both corruption and the lack of respect our government/corporate elites have for the American people. Additionally, what the mortgage crisis exposed was that those who were responsible for this debacle knew that they would receive bailouts and that no one would be held accountable. Let me be clear: I do not see this as a partisan issue. This was a case of the government, dating back several administrations, turning a blind eye to financial institutions that were knowingly approving bad loans, thus cooperating with them. This is the danger when we allow the people with the most money to coerce the government through lobbying to create policies and/or laws that are favorable to them.

Let's begin this analysis by listing the participants or connecting the dots of the agencies or corporations I refer to throughout as the "financial pyramid" involved in the ongoing functioning of America's economy. These agencies are the heartbeat that drives the action/reaction process of the flow of currency, and they are the main contributors to what is now referred to as the 2008 mortgage crisis and the Great Recession.

- Central banking: Also known as the Federal Reserve. Controls the volume of monetary supply and long- and short-term interest rates and analyzes the long- and short-term indicators of America's economic pulse.
- Commercial banking: Institutions that supply the money available to the economy once central banking agrees on economic indicators.
- Wall Street: The hub that connects the buying and selling of public and private investment from the United States and around the world. Responsible for providing perspective and analysis for the sale of stocks and bonds.
- Lobbyists: Corporate representatives who have infiltrated the governmental system to manipulate favorable policies for the companies they represent.

It is unrealistic to think the citizens should be in control of the banking policies as directed by the Federal Reserve or the power of commercial banking or even Wall Street's deception, but we can and must control the influence of corruption within the walls of Washington, DC. It is the government's responsibility to represent the American people, and it is imperative that we come together as a unified citizenry to change the rules regarding the ability of the monopolists to lobby our elected government.

What follows is a step-by-step snapshot of how two polar-opposite economic events collided. The first economic event created hope and prosperity, as well as inspiring people, and the second one destroyed the independent spirit of a citizenry, leaving behind carnage and despair. As I began the process of dissecting what occurred before and after the 2008 mortgage crisis, I realized there was still hope in my heart that this horrific devaluation of the American people's personal wealth was an innocent and tragic event that could not have been avoided. Unfortunately, my findings uncovered an orchestrated collusion of greed and a purposeful cultural shift to forever alter how the American people will live their lives.

Representative Democracy or Empire?

Let's, for just one moment, consider the idea that many people believe there are a few wealthy families that have enough money or influence to control not only America's financial system but also others around the world. I think we can agree there are, without question, extremely wealthy families across the globe who associate with powerful and influential circles. We know for sure there are wealthy dictators living in smaller countries like Saudi Arabia and even larger countries such as China, where the government leaders have complete authority over the monetary system as well as the laws that govern their citizens.

We know the people of those countries have few to no rights regarding their ability to protest. Additionally, using easy-to-find research, we come to understand the government in China and the king in Saudi Arabia are the supreme rulers of their nations' financial systems. There might be a few rogue elements in each of their countries attempting to sabotage or change the laws or currency, but for now, the ruling class has the ability and authority to crush anyone they deem a threat.

The purpose of these two examples is to eventually decipher a clear line between whether we truly exist as a representative democracy or under a false pretense of hidden dictatorship. I understand the desire to discredit conspiracies as hogwash. I myself struggle with the conspirator's thought that a few wealthy families could have singular control over the vast moving parts throughout America, especially a financial system as widespread as ours. But if we step back and analyze the things that we know to be governed by a singular source, such as a few of our large corporations, we see that owners who have mastered the action/reaction process are able to influence large numbers of employees through peer pressure directed by a managed employee culture. This method of managing employee culture is done through what I refer to as "ripple-effect management," meaning the management uses subliminal messaging to make minor tweaks to the policies and procedures that are in place in order not to upset the flow of daily business. If it is a major change in policy and procedure they're after, I call this "the tidal wave effect," which means their aim is to completely alter the flow of the employee culture, with the intent of moving in an entirely new direction.

There are many examples throughout our nation's history of our government's use of tragic events to implement the ripple/tidal wave management technique, helping them change the way we think or what we are allowed to do by law without political backlash. Using the 2008 mortgage crisis, we're going to see how a coordinated effort between government policies and corporate influence used the tidal wave method to completely change our citizenry's sense of independence, as well as to destroy the idea that opportunity and a chance for prosperity are available to all.

Earlier, I listed the agencies that are the major components of America's financial system. The list that follows includes the government and corporate representatives, essentially the main players, who were involved in the creation as well as the resolution of the 2008 crisis. Many of you may recall that, at the beginning of the crisis, we were assured the problem coming our way was nothing more than a ripple, but as time went on, we all learned it was a full-fledged tidal wave.

The Players in the 2008 Mortgage Crisis

Hank Paulson: Paulson was CEO of Goldman Sachs, an investment bank that participated in packaging toxic mortgage debt into securities, prior to taking on the job of secretary of the treasury in 2006. One notable decision Paulson made during his tenure at the treasury was to let Lehman Brothers fail. Additionally, he also is credited with having the most influence on getting the US Congress to pass the Troubled Asset Relief Program (TARP). In 2011, Paulson founded the Paulson Institute at the University of Chicago. The Paulson Institute focuses on environmental and economic policies in the United States and China. He is the chairman of the institute, as well as cochair of the Risky Business Project, which explores the economic impact of climate change.

Ben Bernanke: Bernanke was the chairman of the Federal Reserve during the financial crisis. He is also known as the face of quantitative easing. Quantitative easing reduced interest rates and injected money into the economy for the purpose of encouraging banks to lend and consumers to spend. While many politicians and economists have vilified this practice, believing it ultimately spurs inflation and creates new asset bubbles, others, such as Nobel Prize–winning economist Paul Krugman, supported Bernanke's method of handling the crisis.

Timothy Geithner: When Lehman Brothers collapsed, Geithner was in charge of the New York Federal Reserve Bank. A few months later, President Barack Obama asked him to be treasury secretary. At the time, some on Wall Street decried Geithner as a person who overregulated, whereas other progressive activists viewed him as a tool of the banks. During his time at the Treasury Department, Geithner also was involved in a controversy due to his failure to report and pay income taxes from 2001 to 2004. He is now the president of Warburg Pincus, which is a private-equity firm that runs "loans by mail" outfit Mariner Finance, which makes money from short-term, high-interest loans.

Richard Fuld: Fuld was the last CEO of Lehman Brothers before the collapse. He is best known for navigating the company into subprime mortgages and making it one of the leaders in packaging debt into bonds, then selling the bonds to investors. Fuld claims he did not receive what has been termed a "golden parachute" after his exit from Lehman Brothers, but during his questioning by the House Oversite Committee, he testified that he earned more than $466 million during his tenure. Today, Fuld is the head of Matrix Private Capital Group, a high-end wealth management firm founded in 2016.

John Mack: Then–Morgan Stanley CEO Mack feared the company would be next after Lehman Brothers, so he fought with Paulson, Bernanke, and Geithner to secure a bailout while at the same time trying to cultivate investment from Japan and China. Mack's tough negotiating with policymakers succeeded in helping Morgan Stanley become a holding bank, opening the door to increased liquidity and the opportunity to be part of the bailout. He stepped down as CEO in 2010 but remained chairman of the board until 2012. Mack is currently a board member with fintech companies such as Lending Club, and he is chairman of the board at Lantern Credit.

Lloyd Blankfein: Blankfein led Goldman Sachs. He also was allowed to convert it into a bank holding company, thus receiving $10 billion in government bailouts. In 2009, Blankfein apologized for the firm's role in the meltdown. He is one of the few players during the crisis who retained his position as CEO.

Jamie Dimon: Under Dimon's leadership, JPMorgan Chase was prompted by the US government to buy Bear Stearns as well as Washington Mutual in an effort to promote the feeling of economic stability. JPMorgan Chase received millions from the federal TARP program, yet Dimon insisted the company didn't need the bailout and only agreed to move forward under duress from congressional policymakers. Similar to Blankfein, Dimon held on to the reins of his company as chairman. In fact, after dealing with legal issues arising from crisis-era purchases, JPMorgan Chase is stronger than ever.

Dimon remains chairman/CEO, and in 2018, he signed on for another five years.

Ken Lewis: Taking a similar stance to Dimon's, Lewis told policymakers that Bank of America wasn't interested in major acquisitions, yet after similar persuasion from the US government, Bank of America presided over the takeovers of Countrywide Financial and Merrill Lynch. Lewis was heralded as one of the saviors of the crisis and received the Banker of the Year Award in 2008 from *American Banker* as well as being featured in *TIME* magazine. The truth is, Bank of America almost buckled under the weight of those acquisitions, and Lewis was investigated for the methods he used to gain approval for the Merrill Lynch deal. In the end, he agreed to pay a $10 million settlement and was forced to sell one of his multimillion-dollar homes.

Kathleen Corbet: While there were other rating agencies using practices similar to Standard & Poor's that ultimately helped fuel the crisis, Corbet, who was president of Standard & Poor's up to and during the crisis, is considered the highest-profile individual of the rating-agency leaders. *TIME* magazine listed her as one of the top-twenty-five people to be blamed for the crash. Critics believe Standard & Poor's had a conflict of interest when taking payments from companies to ultimately rate the riskiness of its products. Though Corbet left Standard & Poor's in disgrace—and the company later had to pay a $1.5 billion fine to the US government—she remains on several boards of various companies. Corbet is currently the principal of Cross Ridge Capital, a firm she established in 2008, and a director of MassMutual.

George W. Bush: It's debatable how much power a president actually has over the economy and the markets. However, since he was in office during the lead-up to the financial crisis and the Great Recession, it makes him a major player. Additionally, we all remember him promoting on the campaign trail the idea that every American should own a home. The policy of tax cuts and deficit spending that his administration favored most assuredly helped fuel the eventual collapse. (There is a case to be made, though, that many of the economic problems leading to the meltdown began during previous administrations, and the tipping point was when then-president Bill Clinton signed the repeal of the Glass–Steagall Act, which was responsible for separating commercial and investment banking.)

For the purpose of keeping the explanation of what happened short yet effective, my review of what happened leading up to and the crash starts around the year 1990 and goes until we were notified of the crash in 2008. My goal from the onset was to help us decide whether the tidal wave caused by the mortgage crisis was an accident or happened by design. I chose to start in 1990 because that is when the beginning phases of the technological revolution became a significant part of the American economy.

It is my belief that the financial pyramid and the US government understood early on that the technological revolution was going to be the driving force in a long-term sustained economy. The proof our government knew is evident by the policy changes made during that time period. We know the financial pyramid knew early on because, without banks loaning money to help finance new innovations, there wouldn't be any.

Analyzing which banks were involved in the mortgage crisis, we see there were four major players involved during and survivors after the crisis was over—Bank of America, JPMorgan Chase, Goldman Sachs, and Morgan Stanley. All four were involved with the negotiations of what became the TARP bailout. Although we see the names of Lewis, Dimon, Blankfein, and Mack listed as the CEOs of these commercial entities, we can be fairly certain the banks' top shareholders have the ability to remove any sitting chair if needed. In many cases, the shareholders behind the scenes are actually the people who possess the most wealth. In general, these names are private, but make no mistake, these folks are not just the main shareholders of the banks—they are also the main shareholders of many of the largest corporations around the globe. These are the people I am referring to in my earlier mention of the top players in the financial pyramid.

Throughout history, every vibrant economy was spurred by a revolutionary occurrence. In the 1920s, it was the industrial revolution, and, fast-forwarding to the 1990s, it was the technological revolution. Every one of these potential economic events required wealthy bankers such as the ones I've mentioned to participate in order to provide the necessary capital to fund a business's infrastructure. The most well-known innovators of the recent technological revolution would be Steve Jobs and Bill Gates. Even though they both had amazing ideas that ultimately changed America, neither of them could have made them happen without the support of a banking system willing to invest in their ideas. It can be stated with confidence that commercial banks and the Federal Reserve System are acutely aware of any and all potential innovations that will become a driving force behind a sustained uptick in the American economy.

The Federal Reserve is involved for two reasons. First, it's their job to analyze the income/debt ratio—money collected by government through taxes and debt due to overspending. Additionally, it is their responsibility to analyze the economic indicators to watch for a sudden increase in inflation or deflation. The best way for us to judge how the Federal Reserve views our economy's long-term health is what they do with interest rates. The raising and lowering of interest rates are essentially done for the purpose of heating up or slowing down America's economic conditions. You could say they are analyzing and responding with the action/reaction method, using the interest rate as the power to influence the economy with either a ripple effect or a tidal wave.

In the next chapter, we will review the specifics of what caused the 2008 market crash. But before we get started, for the purpose of building our case, I would like to highlight two unusual things President Clinton did that were not common practice for a Democratic president. First was the controversial signing of the 1994 North American Free Trade Agreement (NAFTA). The idea that a Democratic president supported by America's labor unions would sign into law a program that encouraged American companies to leave the United States for the purpose of finding cheap labor is beyond comprehension.

Clinton's second out-of-the-ordinary move was his 1999 reform of the Glass-Steagall legislation. Prior to this, the law prohibited commercial banks and all other lending institutions from interacting with one another and Wall Street. The reformation of Glass-Steagall essentially permitted these entities to interact with one another, as well as with other financial institutions. The reform ultimately became the framework for selling bundled mortgage products to secondary markets, which ultimately became the nucleus of the collapse. I will explain that process as we continue.

My hypothesis of the 2008 mortgage crisis as likely being a collaboration from its inception and collusion at the end stems from what I see as aligned occurrences from the beginning of the economic boom (how the Federal Reserve and commercial banks agreed to loosen monetary policy) to the federal government's reform of the Glass-Steagall legislation. It is easy to prove that the heated economy from 1994 to 1999 began to restrict the banks' loaning capacity under then-current regulatory policy, so reforming Glass-Steagall allowed banks to sell existing loans, thus alleviating their regulatory lending restrictions. Let's remember that prior to 1999, a bank's lending capacity was limited by the regulatory standard of a 10-percent-capital-to-90-percent-loan ratio, meaning they were prohibited from trading with any other financial institutions. If a bank had reached their lending capacity and wanted to loan more money, they were required to raise additional capital within the bank. The reform to Glass-Steagall specifically gave banks the green light to sell existing loans to secondary markets as investment stocks. Once the banks sold their loans, it gave them a clean slate to start loaning all over again!

I used a simplified classification system to describe what the banks and Wall Street did when selling investment funds (mortgage loans) to the secondary market. The important thing to understand is that allowing the sale of mortgage loans to a secondary market greatly reduced the banks' risk of becoming a victim of defaulting loans. Additionally, it gave the banks the option of picking which loans they wanted to keep on their books, ultimately making them look more attractive to potential investors. As their lending continued, the stringent regulatory policies of the past became lax because the banks no longer had any concerns about scrutiny and/or risk.

The following is a simplified explanation of how the banks viewed potential borrowers and what they did pertaining to selling mortgages as bundled products to a secondary market. Borrowers who possessed good credit (someone with substantial income, little debt, and employed by the same company for two to five years) would be categorized as "A" class borrowers. Risky borrowers (someone with a history of making late payments, short-term employment, and questionable monthly income) would be considered "F" class borrowers.

These, of course, are the two extremes, but what is important to understand is the process that the banks and Wall Street used to bundle these existing loans before selling them to a secondary market. The deception was how they deliberately mixed the two extremes ("A" and "F" borrowers) in order to disguise risk within the investment products they were selling as low-risk products to "A" class borrowers. By disguising or mixing good loans with bad ones, it became much easier for the banks to rid themselves of the high-risk, poor-quality loans that could potentially harm them if they were forced to hold those loans.

The 2008 unraveling began when a few Wall Street hedge-fund managers (including Michael Burry of Scion Capital) began to analyze the actual loans within the bundled products. He became suspicious, realizing the banks had deceptively combined clients with good and bad credit. Once Burry discovered the banks' deceit, he deduced it would not take long before the risky borrowers would begin to default on their mortgage payments. He calculated that once they began to fall behind on their payments, because these borrowers had made little to no down payment when securing their loans, they had little to lose and would ultimately begin to default or just walk away. Burry realized that once the borrowers did this, it would lower the value of the mortgage-related products sold on Wall Street, and once the Wall Street sharks realized the investment funds were going to lose value, they would immediately begin to short the stocks.

Shorting the stock means that rather than investing your money in a company or products sold on the market because you think the company or product will rise in value, hedge-fund operators and Wall Street actually invest money by betting the corporation or investment fund will lose its value. . . and if it does, they make money!

Average people struggle with the idea that there are individuals or organizations smart enough to create and control economic outcomes, yet we know this to be true because that is precisely what the Federal Reserve is designed to do. With the mortgage crisis, the one outcome that was assured was that once the economy ran its course, the citizens would be on the hook to absorb the damage. Because both central banking and commercial banking *knew* the technological revolution was going to provide a sustained economy and slightly higher-paying jobs to the American worker, they anticipated that an increase in wages would ultimately trigger a rise in housing prices and increase demand for appliances, automobiles, etcetera. As the boom began, they understood the risk of inflation, but they also knew how to contain it. That's why NAFTA became Clinton's first achievement as president: because policymakers knew allowing American companies to move south of the border and permitting free trade with Mexico and Canada would ultimately lower the cost of products sold in the United States. Even though wages would rise significantly, because the price of goods and services would remain low due to NAFTA, this would keep inflation in check for a sustained period of time.

Now that we know the reasoning and the framework behind the 2008 crisis, it's time to understand the ramifications that remain. My concern is, given what we know, was the mortgage crisis and the deflation of our assets done by accident or by design? I promise that after reading my thought-provoking analysis on how the crime of the century impacted the boomers' retirement and deflated the value of their assets, as well as examining the plan of allowing free-flowing immigration, the damage to the millennials' future, and the real reason behind the signing of the Affordable Care Act (also known as Obamacare), you will begin to understand that if we don't act now as a united citizenry, there will never be another opportunity for us to do so. Buckle your seat belts!

Action

The action was clearly driven by greed. I hope the information I have provided has convinced you there was without question a coordinated effort among Washington, DC; the Federal Reserve; and Wall Street to collectively orchestrate a long-term economic run the problem is once this run was over, greed was allowed to win the day at the expense of the taxpayer..

It is my belief most of the Washington, DC, politicians were not wise enough to realize that bad policy and Wall Street greed would ultimately deliver a black swan that would forever damage the lives of the American people. Yet their solution to the problem is not to make it right with their constituents, but to further cut deals to enrich themselves while they seal a fate for our citizenry to have limited growth, one that they will dictate.

Reaction

If we open our eyes, what we see are fixed outcomes developing within all our industries. There has never been a greater distance between the haves and the have-nots. I will continue to prove that although the ones who possess the most wealth are greedy as hell, they are not the ones who pose the greatest threat of trapping you into a life of slavery.

As we continue, each chapter will provide a stepping-stone to help you understand what the government seeks to achieve as their endgame for our citizenry. My intent is to build a unified citizenry and to formulate a game plan that will put an end to centralized government and a limited future.

The Aftermath

At the end of every great society, the only resource we have for understanding what caused its demise comes from the historian's portrayal of its destruction. What historians usually provide in their accountings is a significant event that either caused profound change or a particular movement that ultimately delivered the final blow to these once-great societies.

In this chapter and the next, I will continue to present my case that the mortgage crisis was caused by greed and corruption perpetrated by Wall Street and allowed by Washington, DC. I intend to prove the moves that our government made during and after the crisis were, and always have been, to slowly shift our citizenry away from a people built on independence to a people dependent on government.

As I go through the events leading to the 2008 collapse, I want you to remember my goal is to explain why I believe both political parties are knowingly pursuing a centralized government. There are two specific reasons. The first is they have run out of internal surplus cash to pay the interest on our nation's growing debt. The second is they are extremely concerned a political revolution could begin to take shape once our citizenry learns the truth about how they have bankrupted our nation from the inside out.

What I hope to accomplish in the remaining chapters is to explain how we got to the point of insurmountable debt. Then I hope to convince my readers that we cannot and should not allow the government to deal with our debt crisis without our involvement. Lastly, I will explain why I believe the division of our citizenry is an orchestrated attack by both political parties in an effort to deflect us from the truth.

What is the truth? The truth is that when Nixon moved our nation's monetary system away from the gold standard, converting it to our present-day fiat currency, this opened the floodgates to greed, corruption, and insurmountable debt. This is the driving force behind what caused a government that once represented its people to become slaves to Wall Street, commercial banking, private equity, and the monetary system that must have perpetual debt.

The Beginning

Starting in 1980, information found on the balance's website listed our nation's debt at $908 billion. On the same website, they project our deficit at $22.7 trillion in 2019, and by 2021, it is expected to rise to $25.3 trillion.

There is much debate as to which presidential administration is most responsible for our nation's catastrophic debt growth. The truth is that it no longer matters who's most responsible. My goal is to convince you that we must not let the politicians who allowed this to happen to be the people we trust to fix it.

Historical data clearly shows our nation's largest debt increases in comparison with years past began during the Ronald Reagan administration and has continued with every new administration since. The process started in 1984, which was the end of Reagan's first term. What also transpired after 1984 was that the vast number of boomers available to work within the job market and the technological revolution ultimately aligned at the same time to fuel a thirty-year economic expansion, along with a thirty-year accumulation of massive debt.

The first requirement necessary for the technological revolution's success was the availability of an educated workforce to fill the demand for qualified workers necessary to build the infrastructure (underground cable, programming, computer devices, etcetera). What was also significant to its success was that 58 percent of the boomer generation had college degrees, which was a substantial increase over the 24 percent of the prior generation who had them.

What is important to note, and why I continue to stress innovation by our citizenry, is that prior to the technological revolution, jobs such as lawn mowing, house painting, automobile repair, appliance manufacturing, food service, and retail were the main supply of employment available to most Americans. Additionally, it's important to understand the unemployment rate in 1982 was 10.8 percent, the average interest rate to buy a home was 17 percent, and the inflation rate was 13.5 percent. If we compare those statistics with 2017, showing a 1.5 percent inflation rate, a 4 percent average mortgage rate, and 4 percent unemployment, it gives us a sense of how bad things were at the time and how significant the technological revolution was for the lives of the American people.

The Federal Reserve, commercial banking, and the government understood the technological revolution was on its way, and they were prepared to loan money in order to fuel the economy it would provide. They also knew that as the revolution began to heat up, they would be required to control runaway inflation by passing legislation such as NAFTA and reforming the Glass-Steagall Act. Passing NAFTA would help stabilize inflation by manufacturing products in low-wage countries, and the Glass-Steagall reform provided Wall Street and commercial banking the ability to bundle and sell mortgage loans to a secondary market, creating what would become perpetual lending.

As I continue to describe this economic tragedy, please keep in mind that at some point we must collectively decide whether the outcome of the crisis was or was not intentional. So, as we continue connecting the dots, I ask that you keep an open mind about whether the folks who were smart enough to visualize, organize, and sustain a thirty-year economic boom were also smart enough to deflate various economic bubbles once the boom had run its course.

Once the technological revolution began to heat up, just as the economists had anticipated, the wages of the American worker began to rise. Additionally, the effects of NAFTA started lowering the prices of available products, so items such as televisions, appliances, and automobiles became much more affordable. However, there were areas such as housing where inflated prices began to surface, but what saved the day was that, as home prices increased, mortgage rates decreased, so the monthly payment of the average household still worked out evenly or in favor of the buyer.

During this time of economic prosperity, a jubilant America began to fall in love with Alan Greenspan as he kept delivering promising news regarding the state of the economy. He did mention from time to time his concern in reference to inflated housing prices, but he did not foresee a downturn in the economy, so even if the Federal Reserve raised interest rates, they did not raise them significantly. As time went on, many borrowers began to take advantage of the low interest rates and the ease with which the banks were willing to loan money. Many became reckless as they began refinancing their homes, using the equity they had gained from inflated housing prices to buy new cars or vacation homes.

I entered the workforce in 1978, which instilled a permanent impression in my mind of just how bad things can get, so I was one of the few skeptics who felt all the borrowing could not possibly end well. Even though I did extend beyond what I felt was cautious, I always had it in the back of my mind to be careful, making sure I hadn't gotten into something that would ultimately harm my family if economic conditions began to decline.

As the economy remained healthy, the boomers' wealth began to grow, and their investment in the stock market started to become significant. Much of that was due to IRAs or 401(k) pensions. Additionally, the steady growth of home appreciation (averaging from 3 percent to 5 percent per year) created a sensation of wealth beyond what any of us could have dreamed. As time went on, even though home appreciation began to slow, the economy remained strong, so there really wasn't any concern because we all knew home prices couldn't rise forever. Yet something else was transpiring and had gone largely unnoticed. Because of the plethora of jobs created by the technological revolution, the jobs we did as youngsters (mowing lawns, construction, etcetera) were no longer being done by kids entering the workforce. They were being handled by a new base of immigrants who had come to America in need of work.

The End

As time went on and the economy began to show signs of slowing, several thoughts began to formulate in my mind. The first one was, once economic conditions began to decline, what would happen to the people who had borrowed from the equity they had in their first home to buy a second home? Additionally, as the economy slowed and jobs became sparse, how would the next generation be able to afford to buy homes? It didn't take a rocket scientist to see that the immigrants coming to America for jobs were coming from impoverished countries, so the thought of them being potential buyers didn't add up.

It wasn't long after I began to consider how these questions might play out that Lehman Brothers announced that they had filed for bankruptcy on September 15, 2008. The truth is most Americans knew this was significant, but we really had little understanding as to the catastrophe that was to befall the American people. I truly believe most of the folks who experienced what transpired during the technological revolution knew in their gut that the massive borrowing by unqualified loan recipients would end tragically. There was no way any of us could have foreseen this was going to severely decrease the value of our homes', our 401(k) pensions, and cause ten years of wage stagnation.

As my home's value plunged, our businesses suffered six years of hardship, and we lived each day hoping we could survive, I began to think about how a government and a banking industry that had so brilliantly manipulated a thirty-year economic run could be so dumb as to have it end so tragically. Reflecting back to the announcement by Lehman Brothers, there was no way any of us could have prepared for the disaster heading our way. We could not possibly have imagined how many of our friends and family members would lose their homes, jobs, and life savings. The 2008 crash had an immediate impact, but as time went on, the American people began to realize the painful process of devaluation and stagnation would continue for many years to come.

What bothered me more than anything was that America's real estate market crashed because our government unquestionably colluded with the Federal Reserve, commercial banking, and ultimately Wall Street by turning their heads and allowing reckless policy. What is additionally troublesome is that after the crash, the government came to the citizens with hat in hand saying they needed $700 billion to bail out the perpetrators—that is, the financial institutions. The idea was to inject money into the banks so they would begin loaning to creditworthy small-business owners as well as the people who remained in good standing regarding personal credit.

What transpired after the banks were injected with our tax dollars was far from what we were told. Once the government gave the banks the money, the citizens in need quickly learned that the Wall Street banks guilty of creating fraudulent investment products had no intention of loaning money to the people who actually needed it. In fact, the only people they did loan money to were the monopolists who really didn't need it. To make matters worse, we later found out that instead of the banks using the tarp money given to them by our government, for the purpose of loaning to small and medium size businesses, they used our tax dollars as a tool to buy back stock options so they could pay exorbitant bonuses to themselves and their network of thieves!

In summation, the federal government rewarded the banks with a $700 billion bailout, while American families across our nation continued to suffer the plight of foreclosure. What became tragic was as the economic downturn continued, ultimately causing more unemployment, the people who once had good credit as well as substantial equity in their homes also began to falter, ultimately losing their equity and their homes to foreclosure as well.

Adding insult to injury, foreclosed homes often sold for much less than their appraised value, and the banks used the foreclosed homes as comps (comparable pricing) for other homes, ultimately causing devaluation of home pricing throughout our neighborhoods and all across the country. A government or banking system that was sorry for what they had done would have allowed the free-market economic conditions to decide what the real values of the homes were—unless, of course, their plan was to devalue all along.

Let's examine who it was who benefited most from our friends and families who lost their homes to foreclosure. With a little research it's not hard to find that the people our federal government allowed to monopolize are the same people who bought many of the foreclosed homes at a discounted price.

The Rich Get Richer

The Blackstone Group, one of the largest equity firms in the United States (and quite possibly the world), used a subsidiary company called Invitation Homes to buy large swaths of foreclosed homes through local brokers. Corpwatch's Laura Gottesdiener stated in an article written on November 28th, 2013 that the Blackstone Group bought 1,400 foreclosed properties in a single day. Additionally, in 2012, the Blackstone Group spent $7.5 billion on approximately 40,000 foreclosed homes. This is not an attempt to single them out—there were several other equity firms doing the same thing. The point is to emphasize how the 2008 collapse became a tool to transfer wealth from Main Street to Wall Street at a discounted price.

As we begin to understand that powerful real estate portfolios bought many of those foreclosed homes at discounted prices, my question about how the next generation could possibly afford the escalated prices of homes from the thirty-year economic expansion was answered. What became crystal clear was the people who had so brilliantly orchestrated the thirty-year economic run also had brilliantly manipulated a collapse and theft of an entire generation's wealth! As I pondered how the generation next in line could afford our homes, little did I know that the manipulators of money already had a plan in place that would ultimately deflate the value of our homes by 40 percent.

There are a few action/reaction items that I would like to draw your attention to. We don't need to decide yet whether this was a planned attack or bad governing. Please approach the following hypothetical action/reaction suggestions with an open mind. It's okay if you come up with a different view than mine; my only desire is to inspire my readers to avoid passiveness and to see the things you know in your heart to be real.

We must remember the beginning and end of the mortgage crisis happened because a technological revolution aligned with the boomers. Economists understood from the beginning that this generation of seventy-six million was a bubble within America's population. They knew from the start the positives this bubble would deliver and the burden it would create as they began to exit the workforce.

The following boomer statistics found on the Smart Instincts website may surprise, frighten, or enlighten you:

- Boomers make up 28 percent of America's population.
- Boomers are responsible for over half of all consumer spending.
- Boomers control 80 percent of personal financial assets.
- One in three Americans over sixty-five relies on Social Security benefits alone.
- Three out of four claim benefits when they turn sixty-two out of financial necessity.
- In 2010, Social Security paid out more in benefits than it received in payments.

- In 1950, 16 workers paid for each retiree's Social Security benefits. In 2010, it was 3.3 workers, and by 2025, that figure is projected to be 2 workers.

After each chapter, I will present what I believe to be an "action" that was done to either create a ripple or tidal wave that would impact our citizenry. I will also list a "reaction": what I believe they might have been attempting to achieve. There are a few chapters that I offer only a conclusion, because the action/reaction was thoroughly explained within the chapter itself. (By *they*, I mean our government and the financial pyramid. Do I believe they are working together? No. I believe the financial pyramid is driven by greed, and our poorly managed government is trying to hide the truth of how their bad policies and corruption have damaged our future.

The action/reactions I provide are suggestions as to what might have driven their policies. My goal is to engage you the reader to start analyzing the potential outcome of the idea's politicians present on the campaign trail. If we collectively analyze their ideas and stop them before they cause further damage, we can secure a better future for our children.

Action

After reviewing these statistics, we begin to understand the issues that a bubble within a country's population can cause. I mentioned this before, but it's worth repeating: Investopedia says, "There are 10,000 boomers retiring per day for the next twenty years." So the issue becomes, if a bubble exists within a country's population, and the generation following it is smaller in numbers, who will fill the jobs once the bubble begins to age or retire?

Reaction

With the knowledge the government had regarding the potential shortfall coming to our job sector once the boomers began retirement, is it possible their open-border policy was to offset this shortfall? In other words, did the government know they needed a large influx of immigration to fill jobs once the retirement process began? Is it possible they permitted illegal immigration, knowing there would be a budget deficit within the Social Security system once the boomers began to retire? In other words, did they delay enforcing an immigration policy because they knew many of the undocumented workers would pay into the Social Security fund while also knowing they would not be eligible for the benefit? Additionally, is it possible we haven't fixed our immigration policy because it provides jobs for high-paid lawyers who charge hefty fees to immigrants attempting to become American citizens?

Action

How can the government pay for programs such as Social Security and Medicare/Medicaid when it has misused or wasted the surplus dollars that were meant to pay Social Security benefits to its contributors?

Reaction

The solution can be achieved in a multitude of ways. The first is to create conditions that force the potential retiree to work longer. This can be done easily if the retiree's savings is in the financial markets that are controlled by outside forces such as Wall Street. To force the potential retiree to work longer, reduce the value of the money they plan on using to retire—in other words, crash the market. For the folks who are already retired, no longer having enough money due to the market crash, create programs such as reverse mortgages. Although in the beginning reverse mortgages will provide several benefits to those in need of supplemental income. This process will significantly decrease the transfer of wealth from the boomers to their children because most families will not have the resources to pay the debt balance owed by the parents to the bank once their parents are deceased.

Action

What happens when the largest portion of a country's spending begins to slow down due to retirement?

Reaction

As I mentioned earlier, the boomers retiring presents a multitude of problems. The federal government, as well as central banking, fully understands the impact their reduction in spending will have on our nation's economy. Tax revenue will decrease, and our nation's gross domestic product will either slow or be significantly reduced as the boomers become more conservative in their spending habits. Additionally, if what many economists believe that Wall Street's financial markets are overvalued is true, that means much of the boomers' retirement savings have overinflated values and that at some point a correction to the true value of those investments will come. The point I make throughout the book is that those at the top of these overvalued pyramids make their money as it's happening, and when the stock collapses, they simply rebuy their own stock at a discounted price.

Additionally, Wall Street and the Federal Reserve understand that the Treasury Department must sell bonds in order to fund the budget deficit. What I mean is that the federal government spends more annually than it collects in tax revenue. As an example, the Office of Management and Budget estimates, in 2019 projections, the treasury will collect $3.438 trillion and will spend $4.529 trillion. If their estimated budget overrun is correct that means the 2019 annual shortfall of $1.091 trillion must be supplied through the sale of US treasury bonds.

What generally happens in order to fund the budget deficit is the banks, Wall Street, and other countries buy our treasury bonds, thus supplying the Treasury Department with borrowed money to pay its bills. The Treasury Department then pays interest to the bond buyers for the use of their money. What is critical to understand is that the federal government/Treasury Department is not the one paying interest to the bond buyers—you are.

The last piece of the puzzle, which we will discuss in much greater detail later, is the signing of the Affordable Care Act. I believe the economic brainiacs knew the boomers' spending on things such as homes and cars would slow, but the one place they would increase their spending is health care. They will bring a unique opportunity for the federal government to ultimately expand another tax entitlement that will be paid for by our citizenry. I will explain in greater detail later, but I believe that even though Republicans and Democrats pretend to disagree, the Affordable Care Act will eventually be a single-payer system that will be paid for by a mandatory tax.

Conclusion

As we listen to the perpetual outcry from the federal government and our nation's economists pitching their doom-and gloom outlook as it pertains to America's budget deficit, if we analyze the areas I've highlighted, one might conclude this may have been a strategic plan all along.

Let's summarize the aftermath. As the once-prosperous boomers head into retirement, their home values have been deflated, thus making them affordable for the next generation. The open-border immigration policy has supplied a labor force to fill vacant jobs while the federal government has collected Social Security and Medicare/Medicaid taxes from many of the undocumented workers, knowing many will never reap the benefits, thus creating more usable income for the government to spend. The transfer of wealth from the boomers to their offspring has been drastically reduced through the process of home devaluation, a market crash, and the use of reverse mortgages. At the same time, the educational curriculum has significantly changed compared to past generations becoming more promotional or accepting to the idea of government having a bigger role in our daily lives.

It is difficult to prove that people conspired to achieve certain outcomes. It may not be collusion; it might simply be an incompetent leadership that produced bad policies. In the end, the people with the most wealth benefited from the people who had the least.

The federal government under the Clinton administration helped orchestrate (or, at a minimum, participated in) the beginning of the crisis, and the George W. Bush administration replenished Wall Street banks with taxpayers' dollars in the end.

The people who committed this crime are not sorry. Give them another chance, and this time, it won't be just the value of your home and your life savings they will come after—it will be your freedom.

Consolidation/Monopolization

In the beginning of this book, I stated that each chapter would be a stepping-stone to provide logical proof of things that are happening in our nation. I've explained the danger to our independence if we allow ourselves to become sheep grazing in the field of a massive government and a business sector that is predominantly controlled by a few. In this chapter, I ask that you check your partisanship at the door and understand that when I use the term *government*, I'm referring to both political parties. What follows is evidence that our federal government continues to grow in size, and although we hear one party speak of the horrors of debt growth as well as the ballooning expansion of government, the truth is that both political parties are responsible for government increasing in size and scope.

It is my belief that although our elected government gives the impression that Washington, DC, is in gridlock, the things they believe to be important (be it George W. Bush's Homeland Security Act or Obama's Affordable Care Act) always find enough agreement to pass. As a collective citizenry, we must realize that each time we allow the formation of more government agencies, we're essentially letting government increase the total number of people who work for them, and we're giving Congress the authority to create and regulate a larger discretionary spending budget to tax and pay for those agencies.

I must admit it becomes paralyzing when I attempt to use the action/reaction method to analyze the need for more government, as well as its social programs and how we determine when they've become too burdensome. In my view, the first sign a government has become too big is when it needs money above and beyond what it reasonably collects from its citizenry. In other words, when the cost of government exceeds the amount of money we pay in taxes for them to operate.

To be clear, I am in no way attempting to minimize the task of governing or the need in some cases to regulate something. I do believe the government can provide value by being involved in some of our public services. Much of what follows is to help us understand what I mean about maintaining a balanced job growth among private-sector businesses, government, and corporation/monopolization. As we continue, I will explain why I've listed corporate jobs separately from private-sector jobs.

The following information provides a picture of the size and scope of our nation's government. I reviewed several different statistical websites to provide the numbers listed below. These employment numbers change frequently based on budget availability and/ or which political party is in power. The point of presenting this information is to focus our attention on the fact government has become a major job provider.

Total Government Employment

US Department of Labor	2,797,000
Office of Personnel Management	2,059,605
US Postal Service	603,911
Active-duty military	1,345,550
Army National Guard reserves	802,842
Local, state, and federal	12,400,000

If we combine the various agencies, we realize government employs a grand total of 20 million people. Again, after reviewing several different statistical websites there are approximately 128 million full time employees, so combining local, state and federal, this means government is our nation's largest employer, as they employ 17 percent of our total workforce.

When discussing government-run agencies, several things immediately come to mind: waste, inefficiency, bureaucracy, overregulation, lack of accountability. There may be more, but to avoid having this sound like an antigovernment rant, I will stop there. To give credence to the adjectives used to describe government's ineffectiveness, we need look no further than at how the US House of Representatives and the US Senate represent themselves on cable news, displaying to the American people the gridlock and partisanship and their inability to solve problems.

I know there are still some people who believe government is the solution. I will admit I am baffled by the idea of giving more responsibility and more money to something that has already proven to deliver poor results. To encourage an open-minded conversation, I ask the pro-government folks to honestly answer the next few questions:

- If you had a package that needed to be mailed from Chicago to California to someone extremely important to you that contained life-or-death information, would you use the US

Postal Service, or would you use a well-known carrier from the private sector?

- If you needed a heart operation or a knee replacement and you were given a choice of going to a VA hospital or a private health-care provider, which would you choose?

If your choice for either of those questions was not a government-run agency, I must ask: Why in the heck would you want them to handle more responsibility?

In addition to government growth, what seems to have gone largely unnoticed, and thus become a real threat to our country's economic stability, is that the federal government seems to have turned a blind eye to mass monopolization and consolidation throughout our nation's industries. In addition, they have ballooned in size and scope, thus becoming a burden by creating unsustainable debt due to their continual budget deficits.

We must understand what history has proved time and again—that when governments spend more money than they take in, there are only two options to fix the problem: they either cut spending by eliminating agencies or inflict unsustainable taxes on their people. My concern is that it seems we recognize price gouging when it pertains to products or services we buy, but when it comes to government charging too much in taxes due to their poor performance, we've somehow adopted the attitude that it is their right to do so.

There are vast differences between federal government and private-sector businesses as it pertains to providing a service. If consumers think a corporation is engaging in price gouging or providing poor service, the consumers have the option to go somewhere else if they're unhappy. In order for the private-sector provider to earn our loyalty back, they must prove they've done something to alleviate what it was that made us unhappy. They most certainly do not have the option of adding staff and mandating their customers pay an added expense to improve their service. The power of the consumer forces them to find a more effective way to regain the consumers' business. A good example of this would be the near collapse of America's automotive industry back in the late 1970s and throughout the 1980s. Once our citizenry began to realize the Japanese automakers had made numerous changes and were offering superior-quality vehicles at a lesser price than our automakers, America's auto manufacturers were forced to provide better products.

Governments, on the other hand, are extremely dangerous because they can use tools businesses do not have. The first is they have the power to create money through what is known as the fiat system. A fiat system is based on a government's promise that the paper currency they print is legal tender used for the purpose of making financial transactions. Legal tender means that the money is backed by the full faith and credit of the government that issues it. In other words, the government promises to be good for it.

Note the last sentence in the definition of the fiat system states the government promises our legal tender is legitimate. What it doesn't say is the government's promise is actually one that rests on the backs of their citizens. It is a promise that the world investors understand, that should our nation's fiat currency get into trouble, the government will raise our taxes and/or special assess the taxpayers because the real truth is it is our citizenry and the taxes we pay that support the fiat system.

What's important to understand is that when a business forecasts their annual budget, they must meet or beat their budget (spend less) in order to properly cash-flow the business. If said business does not stay within budget, they cannot simply raise the price of goods and services and demand their consumers/customers make up the shortfall.

When our government forecasts their budget, we should take note that the dollar amounts on their budget totals are listed as discretionary spending. The vast difference between the private businesses' budgets and the government's budget is the private-sector business has no choice but to live with the reality of their budget's accuracy and suffer the consequences if they don't. In the case of the government's budget, being close is good enough because they have the power to sell treasury bonds, along with their ability to raise taxes or go to the citizenry for a bailout, as was done in the mortgage crisis. Additionally, if private business continues to spend more than it brings in, banks will stop loaning them money. If the government continues to spend more than it brings in, it prints money and demands more taxes from us. I hope you are beginning to see the light: government is the most dangerous monopoly of them all!

Older readers may understand my concern regarding corporate monopolization more than younger ones. This has much to do with the 1970s educational system and its stressing upon students the dangers of monopolists like John D. Rockefeller, the owner of Standard Oil. Rockefeller was a business tycoon famous for his monopolization of the oil refinery business. The focus of our teaching at the time emphasized the importance of competition and explained in detail how allowing a corporation to monopolize a much-needed commodity could ultimately endanger the citizens' ability to obtain products (in this case, gasoline and oil) at a reasonable price. The fear was, once a private corporation has complete control over a given product or service, it gives them the ability to demand unreasonable or unsustainable pricing for that product or service. The education during the 70's stressed the importance of a free-market economy (a method of creating price competition) through the promotion of small-business innovation in order to fight consumer price gouging by a single corporation.

There has unquestionably been a consolidation or monopolization in American industries. The burden of too much government regulation and the size and strength of corporate America's big-box stores have forced many small businesses to close. A few examples in the construction industry are the Home Depot, Lowe's, and Menards essentially dominating the sale of construction supplies to the novice needing materials for home remodeling. Then retailers such as Best Buy, Target, Walmart, Amazon, etcetera as well as tech giants such as

Google, Microsoft, and Apple are reshaping how we buy products, do business, and obtain our news.

It is nice to have one-stop shopping or click-and-deliver service, but we should ponder the question of what becomes of our individuality and dynamic leadership within our communities if we lose small business completely. What America gained from the system of merchandise and service independence is not just the quality of a service or knowledge of a product. It was a system that produced a wealth of leadership within small communities.

The idea of a small shop and individual store owners is on the verge of extinction. This is largely because they do not have the resources required to meet government regulations or the capital to compete against corporate big-box stores. Because corporations have the resources to sell products to the public on a large scale, they have the ability to buy at significantly lower prices from the products' manufacturers than the small-business owner who sells far less product.

By now, I'm certain you get the point regarding the danger to our nation's free market being compromised through the expanse of corporations consuming small businesses and too much job growth being supplied by federal, state, and local governments. It is my belief that if our country is to remain strong, we must be economically diverse. We must have governing systems in place that are not too restrictive in order to allow our citizenry to innovate. We must understand our nation is not great because its innovations came from corporate giants. Many of these innovations were born in the working trenches of America.

You might have noticed that when I mention corporate monopolization, I commonly include the word *consolidation*. My background stems from the construction industry. What was a diverse construction material supply market has been reduced to just a few suppliers. The few suppliers that remain are large corporations that were not necessarily in the construction supply business, but because they had access to resources and low-interest loans, many began to expand or diversify their businesses. So, what has transpired is a shrinking of available material suppliers and an increase in the cost of materials.

We've also seen this expansion in stores such as Target, Walmart, and other retailers that expanded their markets into groceries, patio supplies, etcetera. Additionally, we've seen the auto industry close a multitude of small dealerships while AutoNation strategically bought the few remaining. Across our nation, we're seeing a process of corporate giants pushing their way step by step to essentially change our free-market economy to a fixed market.

Much of this consolidation has gone relatively unnoticed because after suffering the hardship of the Great Recession, the people of America were left with a mind-set of trying to merely survive, so the idea of the products we needed to live being available—in some cases, at a lesser price—is something we found comforting.

The fact is unless we completely revamp the rules of those who govern, stopping the ability of Wall Street's lobbyists to coerce government officials to turn their heads, our nation's destiny will be no different than those of other failed socialist countries, where merchants are few and government authority is all powerful. We must understand the failure of the free market is not because it's a bad economic system. It fails when competition shrinks, and elected officials who are morally bankrupt begin to dominate the free market system for self-gain.

In order to make my point regarding the danger of a centralized government and a growing consolidation of our merchants' monopolization power, I thought I would start by asking a few simple questions:

- If the largest corporations in America continue to consolidate by buying small independent businesses, and our federal, state, and local governments continue to grow through their expansion into health care, etcetera, who will be the two largest job providers to our citizenry?

- If the free market is transformed into a fixed market, who will have the greatest power to persuade a nation's government?
- What happens when corporate wealth has the power to control the supply of goods and services to a nation's people and the government of those people threatens to increase their taxes?
- If government representatives of a nation's people have free rein to hold positions of power for an unlimited amount of time and those representatives are subjected to the power of money through the system of corporate lobbying, who will ultimately have more influence over the elected officials' decisions, our citizenry or the corporate lobbyists?
- If government officials realize they have no power to increase taxes on the monopolists controlling a fixed market and those monopolists are providing benefits to our elected officials through their lobbyists, whose benefits will the government cut—theirs or the citizenry's?

I believe I've made my point by engaging you to answer these same questions people were forced to face in socialist societies that collapsed under the weight of a ballooning, corrupt government, along with a winner-take-all class of merchants. Let me be clear: my problem is not with the merchants; my issue is with a governmental system in which elected representatives can be coerced through the power of money, ultimately selling the soul of their country's people.

Proof of Government Expansion

As I stated earlier government has become the largest job provider in our nation. The US Bureau of Labor Statistics website reported in January 2019 that America had 128.57 million full-time workers (people working at least thirty-five hours per week). Of that figure, twenty-two million, or 17 percent, work for state, local, or federal government. The remaining 106.57 million is split into job sectors such as health care, tech, financial, retail, agricultural, construction, ectara.

The following information is from the New York State Society of CPAs (NYSSCPA) website. It was published on April 7, 2017:

> For generations, if you were a worker in the United States, it was very likely that you were employed by a small business with fewer than 100 people. In the wake of the economic crisis of 2008, however, this is no longer the case, as large and very large companies now employ a larger percentage of the population than midsize or small businesses, according to the Wall Street Journal. Using census data, the WSJ calculated that 36.2 percent of people worked at either a large (2,500 to 9,999 people) or very large (10,000 or more people) company, versus 38.9 percent who worked for small (100 or fewer people) companies and 24.9 percent who worked for midsize (100 to 2,499 people).
>
> Since 2014, the latest year for which there is census data, this is no longer the case. At this point, 39.2 percent were employed at either a large or very large company, while 26.5 percent worked at midsize companies and 34.3 percent worked at small companies.
>
> The effect has been sharper in some sectors than others. For instance, in 1980, small businesses employed 50.3 percent of all retail workers, while 34.8 percent were employed by large or very large companies. However, decades later it is these giants who now employ the biggest share of workers at 47.2 [percent], versus the 35.6 [percent] employed by small retailers today. And while finance had always had more people working in large or very large companies, employing 38.7 percent of the sector's workers versus 34.4 percent in small companies, the years have widened the gap. The 2014 numbers indicate that

45.4 percent of finance workers now work at large or very large companies, while 29.1 percent work at smaller firms.

While generally one would expect smaller, more nimble competitors to emerge to challenge established giants, the WSJ said this is not happening as much, which could explain why big companies are taking up a higher share of employment than before. In 1980, 12.5 percent of companies were less than a year old. In 2014, this number has shrunk down to 8 percent. The WSJ also pointed to a momentum effect: these big companies have also made large gains in market share in between 1980 and 2014, which means they grow even bigger, and can operate more easily by taking advantage of things like economy of scale.

What the information provided by NYSSCPA proves is that when a corrupt, oversize government can be influenced by a powerful lobby, the citizens are the ones who suffer the consequences. The NYSSCPA data clearly proves the 2008 mortgage crisis changed the dynamic in favor of the haves within American society.

In a later chapter, we will get into more depth regarding the importance of limiting the power of elected officials. Before we do, let's close this chapter with a final thought. The purpose was to focus our attention on a serious threat within our job market and the effects it can have on the survival of a citizenry built on independence. If the largest percentage of the jobs available to American people involve either working for the government or a large corporation that can use its resources to influence government through campaign contributions and/or lobbying, where does this leave you?

The idea of America was to elect fellow citizens to be our representatives to help the citizenry shape our nation's future. Government's design was to help as an equal member of our nation's team to protect our borders and the rights of its fellow citizens. The framers of the Constitution of the United States were careful to create equal branches of government in order to ensure a system of checks and balances for the sole purpose of providing assurance to generation after generation of Americans so their government would never have more power than they do.

America's free market and its spirit of independence allowed people such as Benjamin Franklin, Alexander Graham Bell, Thomas Edison, the Wright brothers, George Washington Carver, Bill Gates, and Steve Jobs the freedom to innovate. To uphold the dream and the spirit of innovation, our government must be strong enough to protect our borders and our rights as individual citizens, but we must be aware and react swiftly to extinguish the formation of a centralized government being coerced by a network of lobbyists rigging our free market for their personal gain.

Action

This chapter proved there has been consolidation of who provides jobs to our nation's people. Additionally, I prove that we are well on our way to a centralized government that will drastically increase its influence on our daily lives. The concept is simple, and it is not new. The idea of increasing the power of government while empowering a select few merchant elites has happened over and over throughout history.

Reaction

The majority of our goods and services will ultimately be controlled and delivered by the policies of corporate America. As they gain strength by eliminating competition, the demand for quality from consumers will take a back seat to ensuring shareholders' profits.

As a central government grows in size, it will need additional tax revenue to supplement its growth. Letting monopolies grow will reduce tax collection from a vast number of free-market businesses, thus consolidating the collection of taxes from corporate America and the people who work for them. The problem with this scenario is that once a corporation has eliminated their competition, they reign over the supply and demand of goods and services to the consumer. Additionally, they will continue to have power over government by using their monetary influence and the system of lobbying.

We've already seen the results: government officials have enriched themselves through backroom deals with lobbyists. The end result will be a heavy tax on the working people in order to pay for the growth in government employees as well as the programs designed for redistribution. The overall impact on our citizenry will be a loss of self-worth and a sense of helplessness to change things.

Private-Sector Job Creation

To begin a discussion about our nation's economy, we should understand that the health of our economy starts and stops with the availability of jobs. Secondary is what type of jobs are available; their pay level; whether they are service, production, or regulatory jobs; and if they have long-term sustainability. America has an amazingly diversified job sector—industrial, financial, clerical, legal, agricultural, technological, construction, retail, food and beverage; the list goes on. Additionally, as diverse as our job market is, so is the pay scale.

I titled this chapter Private-Sector Job Creation to emphasize the importance of creating jobs that help, not hurt, our economy. So when I say, "Productive jobs matter," what I mean is that when we innovate to create industries that will ultimately require a workforce, the intent should be to create as many jobs possible that produce a taxable income derived from goods or services that provide value, not jobs that are regulatory. In short, using accounting terms, goods-and-services jobs should be thought of as an asset (producing income), while regulatory jobs should be thought of as a liability (costing money).

If you concluded from the last paragraph that I do not value regulatory jobs, I assure you that's not the case. I am highlighting the concept of creating jobs that produce goods or services because in general those are the jobs that pay the cost of regulatory jobs. If we use government as an example, we should collectively understand the taxes that you and I pay, as well as the companies where we work, are what pays for the cost of government. Keeping this explanation simple, jobs that regulate something would not exist unless they had something to regulate.

The consequences of the Great Recession unquestionably thinned the herd of small and medium-size businesses. Yet to accentuate the problem because the Great Recession was caused by corrupt behavior, the federal government significantly increased regulations, making it difficult for small and medium-size businesses to return. The result has produced government expansion both in size and scope and a massive influx of corporate mergers and acquisitions throughout our nation's industries.

There are several moving parts within this chapter. The first concern is whether some of our nation's highest paid jobs, which are paid for by the worst parts of society, are there because crime pays. Yet my greatest concern is what happens to our independence if the majority of the jobs available are from government and/or massive corporations. We must remember anything or anyone that controls the majority can and most likely will abuse the minority.

Crime Pays, but at What Cost?

Many readers will, without question, consider the remaining part of this chapter provocative. The truth is how our citizenry will ultimately live their lives in the near future has been compromised by a few in order to control the many. I warn you, some of the challenges I present may seem a bit harsh or conspiratorial. My intent is to have an open-minded conversation, drawing your attention to things we know are problems but have somehow accepted as part of our daily existence. As we continue, I will highlight how the worst parts of our society are funding some of the highest-paid jobs in our country.

Let's start the job-creation conversation with legal and illegal drugs and examine the high-paying jobs that drugs provide. I am continually puzzled by the idea that America is plagued with what seems to be an unsolvable problem of illegal drugs flooding our borders, given the multitude of agencies we have with the ability to annihilate the dealers at their base of operation if we so choose. I'm not trying to minimize the difficulty of eliminating drug cartels, but let's remember, we have the ability to engage the Central Intelligence Agency; the Federal Bureau of Investigation; the US Army, Navy, Marine Corps, and Coast Guard; federal, state, and local police; the United States Drug

Enforcement Administration; and the US Department of Homeland Security to collectively engage in eliminating large-scale drug crime.

Using logic to analyze our drug epidemic causes one to question how it is that with all our resources, the United States is having little to no success in stopping this flood of illegal substances. When analyzing problems such as these, I start with the thought process "for every action, there is a reaction." In this analysis, the action is drugs in America, and the reaction is the carnage the drugs leave behind within our communities. Understanding that drugs cause destruction in people's lives is easy. What is hard to understand is why the action isn't an all-out war to annihilate illegal drugs, but more of a servicing approach to the problem when we consider the resources available to eliminate drugs in America. Suddenly, an eerie question begins to formulate in my mind: are illegal drugs in America because they provide a plethora of high-paying jobs?

I get that this is a terrible thought to consider, but if illegal drugs are not here because they provide multiple well-paying jobs, then that leaves us with the alternative, which is an ineffective, oversize government that is not capable of getting the job done. I have to admit it gives me a sinking feeling to consider the idea that the drug problem in America could actually be intentional. Yet when we consider the politicians and their underhanded deal making in Washington, DC, it leads one to believe it could be possible.

Let's review the jobs that drugs create, starting with the judicial system and the initial apprehension of the criminal or addict by the police. After an arrest, the accused is required to prove his or her innocence within a court of law. The defendant either hires an attorney or requests the state appoint one. Depending on the severity of the drug-related charge, if the defendant is found guilty, they might be sentenced to a local, state, or federal prison. The list of people involved in processing drug-related crimes are prison guards, prison wardens, courtroom security, bail bondsmen, judges, lawyers, counselors, bailiffs, court reporters, parole officers—it goes on and on.

The following statistical information was taken directly from (the Drug War Statistics website, accessed November 15th, 2019) Reviewing the number of drug-related crimes from 2010 to 2017 clearly demonstrates that drugs create numerous jobs in America:

2017: Of the 1,632,921 drug law violations, 85.4% (1,394,515) were for possession of a controlled substance. Only 14.6% (238,404) were for sale or manufacture of a drug.

2016: Based on an analysis of 1,186,810 arrests for drug law violations in the US, in 2016, 84.7% (1,004,762) were for possession of a controlled substance. Only 15.3% (182,048) were for sale or manufacture of a drug.

(In 2016, the FBI estimated that there were 1,572,579 arrests for drug law violations in the US. The FBI's Uniform Crime Report for 2016, for the first time in many years, did not provide a breakdown of that figure by offense type. The FBI did perform an analysis of a subset of its arrest data for its 2016 Uniform Crime Report. The data were reported by police agencies in the US that cover 77.37% of the US population (an estimated population of 250,017,636 people out of a total population of 323,127,513 in 2016).

2015: Of the 1,488,707 arrests for drug law violations, 83.9% (1,249,025) were for possession of a controlled substance. Only 16.1% (239,682) were for sale or manufacture of a drug.

2014: Of the 1,561,231 arrests for drug law violations, 83.1% (1,297,384) were for possession of a controlled substance. Only 16.9% (263,848) were for sale or manufacture of a drug.

2013: Of the 1,501,043 arrests for drug law violations, 82.3% (1,235,358) were for possession of a controlled substance. Only 17.7% (265,685) were for sale or manufacture of a drug.

2012: Of the 1,552,432 arrests for drug law violations, 82.2% (1,276,099) were for possession of a controlled substance. Only 17.8% (276,333) were for sale or manufacture of a drug.

2011: Of the 1,531,251 arrests for drug law violations, 81.8% (1,252,563) were for possession of a controlled substance. Only 18.2% (278,687) were for sale or manufacture of a drug.

2010: Of the 1,638,846 arrests for drug law violations, 81.9% (1,342,215) were for possession of a controlled substance. Only 18.1% (296,631) were for sale or manufacture of a drug.

We've all seen the spiraling effects that drugs have on addicts and their families, as well as on the health and well-being of the American family in general. Almost every person has been touched by losing someone they know or love. Many know the pain of losing their child, parent, spouse, or sibling. We as a people have paid a heavy price with our mental health from the burden of drugs within our communities.

The cost of addiction and crime doesn't stop after paying for the lawyers, judges, and prisons. The impact drugs have on our cost of living and our sense of well-being regarding our family's safety is immeasurable. Drug addiction is a major contributor to crimes such as theft, burglary, and murder. American families have an overabundance of cortisol flowing through their veins due to their concern that one of their family members might become a victim of drug addiction.

Big Pharma Makes Big Money

Everything I've mentioned thus far has focused on the illegal side of America's drug epidemic. We also know many addictions have started from a doctor's prescription of narcotics. People innocently start taking medications to relieve pain, only to find out years later after taking that first prescription of narcotics for pain, became an avalanche of conning their way through the legal network of trying to obtain more prescriptions in order to satisfy their addiction. Many patients go from one doctor to another in the pursuit of new prescriptions.

If we follow the same exercise with legal drugs that we did with illegal ones regarding the job-creation process, we know the legal side produces jobs such as doctors, nurses, psychiatrists, counselors, and pharmacists. We also know there are giant corporations we call Big Pharma that are responsible for employing millions of people around the world.

There is yet one additional reaction to discuss regarding America's drug problem. Again, I walk the line carefully here for the purpose of promoting the use of logic, not in an attempt to be conspiratorial. This part of the discussion is centered on prescription drugs and the practice of medicine. Using the action/reaction process when dissecting all aspects of health-related issues, we find that no matter what the ailment is, there is a pharmaceutical drug available for treatment. Over time, it seems doctors have become less interested in a cure and more interested in a prescribed treatment. I refer to this as "treat but don't cure" diagnosing. Without question, this type of doctoring/treatment has created a plethora of jobs in the medical industry and is most certainly a home run for Big Pharma.

The jobs created through the "treat but don't cure" method start with the Food and Drug Administration; medical science; medical schools, professors, and students; physicians; nurses; administration staff; drug and equipment manufacturers: again, the list goes on and on.

A little research provides a well-known fact that the formation of medical science in America made huge gains when oil tycoon-turned-philanthropist John D. Rockefeller formed and funded the Rockefeller Foundation. Through his philanthropy, Rockefeller was responsible for creating and funding what are now known as the Harvard T.H. Chan School of Public Health, the Johns Hopkins Bloomberg School of Public Health, the London School of Hygiene & Tropical Medicine, and the Max Planck Institute for Brain Research. After his passing at the ripe old age of ninety-seven, his heirs continued to donate money from their foundation to the medical industry. Although we should be grateful to those who donate for the purpose of advancing medicine, we must examine if or when they might have ulterior motives. The Rockefellers' wealth is heavily invested in banks, petroleum, and Big Pharma, so we must be cautious regarding the amount of influence an investor may have in persuading science to achieve research favoring a product they sell.

It's no secret that Washington, DC, is inundated with lobbyists from all sectors of the corporate world, and the pharmaceutical industry is most definitely part of this practice. We should collectively understand that the act of lobbying is either to coerce someone to get something you want or to find out information before others about whether something is going to change. In a nutshell, these lobbyists are wining and dining politicians for the purpose of creating favorable laws that ultimately give them an advantage or maybe inside information regarding changes to a specific law that may happen in the foreseeable future.

This process of job creation and the idea that the government can be influenced by the power of wealth should cause every citizen a great deal of concern. Is there really no way for the most powerful country on earth to stop the flow of illegal drugs from harming our children? Is it wise that our medical industry is heavily influenced and partially funded by people who are the main shareholders of the leading pharmaceutical companies?

Jobs from Terror

Shifting the narrative from drugs while continuing to use the action/reaction process relating to the subject of job creation, the next topic of discussion has to do with terror here in America.

There always has been some form of terror in America; we've seen serial murders, explosions at nuclear plants, and plane crashes. September 11, 2001, changed the way Americans think and severely damaged the independent spirit of our culture, forcing the country to always consider the possibility of terror. Even though we've had our share of tragedies, 9/11 was different because technology caught the entire premeditated attack on camera for the entire nation to see. Though there have been other tragedies, few happened upon our nation's soil that damaged our collective psyche. The only notable comparison to 9/11 would be Japan's attack on Pearl Harbor, but many viewed that differently because Pearl Harbor occurred on an island far away in the middle of the Pacific Ocean. The attack of 9/11 was a successful, premeditated strike on the largest city on the United States mainland.

Yet the effects that 9/11 had on our psyches could be likened to the fear our children have of the boogeyman. Almost every parent has invested countless hours assuring their children that the monster they see in their closet or the imaginary person hiding behind the tree is not real. We turn on their light, and we open the door and walk out into the night to prove the imaginary figure is not there, telling them over and over, "He's not real!" The 9/11 attacks put the boogeyman in all our closets. Unfortunately, eliminating this monster can only be accomplished by creating an impenetrable line of defense in the hopes that we can find him before he can hurt us.

The reality of 9/11 is that it instilled terror in our lives, and it is being used as a political tool to deliver mass destruction to our independence and freedom from intrusion by our federal government. When crises such as 9/11 occur, we should take precautions to assure they can't happen again, but we should tread carefully to be sure we do not overreact. Reflecting back on how carefree travel was prior to the 9/11 attack, it is almost unthinkable compared to the processes we follow today.

The result of the attack ultimately delivered the signing of the USA Patriot Act on October 26, 2001. There was much debate in Washington, DC, as well as among our citizenry, regarding the authority that the signing of the act afforded the government. One year later, on November 25, 2002, the Homeland Security Act was signed, creating yet another federal government agency. The official website of the Department of Homeland Security reports that in 2019 their annual budget for discretionary spending was $47.5 billion, and the agency employs a grand total of 240,000 people.

The Internal Revenue Service Wants Your Money

This last look at job creation is a lightning rod that fuels many debates within our politics. Any idea what it might be? You guessed it: this discussion has to do with taxes—only we're not going to talk about how much we pay; we're going to analyze the plethora of jobs our system of taxation creates.

Accounting WEB is a leading website designed to provide helpful information to people who have chosen accounting as their profession. The website states, "In 2016 the government census reported 1,397,000 people working within the field of Auditors and Accountants." It goes on to say that by the year 2026, the anticipated total of people working in the accounting industry will be 1,537,000. (To provide some perspective regarding how vast employment is in accounting, the Center for Automotive Research states there are a total of 1.7 million people working in the entire US auto industry.)

When we view America's problems, many of us are guilty of saying how we believe something needs to be fixed, yet few invest the time to understand the ripple effect that develops from the solution we create. The truth is, most of the problems we have—growth of government, world population, global warming—are the result of issues that have developed over time, so unraveling these problems becomes a monumental task because many of these problems created from bad policy are engrained within our daily existence.

Most of us understand the job of the IRS, but for those who don't, their main function is to collect a percentage of earned income through taxation of the citizenry and businesses in order to pay the expense of maintaining a functioning government. The (IRS Website states 73,579 full time employees in 2018, with an annual operating expenditure of 11.7 billion in that same year.)

There are many opinions/proposals from financial gurus stating that our tax system is outdated, ineffective, and in need of an overhaul. We've seen over time that as our governmental power shifts from one party to another, although tax rates may change, the system of how we are taxed remains largely the same. There are many intelligent people who believe a flat tax, or a fair tax, would simplify/solve the dilemma of who is or is not paying their fair share of taxes.

Using the action/reaction analysis makes me think of two things. First, if we're to use a simpler method of taxation, does streamlining the system eventually cut the need for people in the accounting industry? Second, if we're to eliminate, let's say, half the jobs in accounting, what kind of jobs could we create that would be comparable for those who become unemployed?

The truth is that this kicking the can down the road that we all complain about in most cases does not have an easy solution. This, to me, is where the rubber must finally meet the road, and lying to the American people by providing Band-Aid solutions must end. With the advancement of robotics as part of our manufacturing procedures and the continuation of monopolization/consolidation in our industries, it is critically important to understand that unless we innovate new technologies and create new industries, we will be left with stagnation and erosion.

I believe the millennials understand that the future will provide robotics or technology that in many cases could replace the need for human participation in some jobs. Yet they must understand this is not something new. Every generation throughout our nation's history has dealt with the fear of being replaced. In the case of manufacturing, the fear is not only robotics. It is also the hard truth that many of our companies have moved their businesses to other countries that have cheaper labor and less government regulation. Much of the concern regarding immigration has to do with our fear of losing our jobs to someone younger who is willing to work for less. The only way to fight this is to constantly pursue new ideas, new technologies, and new industries.

My concern is that if people buy into this push from the so-called brainiacs' idea of "universal basic income" provided by a centralized government redistribution plan, they will have sealed their fate to be governed by the measures of austerity. I've tried to make this crystal clear, but it's worth repeating one more time: allowing a centralized government to become the redistribution arm to our citizenry and allowing consolidation/monopolization by corporate giants to continue will ultimately create paralyzing results for the future of our people.

The point of this chapter has been to build my case regarding the need for us to remain an innovative citizenry. We must collectively understand the importance of creating industries and jobs that produce prosperity. Understanding that the jobs such as police officers, firefighters, and others responsible for maintaining civility and safety, although these jobs are critically important, they are paid for from our taxes. What I mean is local, state, and federal service jobs (such as police, fireman, teachers) in general are paid for by people or companies that produce a profit. To exist within the system of capitalism, it is required that the cost of a product or service provided does not exceed what people are willing to pay for it. Meaning what the service or product sells for, minus the cost to provide, is what determines profit. The bottom line is that in order to survive in the system of capitalism, a business must produce a surplus revenue beyond what it cost to make its product, to determine success or failure.

Conversely, governments are not self-sustaining because they must rely on their citizenry and businesses to provide income through tax revenue to pay their expenses. Additionally, even though government employees do pay income tax, because the government is using redistributed prosperity (or taxes paid to government from profit) to pay them, this means the government itself does not contribute a net gain to the economic system. In fact, because the government has a budget deficit, that causes them to borrow money to pay for their overspending, and the cost of that borrowing reduces the overall benefit government employees pay in taxes. So when I mention the growth of government regulatory jobs and that government giveaways are dangerous, I say this because both are being paid for with added debt. We must understand that as the government grows in size and the system of capitalism supplying prosperity begins to shrink, this is when our economic system can no longer sustain itself.

What's an even greater danger is that Washington, DC, and corporate America have essentially become partners. What should be understood is that through the process of taxpayer bailouts, the government has socialized Wall Street, making them the largest recipient of tax-dollar redistribution. In other words, because Washington, DC, has delivered bailouts to failing corporations by using our taxpayer dollars while at the same time providing massive loopholes to avoid taxation, the corporations have essentially become an appendage of Washington, DC.

Throughout the remaining chapters, I will continue to stress the dangers to a citizenry that is prevented from innovating or creating new ideas. If the supply of our jobs comes mainly from government or corporations, we will have lost our ability to demand quality services and products from those who provide them. Our only chance to remain significant is to be an innovative, inspired people, thus a force of competition, to ensure the corporate giants remain on their best behavior when providing goods and services to consumers.

In the next chapter, you will begin to understand why I am so concerned about allowing our government, the Federal Reserve, corporate banking, and Wall Street to become the main sources of our provisions. If we give them the rope, history proves they will most assuredly deliver our citizenry to the hangman's noose.

Action

I touched on several moving parts that make up our nation's job sector. I've highlighted the importance of creating jobs and industries that are self-sustaining. In other words, businesses that produce excess income beyond the cost of making the product or service it is providing to the public.

Another important point was to analyze whether the leaders of our country see crime, drugs, and other ills within our society as necessary evils for the purpose of providing jobs. The thought we must consider: Is the growth of government jobs happening because we've run out of ideas on how to create self-sustaining industries, or is this an orchestrated effort to grow a centralized government while at the same time allowing corporate monopolization to make government and corporations the two main suppliers of jobs?

Reaction

Freedom and prosperity in America have been sustained because we've been able to maintain a proper balance between effective government lending a helping hand to innovation and effective job creation.

Throughout this book, I will continue to stress the need for us to remain incentivized, assuring ourselves we are actively involved in the creation and innovation of new industries or better ways to do our jobs. We must never forget the importance of cultivating jobs and industries that produce products and services that provide income prosperity rather than jobs that must rely on someone else's prosperity to survive.

In order to preserve the future for our children, it can never be acceptable to think of illegal drugs and crime as part of a necessary evil for job creation. Is it time to bring home our military to help law enforcement rout out the dealers from within as well as the dealers around the globe? The question I have is, why are we not already doing that?

This chapter is not meant to degrade or to imply we do not need regulatory jobs; civility depends on those who maintain it. The point is that we cannot exist or grow as a prosperous nation if stagnation is to be our guide. My final point is this: no matter if you are rich or poor, if you settle for expansion of government and corporate monopolization as the force to guide your future, then whatever your status today, tomorrow they will bring you austerity.

The Government Needs Your Review

For the most part, we live our lives according to judgment related to the consequences of our daily actions. If we drive too fast, we get a ticket. If we show up late to work, we are reprimanded. This review process comes from our peers, our families, and the laws of our land. In this chapter, I begin building my case that our citizenry needs to wake up to the idea that our government needs your review, and it is your right to voice your opinion. Our review is our power, and if we don't exercise our right to use it, we're going to lose the power to do so.

Your Opinion Matters

Our nation has changed drastically in the way we buy products and how we communicate with others whether or not we are happy with a purchase or service. Almost every business in America has a website describing the services they provide, and, in most cases, somewhere on the website is a place where a customer can share his or her experience (a review). The reviews we share with others are important to the retailer, manufacturer, and author because word of mouth is a big part of continued sales. Our review can be complex and even unfair at times because much of what we buy now is purchased through the internet, which means we are not judging the product by itself; we include on-time and undamaged delivery as part of our critique.

The moral of the story is, when we buy our goods and services from private-sector businesses, we have the option to choose from a plethora of different stores competing against one another to earn their customers' loyalty. The satisfaction of your buying experience is critically important to the merchant because the only way they can make you a frequent shopper at their store is to develop a reputation over time that they will do the right thing if for some reason you are unhappy with your purchase. Because of this shift to buying products on a website and having them delivered to our homes, many of the once-powerful retailers who hedged their bets that internet purchasing would not succeed as the new way of shopping are gone.

When the internet launched, many older folks didn't like the idea of purchasing a product without seeing it in a store. They couldn't imagine buying something they couldn't physically touch to determine its quality. The review of a product and questioning the salesperson were done right there in the store. Our reviews have put considerable pressure on retailers to be more attentive to satisfying their customers' complaints. The bottom line is the power of your complaint has forced retailers to improve, and the good news is that, because of competition, they, unlike government, cannot simply raise the price if their competitors are offering the same or better product at lower prices.

This is why I am so baffled when it comes to the argument about whether we should have government or private business be more involved in services to the public and our health-care industry. I ask the pro-government folks to remove your political shield for just a moment and, as a nonpartisan consumer, name one federal or state government agency that has a website providing you with the option to express a bad review regarding the service they provided. Since we know you can't, let's go one step further. Name one instance when you paid for a governmental service and received a refund or credit due to your dissatisfaction? Folks, in my day, this is what we called "a Perry Mason moment," or case closed, because government does not refund your money.

If you gain nothing else from this chapter, other than realizing the danger a centralized ruling government, free from restrictions, that can be coerced by powerful merchants, and a monopolized banking industry, I will feel accomplished. I've promised from the beginning I would do my best to remain free from political bias regarding left or right ideology, and I intend to do the same regarding the subject of government versus private-sector business. I mentioned it earlier in the chapter, but it's worth repeating that the private sector does not have the option of raising its prices in order to provide you a better service. The power of our freedom to support competing merchants is what maintains the strength of the consumer's ability to demand better service.

If we step back to philosophically review our lives, what is it most of us hope for? For me, it's the ability to achieve my life's ambition by having the freedom of choice to do whatever it is I'm passionate about and to fight for others to achieve their life's ambitions because when people are able to excel in the things they are passionate about, the world becomes a better place. Think about the stores you choose to buy your products from or the restaurants you choose to eat in, and ask yourself why you've chosen those specific places. If you are like me, it's generally because the service or provider has gone out of their way to fit your lifestyle. It might be their customer-friendly website or the drive-through accessibility to pick up food on your way home. Whatever the case, you've made a choice to use their service because they went out of their way to make sure you felt comfortable and that you were getting value for the money you spent.

Let's consider how we feel when dealing with large corporations where the competition is much less. Even though there might be other competitors within the industry, because there are only a few, we're left with limited options to find a better product or service elsewhere. The two that immediately come to mind are cable television and the mega-size airlines. In the state of Illinois, one might choose to have their teeth pulled over having a problem with their cable service. By the time you finish reporting your initial complaint, having a technical representative come to your home takes, in many cases as long as a week. It's similar to the dreaded process of changing flight arrangements with companies such as United Airlines or American Airlines.

Ask yourself this question: For consumers buying a product or service, is it wise to empower government or corporate bureaucracies to handle more of the things we need? Have they not already proven the only thing they'll deliver is a sense of powerlessness in response to our complaint?

It is a continual effort on my part to avoid the discussion of government and corporate growth sounding like a rant. I'm certain there are others like me who are fed up with the bloviating between two political parties using capitalism-versus-socialism talking points, not for the purpose of improving how our nation functions, but to divide us into political voting bases. I am not from the world of politics and have no further agenda other than to spark a flame within the next generation of Americans, helping them see the forest for the trees. It is crucial that our next leaders understand that the more centralized government and large corporations expand, the less chance we will have to express our views.

The economic debate before us is being presented through a left-and-right ideological argument, one side presenting capitalism as evil and the other side presenting socialism as life in prison. My fellow citizens, we must not be drawn into the sensationalized propaganda used to divide us. It is not a conspiracy for me to say that the federal government and corporate America are either knowingly or unknowingly using mass and social media as weapons to weaken our ability to unite and make change. It is also not a conspiracy to use logic or the action/reaction process to identify how the creation of disarray and confusion can distract people from ever seeing the core of how a problem began and the simple steps it takes to fix it once you reach and remove its source.

I believe it's time the American people change the way they think about the people we elect. Additionally, it's time for the people we elect to understand they are not elected solely for the purpose of creating more laws to restrict citizens. They should, without question, understand our laws and be able to assist when necessary to change them, but what seems to be missing is the understanding they are also there to manage and maintain the laws and the budgets already in place. The idea of what a representative democracy is has somehow become skewed to the point that citizens and special interest groups believe the only reason they are electing a certain candidate is to deliver their specific needs.

I believe this selfish thinking is what has fueled the growth of special interest groups and the process of lobbying government officials. The problem with a system designed so that each elected representative is beholden to people who have a specific agenda is it will always favor those who have the most money to organize. If we analyze our personal lives as parents or the companies we work for or the businesses we run, we know how important it is to have a good management team. If we think about how we operate in our own lives, we see in most cases the policies or habits we have in place, along with self-discipline as our guide, and there are very few times we need to make more laws or change procedures to be successful.

What has developed in Washington, DC, is nothing more than a daily procedure of debating old laws for the purpose of creating new ones. In other words, the people we elect do not focus on or involve themselves in any of the programs we already have in place to examine whether they are effective or not. The problem is the special interest groups with lots of money *have* examined how our Washington, DC, agencies work, and they buy their way in through campaign contributions to influence the politicians' arguments about how our old laws should be changed and adopting new laws that ultimately help the special interest groups flourish.

Government Leadership Matters

Consider how important management is to a corporation, America's government, or even a sports team. I'm from Chicago, so I'll use the Chicago Bulls as an example.

Most of America enjoyed the run of championships the Bulls achieved (except, of course, a few cities I won't name). The truth about the Bulls is the same team under different management had little to average success. The change of coaches from Doug Collins to Phil Jackson was not successful because they brought in a bunch of new players. The truth is that Jackson was better at managing the team and getting more out of the talent he already had. The reason highly successful sports teams succeed is not because they keep changing their procedures. In many cases, they use the procedures already in place and simply hire a coach who better understands how to get the most out of the available talent.

There are a plethora of examples of sports teams that were loaded with talent yet were never able to win championships. In almost every case, the failure had to do with talented players being individualized as stars. Jackson carefully delivered the news to his star player, Michael Jordan, that the Bulls would never win until he began to share the spotlight with the rest of the team. Once he convinced Jordan to pass the ball, as the saying goes, the rest is history.

Let's examine where we know the government is successful and where they actually use the concept of teamwork. The main four branches of our military are the army, the marines, the navy, and the air force It does not matter which website you pull up; each of their websites displays America's melting pot (all ethnic groups) and the value of unity and teamwork. The leadership in our military teaches teamwork during boot camp, explaining that the number one element to succeed in winning battles is coming together as one team with one goal: sending the message to their enemy that America's military will never divide and will never be defeated.

Something we see among winning teams and businesses is the consistent use of positive messaging to promote the importance of teamwork. Yet, in contrast, we see the destruction of citizen comradery caused by the destructive rhetoric used by our nation's political leadership when it applies to team America. Remaining free from attaching blame to either political party as to which is more destructive, we see that both parties view our citizens as nothing more than a political voting base that is divided into specific identity groups.

Teamwork Wins; Division Is Destructive

As an example, to show just how ineffective Washington, DC's leadership is compared to America's military commanders when leading soldiers to win wars, I will divide the American people into the political identity groups our politicians name on the campaign trail. Let's start by defining the groups, starting with *white privilege*, then continue with black (or African American), male, female, transgender, gay, straight, rich, poor, Asian American, Hispanic American, Native American, Jew, Muslim, Christian, atheist, legal immigrant, illegal immigrant—I think I've listed enough for you to get the point.

I would like you to now envision America at war, but instead of implementing the military's winning strategy of unity, we're going to use Washington, DC's strategy of fighting by dividing their soldiers into identity groups. Once the citizen soldiers are separated, the generals will use their political rhetoric to stir up the anger among the individual groups in order to instill passion in one group to outdo the other. Instead of giving various groups a unified goal as our military commanders do, Washington, DC, brass decides to motivate each identity group by saying something bad about all the other groups as they believe this will cause each identity group to try and outperform the other groups to gain individual recognition.

As war wages on and some of the identity groups begin to falter, some can no longer hold their positions on the battlefield, so they begin to run for cover. Yet as they run toward the foxholes of the other identity groups, what happens next is tragic. Because the Washington, DC, generals have promoted such extreme hatred among them, as the soldiers in need of refuge run toward the foxholes, their fellow Americans begin to shoot at them, yelling with disdain and anger, repeating all the hateful things the Washington, DC, generals have told them. Needless to say, there is no chance to build a winning team under this form of management, and every one of us should be appalled that they are doing it.

Time to Self-Reflect

It is time to look inward, my fellow citizens. I understand this example might be considered extreme, but is it really so far from the truth? Is American leadership creating hatred among us, and if so, should we not ask ourselves why? We should take a moment to reflect on the eulogy Senator Alan Simpson (Dec 5th 2018 at Washington National Cathedral) delivered during President George H. W. Bush's funeral: "Hatred corrodes the container it's carried in." Every American should look into their hearts and consider this. If we allow a two-party political system to work against their people by splitting us into a multitude of identity groups, then we must realize what's really happening is the surrender of our rights and our ability to unify as one people. We must realize unity is our only strength to defeat the potential of an enemy that forms within America.

There always will be winners and losers in a free society. What seems like a lot of work to some may not be a lot of work to someone else. Our goal should never be to deny someone willing to risk or to invest countless hours in order to bring us a new innovation. We must encourage and make easy the process in which innovators create because it is through them that systems of management and jobs get their chance to flourish. If we reflect back on the garages of both Gates and Jobs, could they or anyone else truly have understood the vastness of what they created? Did either of those gentlemen realize Microsoft would potentially employ close to 144,000 people or that Apple would directly or indirectly supply jobs in the area of 304,000 employees?

Before starting the next chapter, I leave you with this thought. There is no question America needs effective government, but as citizens, we must understand what the definition of a democracy by a representative government means. It does not mean a government that receives campaign donations from the wealthiest in order to game the capitalist system with favorable laws or regulations that only the wealthy can afford. It is not for the purpose of government becoming the liaison between the haves and the have-nots, deeming themselves the arbitrators of redistribution within a nanny state. Government in America was designed to assist. It was not assembled for the purpose of restricting. We must remain a self-reliant people, understanding that to deny someone else's success is to ultimately deny our own.

We are not the hate-filled people that cable news displays on their reality television propaganda. The American people are the strength of this great nation despite the corruption and waste we see in Washington, DC. It is not conspiracy to challenge the truth of what we see and feel. In the following pages, I will continue to provide my action/reaction analysis of events. There is a movement toward consolidation happening in America, and the only way we can slow this movement is to stop firing bullets at our fellow citizens and aim our weapon of unity to defeat those who seek to divide the American people.

Action

There are several points to this chapter. The first point lies in its title, The Government Needs Your Review. The fact is that the services government provides are poorer than their private-sector counterparts, and because government is not subjected to the consequences of our reviews, their service will never get better.

The second point relates to innovation and job creation and why I continually stress the importance of our citizenry remaining innovative. If we allow corporations to consolidate, they will no longer need to compete to hold their market share. In other words, because they control the market, understanding the consumer has no other options, you will lose your power to write a review.

Last, I will repeat throughout the remainder of this book that in order for our government to achieve their desired goal of ultimate power, dividing our citizenry is essential. It is imperative to understand that allowing Washington, DC, to divide us into political tribes at war with one another will ultimately deliver a tragic end.

Reaction

What is the final outcome when we lose the power of our review? It delivers an overall sensation of powerlessness to voice our opinions or change the things we don't like. It empowers the government and those at the top of the economic food chain to create a citizenry that is compliant by making it clear they are not interested in your review.

What You Should Know

There's a saying: "A good liar can actually convince themselves to believe their lie is truth." Unfortunately, I believe the things we once knew as truth have been surrounded by a fog of mistrust, doubt, conspiracy, and confusion. It seems no matter what the discussion is regarding a current or past event, we can find two polar-opposite opinions that believe they are representing the truth. I believe the internet has provided tremendous power to the deceivers because it has given them the ability to support the core of a deception as though it is well-documented truth.

In this chapter, we're going to discuss the formation and process of America's economic money supply, which is the core of a multitude of conspiracy theories. My approach to this highly controversial subject will start with a promise. I'm not going to lie by telling you I know the truth. I do not know who has supreme authority to manipulate our currency or economy. What I am going to do is shed light on the subject of what our debt is, who creates it, and who gains the most from our having debt. The truth is that our nation's finances can no longer live in the shadows of deception if America is to exist as a free nation.

I've made my position clear: without question, we need the wealthiest among us to invest in our ideals, so when I research or discuss this subject, it is not from a position of disdain, jealousy, or resentment. Although I do see the rich as a problem, I do not see them as the main problem. It is the deceptive parasites that live in between the rich and the poor who ultimately cause a monetary system to collapse. The problem is, once the system becomes too weighed down, the wealthy simply shake the bloodsuckers loose and move on to greener pastures while the parasites begin to feast on the carcasses of the people left behind.

This conversation must start with the conspiracy and mystique that surrounds the Federal Reserve and the secret meeting in the year 1913 on a small island just off the coast of Georgia, a place called Jekyll Island. The attendees were Nelson Aldrich, A. Piatt Andrew, Henry Davison, Arthur Shelton, Paul Warburg, and Frank Vanderlip. They allegedly orchestrated the formation of what is commonly known as the Federal Reserve and central banking financial system. I have no opinion whether this was the great deception that some claim it to be. For now, it is simply part of the discussion of how our financial system works.

The first thing that should be understood is that the Federal Reserve is owned, operated, and managed by America's government. The president of the United States does pick the chairman, along with six other board members, and the US Senate must confirm the proposed candidates. The central bank creators wanted to give the impression that the Federal Reserve was independent of political influence and that it was not owned and operated by the federal government.

The illusion is that once the Federal Reserve's board is elected, none of the members are required to answer to anyone within the federal government. Additionally, the Federal Reserve is not required to display their assets and/or accounting records to any governmental agency or the public at large. I stress this not for the purpose of creating hostility, fear, or conspiracy. That is simply the truth. I say "illusion" because the federal government can change the rules as to what is expected from the Federal Reserve whenever they choose to do so. Members of both political parties use the Federal Reserve as an unknown or a boogeyman to alleviate responsibility or damage to their political careers, thus separating themselves from bad or corruptive monetary policy.

The confusion behind how or why this Federal Reserve boogeyman was created stems from the historical account of its inception. The idea that elected government met with banking barons on Jekyll Island to secretly craft a monetary system has conspiracy written all over it! Yet the truth is, because of the 1907 bank run and near collapse of the US monetary system, history reveals that banker baron J.P. Morgan singlehandedly saved our nation from monetary collapse. So a meeting between government and private banking to formulate a plan to protect the government, as well as protect private banks from a bank run, was a necessary element to a stable monetary system. Unfortunately, what has transpired since the original intent to create stability has been manipulation and coercion to benefit a few at the cost of many.

The Players Involved

So how do we determine who is the greatest danger to our citizenry? We must start by identifying the various parts of the monetary system and the main players. The first part of the Federal Reserve/central bank game is the type of monetary system that is used. As I mentioned earlier, there is much debate whether capitalism or socialism should rule, but there is also a debate about whether our monetary system should be backed by gold or remain a fiat system. The players involved on the government side are the Treasury Department, the treasury secretary, a multitude of department heads, and Congress.

On the private sector-side, there are twelve regional central banks (which are semiprivate); commercial banks/primary bond dealers; independent banks; Wall Street; corporate K Street lobbyists such as Big Pharma, Big Oil, Big Tech, and the medical industry; and, last but not least, you, the taxpaying citizenry. Of course, there are a plethora of others who could be named, but getting too descriptive will distract us from what is important.

The Federal Reserve is the middle player between how the economy is functioning and monetary policy. Their job is to analyze every daily transaction within the fiat monetary system. They do this with the help of the twelve regional central banks. The reason I listed these twelve banks is because the mixture of information they report to the Federal Reserve comes from information that is provided by private-sector banks and local economies. Additionally, to be a member of the twelve regional central banks, private banks own shares in the central banks; thus, they are a blend of private and government owned.

Why You Should Be Concerned

Within the first few pages of this book, I highlighted what it was that drove our ancestors to revolt against Great Britain. In the chapter Connecting the Dots, I proved there was a dangerous connection of either collusion or pure negligence that caused our lives to drastically change. Next, I highlighted the importance of our citizenry remaining actively involved in the creation of what I refer to as "real jobs" in order to sustain our nation's future. In the last chapter, we discussed the importance of electing leadership that represents our citizenry and protects us from Wall Street greed and government bailouts. What follows is one more stepping-stone to help connect the dots of the dangers that lurk within a government joining hands with Wall Street while they sell your soul to a redistribution economic system that will tragically end in austerity.

It is my belief that our political system is doing everything within its power to create an illusionary war between the haves and the have-nots. What I will explain as we continue is a competition between the people of our nation and a power-hungry centralized government. This competition is based on the question of who is more important to the controllers of our fiat currency: Wall Street or our citizenry. Are the taxes we pay to the Treasury Department more important than the treasury bonds sold on Wall Street? The truth is our taxes and Wall Street are both needed because without us, the government would have no revenue, which would result in a complete collapse of the fiat monetary system. Without us, the government would not have sustained revenue, and without Wall Street aiding the sale of treasury bonds, the government could no longer cover its budget deficits.

The question for us becomes whether Wall Street's purchasing of bonds to help government pay for poor monetary management is more important than a productive citizenry paying $3.6 trillion annually to the Treasury Department. That may sound like a meaningless question to some and a radical one to others, but as we get further into how government operates using our tax dollars, those who think it meaningless may become a tad more radical.

Just in case that last paragraph left you puzzled, let me explain the basis of my concern. The important thing to understand, and the reason I compare our personal lives to the operation of government, is that the people who loan us money should be using the same standards when loaning money to the federal government. The difference is that when a bank analyzes how much income we make as an individual versus how much debt we have, they determine our worthiness of a loan based on our available income after our committed expenses. When the Federal Reserve analyzes the Treasury Department's income to ascertain whether the government can afford to borrow more, the difference is it's not the government that produces their income. The income is produced by the taxes they collect from you.

The problem is that most Americans have lost the understanding that the federal and state tax deductions taken from our weekly paychecks are our money, not the government's. It's critical to understand those deductions are your share of payment for the service government provides. Those payments should be thought of no differently than if you were paying an electric or cable provider for services provided to your home or business. You should be just as angry at the government as you would be at your electric or cable provider if they provided inadequate service.

Let's examine how the government uses its monetary system and compare it with how it functions within our personal lives at home. I might sound ridiculous comparing the federal government to our homes, but I believe it's important to do so in order to explain why I believe it has become the citizens' greatest and most dangerous competitor.

In many households, both husband and wife are required to work if they hope to own a home and send their children to good schools.

Let's use a combined income of $100,000 for our example. The rough estimate of total tax on $100,000 is 22 percent, leaving the family with roughly $78,000 after-tax annual income.

Once the bank establishes your disposable income, they review other debt you might have, such as credit cards, an auto or school loan, etcetera. Then they determine how much they are willing to loan you without risking your defaulting on them.

What most people do not understand is when the federal government borrows money, just as a bank analyzes your personal income to determine how much you can borrow, the design of the Federal Reserve is to analyze the Treasury Department's income (your tax dollars) to decide how much the government can afford to borrow. I'm guessing some of you younger readers thought that if the government needed money, they just printed it. This is true: the government/Treasury Department does print money, but the money they print is increased debt to you.

If you learn anything from this chapter, understand that the only money the government has is the money they've collected from their citizenry through taxes and the sale of bonds. Additionally, the money they spend above and beyond what they collect in taxes is money they are borrowing in our name for us to repay later.

To clarify for younger readers, when I say, "You are to pay back the money government borrows," it's because they are truly borrowing money in your name, not theirs. If we think of this like your student loans, the only difference between your student loan and the government loan is you are on the hook to repay the student loan, while the government pays their loan using your money. If the government does not have enough money to cover their promises, they increase our taxes or sell bonds, thus increasing your debt to make up for their budget overrun. So please remember, when a politician says the US government is going to pay for something, it's not them, but you, who's paying for it.

What Supports Fiat?

We should begin the discussion regarding the circulation of money and who is at the center of loaning it by understanding what money is and how it is supported. In 1971, President Richard M. Nixon notified the American people that the nation's system of banking was temporarily changing from a gold-backed one to the presently used fiat monetary system. Although many economists are pushing for the gold standard to return, there is little chance this will happen because of its restrictive nature limiting perpetual loaning. It is worth mentioning that the gold standard did apply greater risk to the bankers' assets (equity, cash) and less pressure on the taxpayers. But that is precisely why they changed it!

The following is a basic description of what supports America's financial system, also referred to as fiat currency. A fiat currency is not supported by a physical commodity. Trust in fiat is determined by the faith people have in its issuer and the virtue of a government declaration. Fiat, or paper money, is used as payment between a buyer and a seller and is an alternative to the barter system or gold standard. It allows people to buy products and services as needed without having to trade product for product.

The strength and value of a government-backed fiat currency coincides with how well the country's economy performs. Additionally, a government must prove to be lawful when regulating fiat currency in order to inspire confidence in their nation's fiat, as well as proving to investors that their nation's economic system is safe. The power of a nation's fiat currency is determined by what stabilizes its strength during poor economic conditions.

What this means is the taxes the American people pay are the faith and the stabilizing force that support our fiat monetary system. In other words, you, the taxpayer, have in essence replaced gold in supporting our nation's currency. I will drive this point home over and over until every person reading this book understands the power we have as citizens: you are the strength of our nation's economy because your taxes are the main source of revenue that allows the federal government to borrow money.

The next part of money circulation involves the Federal Reserve, central banking, commercial banking, and other lending institutions. The two important factors to understand are that the banks are the largest source of money lending available to our businesses as well as the general public, and they are also integral to our government because the banks are among the largest purchasers of treasury bonds, which in turn provide money to the government so they can pay for budget overruns.

It's important to understand that the Federal Reserve and central banking require banking institutions (commercial banks and other lenders) to hold 10 percent of a client's deposit while allowing them to loan the remaining 90 percent of their clients' money. So if the bank receives a deposit of $100,000, regulation dictates that the bank holds $10,000 while allowing them to loan the remaining $90,000 to the public.

If we apply logic, we begin to realize that when Nixon changed the system from the gold standard, what he really did was remove a *real* asset (gold) that the bank was expected to hold in their vault to a paper currency that was backed by our taxes. What this means is the fiat money is *fake*, but what makes the fake money real is the confidence that the federal government will collect enough taxes or have the power to special assess (bail out) its citizenry in order to keep our monetary system secure.

Applying this logic, we begin to realize a bank's value is not the 10 percent reserve it holds because that 10 percent is merely worthless paper. The value of a bank is its ability to loan the other 90 percent of the fake money so it can collect *real* income. This is paid to the bank in the form of interest on the loans they make to their clients, and their shareholders profit from it.

The Mystery

We next move to the following question: Is the Federal Reserve/central bank privately owned by wealthy families or the federal government? I refuse to go down the conspiracy path regarding who actually owns the Federal Reserve. We own it because it is our tax dollars that keep its doors open. It is true the federal government does not have the right to analyze the Federal Reserve's accounting books, set the rate of interest, regulate reserves/fractional loaning requirements, etcetera. But the government can and does create the laws that the Federal Reserve must follow.

The real element that clouds the issue regarding the Federal Reserve as a privately owned versus government-owned entity is the sale of treasury bonds and the accumulation of government debt. It is debt and the buying and selling of various government bonds that cause the interaction between private banking institutions and Wall Street to be intertwined with the Federal Reserve. All the controversy regarding the Federal Reserve and the federal government being connected or influenced by powerful private wealth stems from our government spending beyond its means and its need to sell treasury bonds in order to pay for it.

The Federal Reserve Is Public

Let's start with what the Federal Reserve does.

- It influences the country's money supply and interest rates. The Fed sets federal fund rates that banks use to borrow from one another. That becomes the underlying rate by which all other interest rates are set, such as the prime rate. The prime rate is important for individual borrowers, since it affects the interest rates that banks use for mortgages, home equity lines of credit, and credit cards.

- The Fed essentially supervises banks and other financial institutions, making sure that they are financially sound. The Fed ensures that consumers' rights are protected.
- The Fed preserves the stability of the financial system. When events threaten the financial health of the whole country, as they did in 2008, the Fed can step in and take steps to contain the crisis.
- The Fed provides financial services to the US government, financial institutions, and foreign central banks. It makes sure the country's payment systems function smoothly.

There are twelve reserve banks affiliated with the Federal Reserve, but they operate independently from it. For a private bank to become a member of a reserve bank, it is required to become a shareholder. The shareholder cannot sell, pledge, or use Federal Reserve Bank stock as collateral. There is much to be learned about how these twelve federal reserve banks operate within the American economy, and there are a plethora of conspiracies/controversies surrounding who the main shareholders are. I promised I would remain free from bias and not promote more confusion that would contribute to the division of the American people, so for that reason I suggest if you want to know more about the Federal Reserve and its twelve affiliated central banks, it is without question worth the time and research.

To continue this conversation, we must first understand the importance of the dollar remaining the international currency for private investors. We should understand that America's debt, who owns it, and the importance of representing stability to our monetary system are the main reasons the dollar is considered the leading international currency for private investment in treasury bonds.

Having said that, let me remind you it is our citizenry's taxes (not the federal government) that are the main support or integrity that instills faith in the dollar being accepted as the leading international currency. Remember, the security our taxes provide to the fiat monetary system is the value and faith that gives a sense of security to other nations' willingness to buy our government's overspending, as well as earn interest on their investment.

On June 15th 2019, 2020 (US Debt Clock.Org) listed our debt as $22.5 trillion. Although these numbers change literally every second on a twenty-four-hour timetable, I've listed approximate balances (compiled from various informational websites) of those who own our debt:

The Federal Reserve	$3.2 trillion (11.2 percent)
US investors	$6.89 trillion (32.5 percent)
US government	$6.2 trillion (27 percent)
Foreign investors	$6.21 trillion (29.3 percent)

The top six foreign investors are listed as:

China	$1.18 trillion
Japan	$1.03 trillion
Brazil	$300 billion
Ireland	$300 billion
Switzerland	$237 billion
Luxembourg	$220 billion

The list of countries buying our debt continues, but what becomes abundantly clear when viewing who owns our debt there's vast difference between what China and Japan have invested compared to the investments of other foreign countries.

Who's the biggest owner of the growing national debt? By and large, it is the citizens of the United States, who own 70.7 percent of the government debt.

There are two extremely important things to understand. The $6.2 trillion listed as the US government is actually you. They bought treasury bonds using the surplus dollars held within comingled trust funds, meaning your Social Security, Medicare/Medicaid, etcetera. For many years, the Social Security Trust Funds have collected substantially more tax dollars than the Treasury Department has paid out to retirees. Instead of the cash sitting safely in a Social Security account waiting to be drawn upon for your retirement, Congress took the surplus cash and replaced it with treasury bonds, or government IOUs. The excess money you paid through tax deductions in your weekly paycheck was used to supplement government overspending. Better stated, it was used to pay interest on the $22.03 trillion national debt.

The second part of this insane process is something every one of us must understand. The government IOU sitting in our trust fund is merely paper, meaning they don't actually have the cash to return to our account. In order for the federal government to repay the money, they must borrow more money. What this means to you is either a higher monthly interest payment due to the increased debt or the need for the government to increase your taxes to pay interest on the increased debt.

To discuss America's budget deficit and its relevance to our strength or weakness as a nation, we must understand why we have debt. The importance of understanding how and why our government increases our debt each year and why you, as a citizen, should be concerned cannot be overstated. I've chosen the year 2017 as an example because the final data has been reported and should be accurate. It represents the year-after-year budget deficit and the danger it presents to maintaining a stable fiat currency.

According to the (Office of Management and Budget website), in 2018 US government totals were as follows:

- The total revenue collected was $3.316 trillion.
- The total the federal government spent was $3.982 trillion, thus adding $666 billion to the nation's deficit. That means they borrowed another $666 billion in your name.

- Additional data shows that, on average, the federal government has overspent by $450 billion per year for the last ten years.

What follows is a layman's view of how the federal government obtains the money needed to pay for their excessive spending. The Treasury Department sells various products such as T-bills or T-bonds on the market through various means such as government auctions. It is important to understand what I just said: when our government does not collect enough tax revenue to pay their bills, they borrow other people's money through the sale of various bonds, thus paying the buyers of those bonds interest for the use of their money. These treasury products sell in different denominations, from $1,000 to $5 million and have various rates of maturity running from six months to ten years.

The Treasury Department sells various bond products each year, all having different expiration dates. The bond amount and the duration they are sold for are based on how the Treasury Department determines the government's long- and short-term cash flow. This is done by estimating our nation's tax collection while analyzing future budget deficits provided through economic data. The Treasury Department's job is to determine in advance when the government will run short of cash to pay for spending in excess of their budget. It's also their job to notify Congress when they foresee the need for more money to pay our nation's bills.

This is where the game of politics and the deception begins. Because the American people clearly reject higher taxes, rather than the government explaining the truth regarding their overspending, they have devised ways to avoid directly asking our citizenry for more money because they know coming to us with hat in hand will cause us to ask questions, thus exposing why they're overspending. This is where the term "kicking the can down the road" applies. It is also when Congress uses their internal authority to deceptively use your money held within the Treasury Department. It is this process that has allowed them to kick the can down the road.

What I mean by internal authority is that in order to fund budget shortfalls, Congress has cleverly created various methods that grant them the power to use surplus dollars held within Treasury Department entitlement reserves. To be specific, the laws governing the surplus held within programs such as Social Security and Medicare/Medicaid give Congress the authority to direct the Treasury Department to issue bonds in place of surplus cash and use the cash for congressional discretionary spending.

As we continue, the following information from the Peter G. Peterson Foundation website becomes critically important for you to understand. As we get further along, it will help you understand why the federal government wants more entitlement programs similar to Social Security, Medicare/Medicaid, and why they would like the Affordable Care Act to become another entitlement program.

> A federal trust fund is an accounting mechanism used by the federal government to track earmarked receipts (money designated for a specific purpose or program) and corresponding expenditures. The largest and best-known funds finance Social Security, portions of Medicare/Medicaid, highways and mass transit, and pensions for government employees.

> Federal trust funds bear little resemblance to their private-sector counterparts. In private-sector trust funds, receipts are deposited, and assets are held and invested by trustees on behalf of the stated beneficiaries. In federal trust funds, the federal government does not set aside the receipts or invest them in private assets. Rather, the receipts are recorded as accounting credits in the trust funds, and then combined with other receipts that Treasury collects and spends. Further, the federal government owns the accounts and can, by changing the law, unilaterally alter the purposes of the accounts and raise or lower collections and expenditures.

Let's discuss how they've used the Social Security fund in particular. First, we should understand that Social Security and Medicare/Medicaid are funded by working people and businesses (including nonprofit organizations) through taxation for every hour of every day an employee/business works. The taxes collected for such insurance entitlements are held in reserve accounts in the Treasury Department. So, what the Peter G. Peterson Foundation website explained is that the surplus dollars held in these comingled federal trust funds can be used at Congress's discretion to pay for expenditures. This means that if more money is collected in a given year than will be distributed in that same year, Congress can use the surplus to pay for anything they deem necessary.

In the past, this benefited Congress greatly because there was a massive overfunding ($2.9 trillion) of the Social Security fund. The problem is, because Congress had the authority to use Social Security's surplus to pay for other things, what has become front and center is the alarming rate at which the boomers are scheduled to retire: 10,000 per day for the next twenty years. Recently, this has caused a lot of political banter on whether Social Security and Medicare/Medicaid can remain solvent to meet the increase in future retirees. This political sparring about the potential collapse or changing the terms of their benefits has angered the boomers because they feel they have faithfully paid Social Security and Medicare/Medicaid taxes their entire working careers.

What is not mentioned in the political discourse is how our federal government deceptively used the $2.9 trillion surplus to pay for the budget deficit, replacing it with treasury bonds. Government officials state that they didn't really take the money because the treasury bonds are the same as stored cash. Additionally, they argue that the treasury bonds are a solid investment for the American people, and they are paying us interest on the bonds while the government makes good use of our money. Economists and high-ranking government officials corroborate this deception by saying the dollar value in our trust accounts hasn't changed; they simply replaced the cash with treasury bonds. Many economists repeat the mantra that treasury bonds are the safest IOU in the world and that the American people are receiving a decent return on investment for the use of their money.

Let's analyze this statement logically. The government uses our surplus cash to pay for their overspending, then says not to worry because they're paying us interest on the money they borrowed. My question is how are they paying us interest? If the only money they have is money they collect from us, and they're not collecting enough from us to pay for their overspending, then how can they pay us interest on the treasury bonds if they don't have a surplus in income?

Let's go one step further. If the government continues to run a $600-, $700-, $800-, or now the $984-billion deficit the Congressional Budget Office is reporting for 2019, how will they ever pay us back the original $2.9 trillion? The truth is, because the only money the government has is our money, on the treasury bonds they claim to be paying us interest on, we are actually paying the interest ourselves on money they borrowed from us and on which they would be required to raise our taxes if they tried to pay us back.

Are you getting this, people? Let me explain why I think the preservation of our freedom has fallen upon its final judgment day due to what I believe has become a competition between our representative government and our nation's citizenry. The fiat monetary system will eventually collapse under its own weight. History has proven this. There has never been a successful case in which a central bank using such a system sustained a government's excessive overspending. History also proves that after a monetary collapse, the country suffering the collapse still exists, but it is the deceptive government causing the crash that gains strength while their citizens are doomed to a life of austerity.

Where I feel I am different from other folks that speak about doom and gloom regarding our fiat currency and fractional lending is I'm not proposing we change from using the fiat system. If the fiat currency collapses, there are only two groups who will survive: a centralized government and the wealthy people at the top who control the money game. What happens to the American people? The folks lucky enough to be politically connected will secure jobs working for the central government. Some might find low-paying jobs working for a massive corporation while the majority will live their lives under a government redistribution program.

In order to ensure that our citizens can prosper, we must be proactive in making sure our fiat currency does not collapse, which means we need to educate ourselves about the things that can cause such an event. That's why I'm reaching out to you now as a concerned citizen, because a collapse of our fiat monetary system and an end to the dollar being the leading international currency will deliver a tragic fate to the American people. I may not have all the answers, but my hope is to ignite creative ideas that will preserve the value of our financial system and the future of our children.

So if we understand the Peter G. Peterson Foundation statement that Congress has the authority to use the surplus dollars held in federal trust funds, then we begin to understand how and why our lawmakers are always attempting to create laws or programs that will ultimately fit into the tax-funded comingled treasury account category.

If we understand that the government and the citizens are both borrowing money from the same people, it should be understood that the banks, Wall Street investment funds, and countries buying US Treasury bonds as an investment are analyzing the government's ability to pay, just as they do ours when we borrow money. As we continue this discussion regarding new laws or new programs such as the Affordable Care Act, we begin to understand the bigger picture. When government needs to borrow more money, the banks and countries buying treasury bonds pay attention to how much tax income and how much debt our government has. So as our nation's debt increases, it becomes critically important for lawmakers to increase tax collections, so the need to create programs such as the Affordable Care Act become crucial. If you're baffled as to why, it's because such programs are designed to generate surplus dollars through taxation in the future.

If we again apply logic to the signing of the controversial Affordable Care Act, one could surmise that as the boomers retire, they will most likely spend less money on cars, houses, etcetera. Conversely, they will likely spend a good portion of the money sitting in their Wall Street 401(k) retirement accounts on health care. So how convenient is it that the government will have 100 percent of the boomers' health-care expenditures funneled through the Treasury Department? Additionally, because the boomers will collect Social Security in vast numbers, this will halt the accumulation of surplus dollars and will more than likely require the government to start repaying some of the $2.9 trillion borrowed from the comingled funds. In other words, they need more money, and they need it now.

Make no mistake, folks: Wall Street and the government have known they'll need another source of income for quite some time, and it needs to be created through taxation on a permanent basis. That's why designing more programs similar to Social Security and Medicare/Medicaid where government can create surpluses within comingled treasury accounts are of the utmost importance to the lawmakers. Congress needs access to more comingled trust funds so they can keep kicking the can down the road.

I hope you're beginning to see the light as to why I consider this a battle between our government and its citizens. Fiat currencies collapse because printing too much money eventually creates unsustainable debt. Governments that run up unsustainable debt become desperate to create new ways to generate tax revenue because they must keep up with the rising cost of interest on the money they've borrowed. When runaway debt consumes governments, they no longer focus on needed improvements, such as infrastructure or reducing wasteful spending. They're forced to be deceptive in order to hide what they've done, all the while knowing they must facilitate another way to get more of your money.

The following statement is said to have come from one of the early powerhouse banking families in England. I believe it is safe to conclude that Wall Street and the special interest groups such as Big Pharma, Big Oil, and Big Tech that lobby our politicians today understand the truth of Mayer Amschel Rothschild's statement: "Permit me to issue and control the money of a nation, and I care not who makes its laws!" Whether Rothschild actually said that or not is irrelevant. We would be foolish to believe that the power of money is not and has not been influencing the policies of Washington, DC.

Why Rothschild's Statement Is True

It's important to understand that the folks in the upper echelon of finance and the power-hungry demagogues of Washington, DC, are carnivores. They play by the rules of "kill or be killed," and they take no prisoners. If they see you as necessary to their survival, they will seem friendly. If you expose that you have a weak hand or they find they no longer need what you have to offer, you will be thrown to the wolf pack.

The relationship between Washington, DC, and Wall Street is one that both parties see as a necessary evil. The banks need the government for the assurance of taxpayer bailouts, and the government needs banking/Wall Street for their system of buying and selling treasury bonds. Although the government can create laws that reduce corporate profits, because the government is spending far in excess of what they take in, they have relinquished their strength and become subservient to the power of Wall Street, commercial banking, and private equity.

To better understand this interdependent relationship, it's important to realize that Wall Street, the Big Six Banks, and private-equity firms are significant buyers and sellers of treasury products. Second, it should be understood that much of Wall Street's buying and selling of bonds is done with the retirement money in your 401(k) or IRA. Yet the relationship became significantly closer when the Federal Reserve purchased $2.5 trillion worth of treasury bonds and $1.5 trillion in mortgage-backed securities. The result provided liquidity to banks that were in trouble and aided them in falsifying the value of their businesses.

It is significant to understand who buys treasury bonds because our government is selling those bonds because they need money to pay for their overspending. It is important to understand when we hear the Sunday talk-show analysts discussing the danger of printing all that money, this is what they mean. If we compare the government's bond selling to our personal lives, it would be akin to us running out of money to pay our bills halfway through the year and then using our credit card for the remainder of the year to cover our expenses. The difference is our credit gets shut off once they figure out we are spending beyond what we can afford while the government has the means to keep increasing debt.

This process is what empowers the financial sharks who buy and sell bonds, and it weakens the hand of our government, which ultimately diminishes our sustainability as a nation. You see, if the government was selling bonds because we collectively decided it was time to rebuild our nation's infrastructure, the world would view this as our selling bonds from a position of strength. The fact that our government is selling bonds because their everyday spending exceeds their annual budget is a signal to all those who budget their money wisely that our treasury bonds are being sold from a position of weakness.

How does all this tie in with Rothschild's idea that controlling money eventually means controlling governments? In our case, it proved to be accurate when our government committed the cardinal sin of using the surpluses from our treasury reserves instead of buckling down and cutting spending to balance their budget. What transpired after they burned up our surplus cash meant they ran out of options to use money internally. Once that happened, it became necessary for our government to develop a closer relationship with the sharks on Wall Street and their system of buying and selling bonds. In other words, because the government mismanaged their budget, ran up massive debt, and then paid for it by drying up our reserves, it left them and us exposed to cutting deals with the sharks at the top of the financial food chain.

We Became Chum in Their Shark-Infested Water

Once we begin to understand the moving parts of the fiat monetary system as well as the main players sitting on the throne of the financial pyramid, we can begin analyzing with logic who it is that sits at the top of the financial pyramid. We know the Big Six Banks, Wall Street's massive hedge funds, and private-equity firms are actively involved in buying and selling treasury bonds. They are also significant shareholders in every major corporation around the world. The depth of their power and influence cannot be overstated. These folks are still at the top of the financial pyramid even after powerful governments have collapsed.

Even people such as Bill Gates, Steve Jobs, and Jeff Bezos need (or needed) a banking relationship in order to get started, as well as to have cash flow for the businesses they operate today. It is because businesses and governments need money that banks are always involved from the ground up in any new innovation or technological breakthroughs. Those at the top of the financial pyramid are always in the know because they always are needed to get the ball rolling. I guess you could say if this were a game of poker, they hold in their hands a royal flush.

Now that we understand the banks have a royal flush and that our representative government did not play their cards well, it's time for us to collectively agree that our nation's government is in complete disarray. Additionally, we should agree this is a failure of leadership from both political parties and is something that has occurred over a long period of time. Both Republicans and Democrats have grown the size of government and expenditures, and both are responsible for increasing our nation's unsustainable debt.

It's time we recognize and agree that our two-party system is defunct and in need of replacement. Each year, candidates from both sides campaign on the doom and gloom of our growing debt, yet behind the scenes, both do all they can to grow government by creating departments such as Homeland Security, Social Security,

Medicare/Medicaid, and, what will most likely expand next, the Affordable Care Act. There must be consequences for politicians who condemn America's $22 trillion debt on the campaign trail, yet covertly do all they can to grow more government programs that ultimately create more debt.

Understanding these truths leaves us with questions that must be answered. Since we know the foundation of the fiat monetary system is built on the strength of the American taxpayer, does this not put our citizenry in a position to demand a better deal? Additionally, if the folks at the top of the financial pyramid have few of their personal assets at risk in comparison to ours, is this not something we should collectively be concerned about? Last, if the fiat monetary system is really nothing more than paper with its strength derived from the collection of our tax dollars, should we not demand more accountability from the perpetrators who abuse it?

Rothschild's theory of money control delivering ultimate power only rings true when governments become infiltrated with unethical, greedy, weak leadership. One should remember it is not money that is the root of all evil; it is what people are willing to do for it that gives money its bad reputation. If we continue to allow ourselves to be governed by people who put their own self-interests before personal integrity, then we have contributed to our own destruction. If we allow our government to spend beyond their means, this establishes a position of weakness and lets others dictate the terms of agreements. We must never forget that in the shark-infested waters of world finance, cash is king, and those without it will relinquish their power to the throne.

Conclusion

As we go on, I will continue to remove the veil of confusion regarding the moving parts associated with the fiat monetary system and the truth about the Federal Reserve. Once we comprehend our debt is nothing more than digits that are recorded on the Federal Reserve's accounting ledger and that our monetary system and fractional loaning are designed to convert fake currency into real money through collecting interest payments on debt, we will consider whether our $22 trillion debt is real or simply an accumulation of digital transactions that are designed to create an ever-increasing payment of interest. Put another way, is the Federal Reserve's accounting of $22 trillion debt really debt, or is this figure merely a digital mirage that our government uses as justification or a scare tactic to collect more taxes? Could it be that the interest we pay on internal debt ($6.2 trillion in our reserves or the Federal Reserve's $4 trillion bond purchase) is really nothing more than a tax sold to us as an interest payment on debt?

What we know for sure is that the Federal Reserve/central banking, the government, and Wall Street, along with their affiliates, have created a multitude of moving parts to our monetary system. They have deceptively passed laws and mechanisms such as the use of comingled treasury accounts, the Glass-Steagall Act, and a multitude of others in order to hide and secure backup for themselves should their greed or lawlessness cause potential damage to the confidence of the dollar remaining the international currency. What is the backup I refer to? It is that your tax dollars will be used as a bailout each and every time a financial crisis occurs.

Why do they create more single-payer tax-funded programs? Because programs such as these give the government the power of money manipulation internally rather than having to sell bonds externally. You see, singular taxing mechanisms (or single-payer systems) give the government the authority to adjust on an as-needed basis, meaning they give them the power to increase your taxes if they deem it necessary to do so. The power of these comingled accounts is their potential to produce excess tax revenue, thus giving the government another monetary resource to be used as discretionary spending.

In summation, what should be understood from this chapter is that the strength of America's fiat monetary system is you, the taxpayer. Allowing any government to continue creating tax-funded entitlements in essence gives them an incentive to create surpluses in those comingled trust accounts. It should be understood that allowing unregulated government authority over our entitlement programs essentially gives them a built-in mechanism to raise our taxes and the ability to increase our nation's debt without asking for permission.

Finally, if we continue to empower the government to be the primary source of our retirement or health care, we should understand that by doing so, we've essentially traded our individual choice for one that is dictated by the policymakers in Washington, DC. The results of surrendering the personal management of our lives to be mandated by them will destroy our freedom and prosperity.

The Story of Babel

After the Great Flood, God told Noah and his family to go travel and live around the world. But soon, the people began to think that they knew better than God, and, consequently, pride filled their hearts. They wanted to make a name for themselves. To show off their power and importance, they decided to build a great tower.

God didn't like that His people had disobeyed Him and that pride had filled their hearts. God knew that if the people couldn't communicate with one another, they wouldn't be able to work together and finish their tower. That's why He confused them by giving them all different languages and scattering them throughout the world.

Not to worry. I am not taking this in the direction of religion being the only solution, although I do believe it can help. My goal is to expose the stepping-stones of how our government has gone from one that represented their people to one that seeks power to control their people.

As I watch cable news, the question that keeps entering my mind is "Why do the supposed leaders of our government continue to use identity/victimization politics?" Why would politicians, along with America's media, sensationalize current events for the purpose of highlighting our differences? How could a government that promotes unity within our military believe it's wise to promote division and hatred among our citizens?

That's when the story of Babel enters my mind. As the story goes, God had once destroyed a world filled with disobedience with the Great Flood, but as He observed Noah's descendants, He knew they already had forgotten. He saw the natural forces of narcissism and self-pride at work and knew He must act with haste to again change the course of man's self-destruction. Scripture says God destroyed Babel's inhabitants' ability to communicate by changing their language. By doing this, He was assured His people could not change His plan for their future. Could it be America's imperial government see themselves as our God, attempting to remove our self-reliant nature in order to control the path of our future? The question we must ponder is "Could it be that voting bases and identity politics are solely for reducing our strength to unify as one people?"

The immigration in America's past is really not much different from what's happening today. Even though most of our earlier immigrants came from Europe, the fact is most of them spoke different languages, and although they were predominantly Christian, the differences among their religious denominations were significant enough to cause a feeling of total separation. What is drastically different in our present situation is not who is coming to America, but the political messaging we're receiving regarding their arrival.

On February 20, 1907, President Theodore Roosevelt signed the Immigration Act of 1907. (Before Roosevelt died on January 6th 1919, he wrote the following letter on January 3rd, 1919.)

> We should insist that if the immigrant who comes here does in good faith become an American and assimilates himself to us, he shall be treated on an exact equality with everyone else, for it is an outrage to discriminate against any such man because of creed or birth-place or origin.

> But this is predicated upon the man's becoming in very fact an American and nothing but an American. If he tries to keep segregated with men of his own origin and separated from the rest of America, then he isn't doing his part as an American. There can be no divided allegiance here...

> We have room for but one language here, and that is the English language, for we intend to see that the crucible turns our people out as Americans, of American nationality, and not as dwellers in a polyglot boarding-house; and we have room

for but one soul loyalty, and that is loyalty to the American people.

Of course, when Roosevelt gave this speech, it was a very different time in America's history, but it should be understood that the sentiment of the American people was not to welcome immigrants with open arms. Most of the Europeans who arrived during that era still suffer from the brutality of the derogatory nicknames given to them by the Americans who saw them as invaders. There was much nation-building to do at the time, and Roosevelt knew his messaging must be one that assured the disgruntled Americans that the federal government would pressure immigrants who did not speak English to assimilate into American culture and learn the language. Roosevelt's messaging was tough, and even though he lost the next election, his hardcore delivery regarding the importance of nationalism and the people being united as one nation was a message that carried on for many generations to come.

What Has Changed Since Roosevelt?

What is the difference between Roosevelt's era and today's political dialogue? Roosevelt was attempting to unify our nation because he realized the danger that division and hatred were to civility if it was not dealt with properly. He chose to highlight that America was the people's common link, using our nation as the glue that would unite our citizenry.

Yet today, the greatest danger to our country is the divisive rhetoric used by both Republican and Democratic politicians. Additionally, it seems the federal government is knowingly using this divisiveness to achieve similar results to the Bible's depiction of what God did to the city of Babel.

Just for a moment, let's remove ourselves from the bias we read and hear on talk radio and political commentary on cable news and focus our attention on the achievements of America's government. Whether you identify as left or right politically, are you really satisfied with the use of your tax dollars, or do you feel completely left out of the decision-making happening in Washington, DC? Do you have a sensation of powerlessness? If you identify with any of these negative feelings, it is important to understand that the sensations of dependency and hopelessness are precisely what a central government hopes to achieve. Because scattering the idea of unity and creating hatred and envy among identity groups ultimately allows them to become the mediator or peacemaker to regulate our differences.

We must ask ourselves why it is that both political parties seek division. It's easy to conclude that many politicians have a thirst for power and want as many voters as possible for reelection, so the division they create could be for the purpose of poll-tested messaging in order to gain a percentage of voters within each group. One must ponder whether this divisiveness is simply for votes or is done to fuel anger among America's people in order to achieve a much larger political agenda. History provides clear results of countries once perceived to be indestructible that became weakened and divided as a centralized government became nothing more than a ruler of redistribution and an arbitrator of fairness among a divided people.

Is America divided and directionless because we've become a country inundated with immigrants no longer assimilating into American culture, or have we become a citizenry that has lost our passion and grit to achieve, succumbing to a government that decides for all? Reflecting on immigration during the Roosevelt administration, even though most of them came from Europe, they were not treated with any less animosity than the immigrants joining us today. America was built by tough people, and the demand on every new immigrant base always has been harsh. The good news is at least the treatment of newcomers has been consistent, meaning all immigrants have been treated just as harshly as the groups that preceded them. The Irish were micks, the Italians were dagos, the Spanish were spics, the Polish were Pollack's, the Germans were krauts, and the English were tommie's; the list of derogatory names goes on and on. The names and conditions they endured were harsh, but each group did get past the stereotypes and went on to succeed in America.

Some of you might feel a central governing force is the only way to deliver fairness to all, but the truth is such governments have consistently destroyed the independent and innovative spirit of their citizens. Just as an employee working on an assembly line has a sensation of powerlessness to change corporate policy, so does a citizenry that is ruled by a centralized government. This sensation of powerlessness is consistent because, as central governments control the lives of their people, they begin confronting and silencing dissenters. They viciously attack those who speak out, displaying them to the public as sacrificial lambs to deter others from challenging their authority.

The problem is all central governments eventually fail because they become victims of the same fate that destroys massive corporations once deemed to be indestructible due to losing the grit and the vision of what it was that made them strong. As they grow in size through decades of success, the succession of generational leadership no longer understands that an inspired citizenry or workforce played a large role in the success. Additionally, what develops is a leadership that no longer understands the value of money or the necessity to be productive to earn money. As generational leadership changes over time, the inheritors of these large corporations (or governments) no longer have a connection to the founding CEO (or patriot) who received little more than the food on their table and a roof over their head as their payment.

Expectations Begin to Replace Earnings

The following information displays how generational compensation has changed over time for America's government. The list below is exclusive to the Senate's yearly salaries, but it should be recognized that the House's rate of pay and increases are similar to the Senate's. What this example proves is that as central governments grow in power and size, so does the amount they distribute to themselves. As the payers of governmental salaries, each of us should examine whether we are happy with our politicians' productivity or their thriftless behavior with our tax dollars.

The following is a list of a US Senator's base salaries from 1907 through 2019:

- 1907–1925: A US senator's annual salary was $7,500.
- 1926–1932: A US senator's annual salary was $10,000.
- 1933–1935: A US senator's annual salary was $9,000.
- 1936–1947: A US senator's annual salary was $10,000.
- 1948–1955: A US senator's annual salary was $12,550.
- 1956–1965: A US senator's annual salary was $22,500.
- 1966–1969: A US senator's annual salary was $30,000.
- 1970–1975: A US senator's annual salary was $42,500.
- 1976–1977: A US senator's annual salary was $44,500.
- 1978–1978: A US senator's annual salary was $57,500.
- 1979–1983: A US senator's annual salary was $60,662.
- 1984–1984: A US senator's annual salary was $72,600.
- 1985–1986: A US senator's annual salary was $75,100.
- 1987–1987: A US senator's annual salary was $77,400.
- 1988–1989: A US senator's annual salary was $89,500.
- 1990–1990: A US senator's annual salary was $98,400.
- 1991–1991: A US senator's annual salary was $101,900.
- 1992–1992: A US senator's annual salary was $129,500.
- 1993–1997: A US senator's annual salary was $133,600.
- 1998–1999: A US senator's annual salary was $136,700.
- 2000–2000: A US senator's annual salary was $141,300.
- 2001–2001: A US senator's annual salary was $145,100.

- 2002–2002: A US senator's annual salary was $150,000.
- 2003–2003: A US senator's annual salary was $154,700.
- 2004–2004: A US senator's annual salary was $158,100.
- 2005–2005: A US senator's annual salary was $162,100.
- 2006–2007: A US senator's annual salary was $165,200.
- 2008–2008: A US senator's annual salary was $169,300.
- 2009–2019: A US senator's annual salary was $174,000.

What I find interesting is that from 1925 to 1969 (forty-four years), a senator's annual salary increased by a mere $22,500. Then, from 1970 to 1975 (once Nixon removed the gold standard), their annual salary grew by $12,500 in five years. From 1975 to 1990, we see how inflationary characteristics affiliated with a fiat currency begin to kick in, increasing the salary another $55,900. The final stage of wage growth increased by $75,600 by the year 2009 and has not risen since. One must assume that after 2009, to avoid the appearance of government greed while the American people suffered the devaluation of their assets brought on by the mortgage crisis and the Great Recession, our unscrupulous leaders found other ways to enrich themselves.

Comparing an inept, oversize government to a failing corporation is built on the concept that neither of them understand the painstaking process of accountability that was required in their early development to be successful. As the corporation's founder gradually shifted ownership to their children, the sense of urgency and passion once required in order to survive changed to a routine of managing and sustaining. The uncertainty and fear that existed for the founder hoping to achieve a weekly paycheck became an expectation of a large yearly salary by their inheritors. The sleepless nights of concern due to the uncertainty of whether the business could be sustained became a business with a proven track record of providing security to many. The point I'm trying to make is that a successful business or government is born from an inspired idea and is most often driven by the fear to survive or be successful. The expectations of the inheritors of the business or governmental system lessens because success and revenue is already established so the element of fear the originators had is substantially diminished.

In most cases, businesses that were once successful do not fail because their product is no longer pertinent. It is generally they fail because the lack of initiative to keep current by maintaining a competitive spirit in the marketplace. What transpires from long-term success is the expectation that the corporation will be successful because it always has, replaces the fear to survive, which ultimately becomes the corporation's destruction. The inheritors of high-end salaries lose the sense of accountability to be productive, instead focusing on the luxuries the corporation provides. The daily struggles or changes in the market become secondary to their concerns because staff was hired to handle those issues. The urgency with which the corporation's founder solved problems becomes smothered within layers of management. Instead of rolling up their sleeves and attacking the problem as the founder did, the clueless inheritors hire a management firm to figure out why the business is failing.

The problem when comparing a government that has grown too big to a generational business that has been passed on to the founder's children is that ineffectiveness destroys corporations much sooner because the free-market competition swiftly prevails over businesses that have ineffective leadership. On the other hand, when governments such as ours become stagnant and lack the free market's pressure forcing them to be more efficient, they begin to add layers of management, ultimately becoming a massive cost to the taxpayer.

The Dangers of Fiat and Media Propaganda

The problem for us is our government has unique tools to disguise and deflect our attention from the truth by using several deceptions:

- The first deception is the illusion that government is using their money, not ours, to pay for their expansion.
- The second deception is the cooperation the politicians have gained from our nation's media, as the latter is assisting in creating the illusion that government programs are the only solution to our nation's problems.
- The third deception is the use of surplus dollars held in reserve for entitlements that are at the government's disposal for discretionary spending.
- The fourth deception is that the government can create money in your name in order to supplement the cost for the added layers of government growth.
- The last and the most dangerous deception is the two-party political system and the "representative democracy" used to govern our citizens. This form of governing becomes extremely dangerous to its citizenry once the monetary system has been corrupted. Coupled with the plethora of divisionary tactics used by today's politicians and the collapse of a monetary system, they can achieve results similar to what God did in the city of Babel.

Division Ensures No Change

The politicians are concerned that once the people get wise to this "robbing Peter to pay Paul" method of managing our finances, this could become the lightning rod that stirs our citizens to unite and demand change. Their fear of the financial debacle, among other things, such as their dirty backroom deals with lobbyists and allowing corporate monopolization, might soon be revealed as what drives their plan to divide. If they can create deep-seated resentments among the American people, this would ensure against us coming together with one voice. Just as God stopped His people from communicating by forcing them to speak different languages, the politicians are doing the same thing by creating hatred.

This is not conspiracy, folks; these are thoughts we should consider.! We must understand that if we remain divided, the US government, the Federal Reserve, and the financiers have dealt us a losing hand in a rigged game. Regardless of which side we favor politically, each of us knows within our heart something has gone terribly wrong in Washington, DC. If we hope to remain free, we must put an end to the division and sensationalized distractions that are keeping us off balance and preoccupied. Their goal is to prevent us from seeing the forest for the trees. The following is the subliminal messaging we receive daily:

- We are depicted within the following identity groups: race, gender, religion, sexual orientation, political, financial status, legal, nonlegal, pro-choice, antiabortion.
- The media destroys celebrities who make or have made controversial statements. The idea is to use sacrificial lambs to pursue "political correctness," thus silencing of the outspoken or opposing voices.
- A lack of trust is created among minority groups and law enforcement, fueling fear to the point of possible civil unrest.
- Class warfare between rich and poor, black and white, and male and female is promoted.
- Immigration and open borders are sensationalized.
- Could it be terror is used to keep the American people in a state of fear? That just maybe the endgame is to create a federal police force funded through a single-payer taxation?

Do you find it curious that our media chooses to report on nothing but negativity? Are there really no acts of kindness or generosity that could be highlighted to promote a sense of security or unity among us? Is it really possible that we hate one another as much as they lead us to believe? If so, how is it possible that we function every day with people from different backgrounds and different skin colors, and we seem to get along just fine? Is the media portraying the country we know, or have they become paid propagandists, used by our political system as a tool to divide our nation?

Just for a moment, take a deep breath and ask yourself, "What do a government that has deceived their people and a monopolized Wall Street/financiers have to gain by dividing our nation's people?" To answer this question honestly, we should collectively agree this divisive rhetoric is not specific to one political party more than the other. Both Republicans and Democrats are using political talking points to stir up emotions. The question is whether this could possibly be a *unified* political strategy by both Republicans and Democrats to ultimately weaken the strength of a unified people.

Our government has lost their way and needs our help. The reality is they are being manipulated by extremely shrewd businesspeople who always get what they want because they control the rules of the game. For the financiers, the goal is to control the flow of money and the interest rate and to monopolize the flow of goods and services provided to the largest economy ever to exist. Yet as powerful as they are, their financial pyramid cannot be sustained unless it is supported by the American people's taxes. There are 326 million of us; we are the volunteer military, we are the massive workforce, and we are the basis of the most powerful financial system in the world. The stakes of this poker game are extremely high. It is time for the American people to call Washington, DC's and the financiers' bluff and let them know we are the dealer of this game, and it is unified citizenship that controls the people's house.

Conclusion

Politicians and the media are collectively sensationalizing news events to exploit far-left and far-right extremists, giving us the illusion that such groups represent American society as a whole. What they accomplish from this extremism is to shift our focus away from the lawlessness and systemic failures of their governing. Using this process delivers a sense of despair while providing the illusion that radical behavior is the new normal.

The ultimate goal for the politician is to continue the two-party political system that divides the population in half, then to further break down their voting base within their collective political party. The final goal is disarray through mass division, creating the sensation our citizens have nothing in common. What this process delivers is a segmented citizenry, each feeling the only way for change is with the help of government.

It doesn't matter whether it was an orchestrated effort by a deceptive government or simply reckless, inept policies that caused these dire conditions. What matters is that we approach a solution to solving our problems as one people, using logic and not emotion. This reducing of our strength as a citizenry through division has eroded our power to demand change from our representative government.

There are many things, such as war and natural disasters, that can alter our lives in a moment. We must collectively understand that whenever tragedy occurs, it will require a stable monetary system to help us get through these events. The erosion of our monetary stability is due to the significant rise of unsustainable debt that largely has been driven by unregulated fractional lending and reckless, speculative greed. We must stop the division of our nation's people and join hands to remove the corruption within that is thriving on the back of America.

Immigration

Like identity politics and economic classification groups, immigration is another hot-button issue being used to divide the American people. Not to minimize what's happening at the border, but I see this entire situation as a complete farce.

I mentioned this earlier, but it is worth repeating—there are 10,000 boomers retiring per day for the next twenty years. Let's do the math:

10,000 people x 365 days = 3,650,000 boomers retiring per year

3,650,000 boomers retiring per year x 20 years = 73,000,000 retired boomers

Let's say 70 percent of the boomers are presently employed. That means slightly over 51 million people are exiting America's workforce.

The truth regarding immigration is that we do need new people coming to America so we can properly train and assimilate them into our workforce and our way of doing things. This is not new, and it should not be controversial. Even though most of America's early immigrants came from Europe, many of these people had very different cultures and needed time to adjust to the American way of life. What is different when comparing past immigration with the present is that we did not have political demonizing, and we did not have political leaders supporting lawlessness regarding our federal immigration policies. The real problem regarding immigration is how both political parties have decided to sensationalize and propagandize it for the purpose of creating more division.

What should be of major concern to all of us is that something as simple as counting how many people America takes in and how many are retiring and/or leaving seems to be beyond our government's capabilities. We should agree on two things. The first is we should know who is entering and who is leaving our country. The second is we should ensure that our nation's finances are solid and that we're making informed decisions about whether or not we can afford additional immigration. I find it hard to believe that any of us would define those two points as controversial.

The real question is why we don't have a functioning immigration policy. Seriously, how can it be that America does not have a set policy, and how can it be that a government full of lawyers can create a policy in a matter of weeks? Let's remember these are the same people who constructed the Affordable Care Act in order to provide 326 million people with healthcare. Heck, after 9/11, they created an entirely new division of government that employs millions of people in the same amount of time.

Sorry, folks, I am not buying that they cannot find a solution to our immigration issue, especially when it is upsetting so many people across America. This is simple: our government is manufacturing a crisis, and they are sensationalizing immigration to intentionally upset us. It is absolutely shameful what they're doing, and it's even more shameful to make America look as though we are a bunch of fools who can't get along or that we are unkind or unwelcoming to immigrants. There is no place on earth that is more welcoming or more generous than America when it comes to immigrants.

I'm not sure about you, but I am embarrassed by and angry with America's leadership. Our government's responsibility is to ensure our safety and to help create an infrastructure that assists a free, innovative people improve a free-flowing prosperous economic system that builds safe communities. Additionally, their job is to make sure we have a diverse (monopoly-free) supply of goods and services in order to sustain balanced job creation and stable pricing on a long-term basis. Instead, America's citizens are left to argue who is worse at their jobs: Republicans or Democrats. They're both incompetent, and they both have made an absolute mess of our country.

Here's what we as a people need to understand about immigration and why it is actually good for America. The rich people know its importance, only their view is based on profit rather than what it does for our society. I see immigration as necessary to keeping long-term inhabitants of countries such as ours competitive. It is the solution to stagnation, and we should welcome anything and anyone that stops our country from becoming stagnant. If we analyze what it is that causes unions, governments, and corporations to fail, it's not that the original concept went bad. They fail because people become too comfortable in their jobs, and they are left unchallenged. Failure happens when people begin to think their paycheck is something that's owed rather than something they need to work for.

There is no better example of stagnation than the performance of our government. When the number one quality of a nation's government is their ability to conjure up campaign donations to ensure they keep their job, that's when you know things are bad. When governments become too comfortable, they begin to do whatever they want, whenever they want, and that is when destruction begins. The main reason we've remained strong as a nation is because the citizens have consistently gone to work. Most of us understand that if we are not effective or we become unproductive, we will be replaced by someone new. This should not be viewed negatively because this is what helps us remain vitally important to our employers, keeps us from becoming lazy, and, in the end, helps provide stability to our families.

Having said all that, I promise you I am not naive about the destruction that unchecked immigration can bring to our communities, our culture, and our nation's finances if we do not handle it effectively. In my opinion, it is important that our government prove to our citizens that they have a handle on who is coming and who is leaving this country. It is even more important that the people immigrating to America know that we have policies and procedures that track who's here and that these procedures include a fair, regulated process for them to obtain legal citizenship in a reasonable amount of time.

Our current president, Donald J. Trump, popularized the political slogan "Make America Great Again," which can be considered offensive depending on your circumstances. There are two problems with his slogan. The first is the deliverer of this MAGA message is a hardline real estate developer from Manhattan, New York, so his style of delivery is offensive, especially to younger Americans. The second part of the message that is controversial and seems to be a lightning rod for anger is the word *again*. This word has upset many African Americans because *again* could be construed as the president meaning they should be enslaved once more. The immigrants coming to America might view *again* as though the president is suggesting that before *they* came to America, everything was just fine. The truth is for every American—whether Asian, European, African, South American, whatever it might be—if their family didn't come to America as an English noble, the word *again* could be considered offensive.

No matter where your ancestors came from, at some point in history, they were treated as the low-class dregs of American society. We should realize that America's progress comes from the fighting spirit of our ancestors' mistreatment and that the attempts to right the injustices they suffered as a people are what make America great. Our labor unions and our criminal justice system that is designed to represent everyone were built on the abuses of those who preceded us. This word *again* doesn't have to be affiliated with abuse. It could be applied to a point in time when our money was worth more or there was less crime in neighborhoods or maybe in reference to when our television programming had less violence.

It is time for us to reflect and decide as a people where we go from here. Have we become a country so divided and so self-centered that a carelessly used word like *again* can bring us to our knees? We must remember that no matter how bad we think we have it now, our ancestors had it much worse. The thing about America is it has been in a state of revolution from its inception—it is who we are. We should keep in mind when people protest or get upset when fighting for what they believe in, this push-and-pull process should be viewed as nothing more than political left and right forces pushing on each side of a political pendulum attempting to find balance.

Citizens exercising their right to protest is what caused a shift in fairness toward those who were once abused, oppressed, or excluded. It is a system that works as long as the opposing forces are able to voice their side of how a change may affect them, thus feeling satisfied their voice was heard and represented as part of a solution. It is when one group attempts to silence another or when one group wants to take something of value from someone else that cracks start to surface in the walls of freedom.

Freedom in America has a lot of moving parts, and they are dependent on one another in order for us to remain an independent people. The size and cost of government must be efficient in order to collect reasonable taxes from its citizens. The systems that provide the American people our goods and services must be supplied by a vast number of independent, diverse merchants to ensure a monopoly cannot force us to pay excessively for what they provide. Our government must be free from the lobbyists' tentacles of coercion and corruption. Our immigration policy finally must be balanced by what our budget allows and what our workforce requires after we are certain we gave people who already are here an opportunity to succeed.

We must respect the natural process of death in our aging population, and we must be prudent with our economic projections, understanding that a well-balanced, effective economy is the only way we can ensure America can sustain its existence. Like it or not, we are subject to the reality of economics. America has offered the world much in the way of help, and if we want to continue helping others, we must follow the law regarding the policies and procedures we have in place or change them expeditiously.

Before we allow an overabundance of immigration into America's workforce, we must first ensure we've educated and given every person a chance to be part of our system. It is not okay to imprison some of our citizens in neighborhoods littered with crime and give them just enough money to live but not enough to leave impoverished conditions. You see, a free society for all must be built on truth and not deception. We have governmental systems in place that have knowingly abused and restricted some of our citizens from having a fair chance to prosper. They've built pockets of poverty throughout our nation, knowingly creating a government-dependent culture that will never have a chance to prosper. What should anger all of us is that instead of trying to elevate the poor who are already here or expediting citizenship for the immigrants who have been waiting in line, they allow a system of lawyers to extract vast sums of legal fees from immigrants trying to gain their citizenship legally. All these terrible things are happening while our Washington, DC, bureaucrats fight for the rights of those who came here illegally.

Imagine how angry you would be if you bought a high-price ticket for a ride at Walt Disney World, and just as you got close to getting your turn, a whole new line of people who got free tickets lined up in front of you. One can only imagine how angry the folks who have lived in America for years who follow immigration laws and are paying massive fees to lawyers by working low-wage jobs must feel. They came looking for the American dream, only to find a system built for lawyers to pilfer money from them with little protection.

My message is not given with a hard heart toward the undocumented immigrants who are caught in a system that promoted illegal entry. My heart is hardened toward a government that knew exactly what it was doing purely for monetary gain. We have a failure in leadership at every level where government is involved, and in every case, these failures are due to corruption that has been influenced by special interest groups and their lobbying power. The problem at our border is not the legal or illegal immigrants' fault, nor is it the fault of the American people. Our government has used immigration as a tool to fuel anger and division. It is time to direct our anger toward the perpetrators of disarray, and it is time to address the incompetence, coercion, and corruption of those who are supposed to lead.

Conclusion

This experiment known throughout the world as the United States of America is a nation like no other. The argument that this "united" concept only worked because it was formed by predominantly white people built on Judeo-Christian roots is not true. It worked because our nation's leaders understood that in order to build an infrastructure, they needed people from entirely different backgrounds to work together.

The only difference between immigration today and past immigration is the messaging we receive from our leadership. What I mean is instead of our politicians using the networks or social media to explain to the people why we need immigration, they chose to use it as another tool to divide. Let us for a moment consider the positive effect if a congressperson or even a president used a one-hour time slot on national television to explain why we need immigration. Imagine if they communicated to the public a detailed plan that explained there are still 70 million boomers scheduled to retire, and that at least half of those boomers (35 million) are still in our workforce. A statistic in Pew Research states that 5,900 boomers (5900 represents how many boomers are in the actual workforce of the 10,000 boomers retiring daily) are exiting our workforce every day.

Now let's imagine a leadership that constructively explained to its citizens that the boomers' retirement is going to provide opportunity to those who are living in substandard conditions; detailing a plan to educate and notify which industries will have the greatest need for employees; and then presenting a plan explaining why we need immigration, how many immigrants they plan to bring in, and how doing so will affect our nation's budget.

Instead, they've chosen to demonize, divide, alienate, and create fear because they feel an informed citizenry is one that is dangerous. We are all immigrants, and the only thing our ancestors had in common was they came to America because it offered people coming from oppression an opportunity to work and the chance to provide a better life for their families.

Owning a Slice of the American Pie

Why is it immigrants coming to this country are willing to leave their place of birth and their ancestral heritage in order to become American citizens? Is it, as some would have us believe, because they want free things, or is it something much greater than that? I believe the majority of those who come here have the same idea as our ancestors did: they want a steady job and a chance of owning what's referred to as a slice of the American pie.

"Owning a slice of the American pie" is a phrase that can be used to describe many different scenarios. It could be used by a highly successful attorney who has built a substantial client base, helping them become a partner in their law firm or a factory worker who became valuable because they thought of an innovative idea responsible for increasing their company's production of goods and services. The point is the inspired lawyer and factory worker both want to be more than just an ordinary employee. Their goal is to have more control over their future within the company they work for.

For our ancestors, owning a slice of the American pie simply meant the same thing it means to today's immigrant, which is a chance to own the house they call their home. Owning property was not possible where most of our ancestors came from, so what America offered then (and now) had significant value. What developed from this land ownership was a sense of pride and an inspired people, giving them a sense of worth and a stake in a country that was worth fighting for. Are the immigrants joining us today any different from those who came generations earlier? I believe their motives are no different from those who have been immigrating for the last two hundred years. They want jobs, freedom of religion, law and order, and to one day own a slice of the American pie.

What I fear is the dream of home ownership that still exists in the immigrants may have been cleansed from our children's DNA. Their willingness to lose their independence if someone else will provide for them goes against everything it means to be American. In other words, because America presents extraordinary opportunities to those willing to work, this always has attracted a courageous, independent-spirited people, regardless of what country they came from.

To create a visual to best describe what I mean by spirited American DNA, envision a field of wild horses on fenceless open land, allowed to run unimpeded for miles. Now imagine cowboys chasing after those wild horses, seeking to capture and corral them so they can bring the horses back to the ranch for branding. Some of the horses they catch will be easily tamed, while others will fight until near death before allowing the cowboy to put his dreaded bit into their mouths. That spirit that exists in that horse fighting to be free of the bit is the spirit I speak of when highlighting the common thread of what resides in us collectively as a people.

Simply put, the majority of immigrants rejected oppressive governments that sought to corral and tame them into a life of destitution. What is the common denominator between the immigrants of today and our ancestors? It is and it was a courageous spirit that was willing to risk it all for the idea of freedom—so courageous, in fact, they were willing to leave behind their families and the only culture they knew, all for the idea of hope and opportunity. My concern is citizens lucky enough to have been born in America may have lost this wild horse spirit and seem to be content with grazing in someone else's field of green grass.

Confusion Delivers Indecision

Because America is no longer a simple country, the variety of distractions we face daily has caused this wild horse spirit to be disturbed and, in many cases, filled with anxiety. We face an ongoing barrage of subliminal messaging delivered to us through mass media and political rhetoric, and it has put many of our citizens in a state of dysfunction, leaving them overwhelmed or paralyzed with indecisiveness. What transpires from this overload of negative messaging is that people begin to think that there are just too many obstacles in their way to succeed, leaving them debilitated and unable to formulate a path to success.

Just so I'm sure you get my point, let's imagine entering a Walgreens or wherever you buy your medicine. Now envision standing in the aisle looking at the plethora of products available while trying to decide which medicine would be best to treat a headache or cold. As we look at all the different labels, we begin to remember the various television commercials all claiming their product is better than the other. This anxiety has crept into every aspect of our daily lives. What brand of car should we buy? What career should we choose? What foods are healthy? Which foods cause cancer? What is the latest fashion? Which is the best weight-loss method? What is the stock market doing today? These distractions go on and on.

Many of our citizens are confused when they see the stories of people coming to America and becoming successful in a short period of time. The truth is most of those success stories happen because the immigrant is not yet tainted by the distractions or the onslaught of subliminal messaging. In other words, they are focused on achieving the dream of freedom using every available resource to capitalize on the opportunity America provides. While we are distracted by the daily circus of events clouding our judgment, the newcomers keep it simple and stay focused on achieving their dream.

Home Ownership Delivers Pride

My goal is to remove those distractions and to prove that the one key element every American should be focusing on is achieving home ownership. Not only is owning a home a good way to protect our families and our personal wealth, it gives us a sense of partnership within the communities we live in. If the majority of Americans become renters, we will lose our sense of pride in maintaining our homes, communities, and schools.

Additionally, this slice of the American pie gives our military the feeling they have something worth fighting for. If we allow ourselves to become nothing more than renters, what follows is deterioration. Why? It's simple. When people don't own their homes, they have no sense of pride or feeling they could be losing value by allowing their homes to deteriorate.

A Home Provides a Safe Harbor from Wall Street

There are multiple books that explain in great detail how to get rich through real estate investment. Although it is true there are many who have done well in that industry, that is not what I'm proposing to you. I've dedicated a good deal of time to explaining how I feel about the dangers of an inflated government surviving from the money they take from our trust funds. The truth is that when—not if—the fiat system collapses and our monetary system is replaced with a different financial system, the people who control the present monetary system will control the new one. Owning your home provides you with security against financial collapse and should be viewed as built-in protection to ensure your family has something of value during turbulent times.

401(k) Is for Wall Street—Not You

I've presented a plethora of examples proving the Big Six Banks and Wall Street are extremely powerful, so the question is how can we have something that they do not control? To be clear, the term *they* includes banks, Wall Street, private equity, the US government, and the lobbying network. It has been proven beyond a reasonable doubt they all had their hand in the mortgage crisis, yet what's not discussed is the people who created the black swan (meaning an unforeseeable result or reaction) are the same ones who are the main stockholders in every corporation throughout the world. What does this mean to you? It means the money you have in your pension, IRA, or 401(k) is controlled by the same individuals responsible for the mortgage crash.

When considering our personal wealth from the perspective of ensuring it will maintain its value, the value of owning our homes debt free cannot be overstated. If we think about the way the system is set up, it surely wasn't done with our best interests in mind. What I mean is, in most cases, people who buy a home do so by signing a thirty-year mortgage that is designed so that the borrower pays mostly interest for the first several years of the loan before their payments begin to reduce the principal. The chart below shows that after 180 payments (or fifteen years) that just under half the payment is still repaying interest to the bank.

Payment	Principal	Interest	Principal Balance
1	$99.55	$500.00	$99,900.45
12	$105.16	$494.39	$98,772.00
180	$243.09	$356.46	$71,048.96
360	$597.00	$2.99	$0

Let's Create Another Option

There is a long, complicated history regarding pensions and investments and how we got to the point where we are today regarding our tax-deferred retirement savings. In the 1970s, the federal government passed a law allowing owners of corporations, and eventually their employees, to take tax-deferred deductions from earned income in order to incentivize people to save money for their retirement. *Tax-deferred* means a person can delay paying income tax on their earned income until the money is used later during their retirement. The original concept was designed to benefit wealthy people who wanted to avoid paying what was then a high tax rate, using a "wait and see" approach in the hope that the rate would be lower once they retired. This gave people with expendable income a chance to gamble and potentially beat the odds of paying high taxes.

Once we begin to peel back the layers of what deferred retirement tax offers, it becomes evident we have been participating in a rigged game, and as usual, we support the entire system. I find it ironic that we are offered tax-deferred income to fund our retirement yet Wall Street and government agencies are the only entities we can invest our money in. Additionally, the laws that govern retirement law, such as age, tax rate, and estate tax, are all decided by the federal government and can be changed at any time they deem it necessary. So we save our entire working career, pay huge service fees to Wall Street for managing our accounts, ride the ups and downs of an industry known for its corruption, and once our working careers end at the designated age of sixty-seven, our remaining life span is ten to fifteen years, in which most of our money will be spent on health care. If the tax-paying citizen is truly what supports the entire fiat currency, should we not have more control, or at least be able to stop the government's ability to change the rules that apply to our lifetime savings accounts? Or maybe we should demand better options?

Earlier, I highlighted how long it takes before our mortgage payments actually start reducing what we owe the bank. Let's review how much interest we pay on a typical fifteen- and thirty-year home mortgage:

Mortgage Loan	Interest Paid for Fifteen Years at a 4 Percent Interest Rate	Interest Paid for Thirty Years at a 4.5 Percent Interest Rate
$200,000	$66,000	$164,813
$300,000	$99,931	$247,220
$400,000	$132,575	$329,627
$500,000	$165,719	$412,034

When I say let's create better options than tax-deferred retirement income that's funneled into Wall Street investment products, I can think of nothing more beneficial than offering the same tax deferment to homeowners attempting to reduce the overall cost of paying off their home. If the government's goal really is to ensure people can obtain financial stability in their retirement years, what better way to help than to reduce the cost of their mortgage? Some policymakers might say present tax law does allow deductions for interest on our tax returns, but I believe many homeowners would prefer to use the tax-deferred option to pay off their mortgage rather than placing their retirement money in a market controlled by Wall Street sharks.

Have Our Children Been Set Up to Fail?

The following example is the reality our children face as it pertains to the cost of their education and the burden of debt. The information provided is not an attempt to persuade young adults in their choice of career or deter them from advancing their education. The example simply provides the ramifications of overloading our children with educational debt. I believe you will find this information helpful, as well as staggering.

Since I am familiar with Chicago's trade union wages, I chose to use a union carpenter's salary for this comparison. What follows is the carpenter's wage starting as a first-year apprentice and following through to the status of journeyman. The chart represents ten years of wages, including the benefit package provided to a union carpenter. To make the information easy to understand, I did not include potential wage increases that are generally assumed when participating in collective bargaining agreement.

Ten-Year Chicago Union Carpenter Wage Chart

Skill Level	Pension Contribution	Gross Wages	After-Tax Pay
First-year apprentice	$18,170	$40,000	$32,000
Second-year apprentice	$22,713	$50,500	$37,500
Third-year apprentice	$29,500	$65,670	$47,280
Fourth-year apprentice	$36,341	$80,787	$56,500
Journeyman	$45,427	$100,984	$70,688
Journeyman	$45,427	$100,984	$70,688
Journeyman	$45,427	$100,984	$70,688
Journeyman	$45,427	$100,984	$70,688
Journeyman	$45,427	$100,984	$70,688
Journeyman	$45,427	$100,984	$70,688
Total	**$379,286**	**$842,861**	**$597,408**

As a comparison with a young adult choosing the college option, I've used being an accountant for a career choice to determine the average cost of college, as well as the expected wage growth. The numbers used for the cost of college vary from school to school, but in general, these figures should be in the ballpark. Although some young adults may be fortunate enough to have their parents pay for their education, most are not. For that reason, I included the cost of education along with the average interest paid per student loan. The following charts represent four years of education and six years of working in the accounting industry.

Four-Year Cost of College

Degree	1-Yr Tuition: State School	Total Tuition	Total Amount of Ten Years of Interest	Total Cost	Monthly Payment for Ten Years
Four-year bachelor's	$10,000	$40,000	$13,289	$53,289	$444

Degree	1-Yr Tuition: Out-of-State School	Total Tuition	Total Amount of Ten Years of Interest	Total Cost	Monthly Payment for Ten Years
Four-year bachelor's	$25,600	$102,400	$34,048.57	$136,448.57	$1,137.07

Degree	1-Yr Tuition: Private School	Total Tuition	Total Amount of Ten Years of Interest	Total Cost	Monthly Payment for Ten Years
Four-year bachelor's	$34,700	$138,000	$45,849.95	$183,849.95	$1,532.08

Six-Year Post-College Employment Wages

Accountant	401(k) Contribution Plus Employer Match	Gross Wages	After-Tax Pay
Year one	$2,000	$50,000	$40,000
Year two	$3,000	$57,000	$46,740
Year three	$3,000	$65,000	$50,700
Year four	$4,000	$78,000	$60,840
Year five	$8,000	$100,000	$78,000
Year six	$8,000	$115,000	$89,700
Total	**$28,000**	**$465,000**	**$365,980**

Based on current publications, I used $50,000 as a starting wage for a first-year accountant with a bachelor's degree, then substantially escalated his or her wage over the next six years. Additionally, I doubled the employee's 401(k) pension contribution because many employers offer to match their employees' retirement contributions. Admittedly, I am conservative regarding how much the young accountant is able to contribute to their 401(k) retirement plan. I did this intentionally because I knew the accountant had, at minimum, a ten-year education loan that would range anywhere from $444 to $1,532.08 per month. My thinking is that with living expenses such as rent, car payments, gas, and insurance, it would not be possible for the employee to contribute more.

What we learn from this comparison is staggering. After ten years, the union carpenter has a combined after-tax income and pension benefit of $976,694, compared to the accountant's $393,980. To add insult to injury, the accountant's overall income is reduced by the cost of education depending on their selection of state, out-of-state, or private school. Of course, the earnings I've listed can vary, but for most young adults entering the job market, this is a true depiction of their reality.

We must find agreement. The battle waging in America is not and should not be between our citizens. The uphill battles we face as a nation are largely due to a monetary system that can only survive if it creates perpetual debt, so when politicians blather on and on about the atrocities of the debt left to our children, they know full well that without the continuation of debt, the system collapses.

It is for these reasons that I dedicated an entire chapter to the importance of owning our homes debt free. Regardless of how well our economy or stock market performs, if we own our homes, this can and will provide stability to our families, giving us the ability to weather long- or short-term economical storms. Additionally, focusing on paying down our mortgages rather than filling the coffers of Wall Street by paying fees on financial products helps us insulate ourselves from Wall Street's risky behavior. The fact is our homes provide shelter to our families and should be considered a stable asset for us personally, regardless of the rise and fall of our nation's economy.

Let us never forget what the controllers of wealth did when people all across America lost their homes. They bought those homes at a discounted price, and our federal government helped them do it! What transpired from the mortgage crisis? The wealthy became landlords to the masses while continuing the narrative that long-term investment in the stock market is the only way for the average citizen to achieve prosperity.

Action

A quick web search provides numerous data that show in 1947, finance, insurance, and real estate accounted for approximately 10 percent of our nation's total gross domestic product. In 2019, a similar search shows those same industries have increased to 20 percent of our GDP. Because these industries are highly lucrative, they are among the leading lobbying groups that have the power to persuade Washington, DC. They are also in the know about speculative deals that can help politicians who are willing to cooperate substantially enrich themselves personally.

Wall Street's power developed for two reasons. The first significant event was Congress passing the 1978 Revenue Act, which resulted in the tax-deferred 401(k)/IRA/pension retirement system. The second was the repeal of the Glass-Stegall Act, which allowed companies working in the financial industry to integrate their operations and invest in one another's businesses as well as consolidate.

As a side note, I should mention that Democratic presidents signed both these acts into law. I highlight this not as a partisan to the Republican Party, but to prove the point that I've reiterated throughout this book that both parties have clearly joined hands with the financial wealth that controls Wall Street.

The result of these changes helped convert our nation's economy, or gross domestic product, from one built on agricultural and industrial companies to a giant in the financial industry. I don't say this with malice toward that business sector. We should be grateful for the brilliance of the financial engineers helping America lead the world in finance, as well as the opportunity the industry offers for good-paying jobs. Yet the finance industry helps give credence to the phrase "For the love of money is the root of all evil." But as we've learned through our analysis, it is not money or prosperity that is evil. It is what people are willing to do to obtain money that makes it evil.

Conclusion

The results of these changes have produced both good and bad things for our country. The good is that it has opened endless opportunities to our citizenry by producing high-paying jobs, as well as financing for our homes and businesses. The list of benefits goes on and on.

The bad is that because the financial industry is highly lucrative, it has the power to corrupt and manipulate. Additionally, because governments are always in need of money, especially those that run budget deficits, they can become vulnerable to manipulation when in need of selling bonds in order to fund overspending. Selling bonds to pay for overspending is the beginning and the end of how corruption and collusion begin to formulate.

What I hope you gained from this chapter is the understanding that Wall Street is operating a rigged game. It is essentially a pyramid that a few win at the expense of many. I understand there are many people who believe in the market and have done well, but there are also many who have not. The truth is that Wall Street has grown from 10 percent to 20 percent of our gross domestic product because they were able to influence the government to create laws that would ultimately consolidate our wealth into Wall Street's system. The results have produced innovation and prosperity, but they also have destroyed the reputation of capitalism.

I've made it clear; I am a proponent of capitalism, and I believe in effective yet limited government. What transpires on Wall Street has become rigged capitalism aided by either an inept government or compromised political integrity due to the manipulation of money. The solution is not to take the opportunity of capitalism away from us; the solution is to put a stop to those who are abusing it.

Home ownership is essential to the spirit of our nation's citizenry. It gives us a stake in partnership, helping our people feel we have something worth fighting for. If we become nothing more than tenants to wealthy tycoons, this will create a sense of despair and in the end will deliver stagnation. Providing a home for our families is more than a financial investment. It is a sensation of accomplishment, and it is an asset that can offer security to those we love. Demanding that our government add the tax-deferred option as a method to pay off our mortgages gives us another option to build a nest egg and avoid paying ridiculous fees to Wall Street for managing our retirement accounts.

Dare to Challenge the Status Quo

If you haven't figured it out yet, you will after this chapter. If we want to remain the leading economy in the world, this can only happen by having an inspired citizenship. Allowing our government to balloon in size, crushing innovative ideas with legal roadblocks while letting a few dominate, has time and again been a recipe for disaster. There is proof throughout history that government overregulation and monopolization of industries will always produce stagnation and a bleak future for the working class.

Why has America become a successful country, boasting the largest economy in the world? Is it because we have a multicultural citizenry or that we're smarter than other countries? Although I do believe a diverse culture will produce a greater variety of creative ideas than one that is homogenized, it's not our diverse culture or our brains that separate us from others around the globe. It is, and always has been, our freedom to have unrestricted creativity.

Depending on which statistical website you use to analyze education data, the United States' highest rank on the list of IQ achievement is fourteenth... In fact, on January 14, 2020 (World Data Info's website lists the United States as number 27 on their list.) Yet even though we are not among the top ten, America still has the greatest economy and the brightest innovators of any country in the world. There are many contributions to consider when discussing America's success (natural resources, etcetera), but unrestricted creativity has allowed innovators to best use our nation's resources in ways no one else has. It is no accident that other countries with similar resources, along with a higher national IQ, are less successful and less motivated than we are.

If we analyze this through a political-ideological microscope, we see that the countries ruled by totalitarian governments have far less success because their people—a key resource—are not allowed to contribute their free-flowing, creative ideas. Their citizens are fearful of speaking out because of the rigid, restrictive society that dictates from a few at the top. America is different because freedom has harvested an inspired people who are willing to speak out and share their thoughts.

As we continue, I'm going to share my ideas for addressing current problems in America. I am certain there will be some who scoff at them—and that's okay. My only goal is to be the warning shot to America. If we do not stay an inspired, passionate, innovative people allowed to participate in the progress of America's future, we will surely fail as a country. We are the nation's greatest resource, and if we allow a few at the top to eliminate our input through restrictive laws that squash our ideas, we will end up the same as every other country overcome by a repressive government.

I must reiterate, my issue is not with the people who have the most money. Like many of you, greedy demagogues who believe the members of the common citizenry are nothing more than sheep roaming in their fields repulse me. The fight we must wage is to be recognized for our value and the contributions we provide. We must ensure that government regulations don't impede the masses who have little money, thus empowering those who do.

I've managed and inspired people from many different countries. The hardest thing to overcome in the human spirit is the feeling of helplessness that develops from the crushing weight of too much red tape due to overregulation. We must fight against being programmed that rules apply to us and that opportunity is only available to a few. As I present my ideas, I ask if you don't like them, don't laugh at or mock them. Create better ideas! Whatever you do, don't adopt a defeatist mind-set that only a select few can deliver ideas to guide our lives.

Ideas for change

Okay, this first idea's a doozy! Nielsen's ratings list the show *Shark Tank* as having five million viewers. For those who have not seen the show, it's essentially a few well known rich people that star in the one-hour program, in which a handful of select innovative people get to present their idea or product in hopes of winning a monetary prize while gaining investors to get their enterprise up and running.

With that premise in mind, what I propose is to impose a small tax on the wealthiest corporations and banks that do business outside the United States, then use those dollars to pay for a national television show similar to *Shark Tank* called *America Has Ideas*. In addition, offer to patriotic Americans a pretax voluntary donation as their "innovate contribution" as another method to help fund the cost of the show. Collecting tax contributions from businesses operating outside the United States would eliminate increasing the costs of the products we buy here at home. In other words, we would pass on the cost of our innovation to the consumers beyond the United States.

The concept of taxing worldwide corporations to fund *America Has Ideas* essentially forces them to pay for the assurance that they have competitors here at home. It is critically important to understand: if we do not have continued innovation and small businesses competing with or challenging corporations' way of doing things, the result is that just a few will provide the products or services we buy. When this happens, because the few do not have competitors, there's no pressure for them to improve their product or service. Additionally, if they have complete control of an industry, any increased cost to them is passed on to you, the consumer. It is imperative to make sure these large corporations have competition in order to keep their pricing and quality at their best for the consumer.

Back to the show. The details to govern the program (assuring money is not used for anything other than the promotion of innovative ideas) could be handled by a straight-shooting Hollywood production company. They would be required to detail expenditures to produce the show, and the results would be made public through open-book accounting for our review. The guidelines would be one show per month, and there would be a total of fifty contestants (one contestant from each state) at the start of the program. The winner would be decided not by a panel, but by computerized online voting by the Americans who watch the show. So, essentially, the citizens would pick by majority the innovation we choose to invest in.

The winner would get a cash prize and an interest-free loan for a certain period of time (maybe three to five years). The company's financial information would be accessible for public view as long as the company was receiving the interest-free loan. Once the loan promotion ended, the newly formed company would no longer be required to make public the business's financial information. In many cases, handling it in this manner would speed up the repayment of the loan because most people do not want to expose the way they operate their businesses to public scrutiny.

I realize this may be a wild idea, but that's what's great about America. A person still has the opportunity to openly present their thoughts. This is precisely what fueled unrestricted innovation here. The results the show would deliver would inspire citizens to be resourceful and to begin thinking outside the box. We must remember that before Gates and Jobs, America's future was lost to stagnation. Their creative ideas have fueled a thirty-year economic expansion. Before the rise of technology, America was mired in slow growth from the innovations of the past. We must never lose the thought that the end of one era must always be the beginning of a new era.

We must never forget the reason successful countries or businesses fail is that they begin to lose their lack of urgency to remain effective. If we continue allowing corporations to consolidate and the federal government to expand by the creation of low-level regulatory jobs, this will produce catastrophic results—not for the wealthy or those who govern, but for you, the American people.

Since America is still a place where a citizen like me can openly comment about how I feel about the performance of our government. I'm going to share my thoughts as to how I feel our present government functions while it's still possible.

I've clearly communicated my concerns regarding the dangers of a central government growing in size and reach in the lives of Main Street America. I've also shared my belief that staged left and right political theater is being used on network media as a divisional tool to point out our differences rather than to promote what we have in common. In my opinion, we cannot blame one political party more than the other. They are both dysfunctional, and both are driven by outside influences from corporate-sponsored money. In other words, instead of representing their constituents, they are representing the powerful people who give them shiny trinkets.

It would be easy for me to use the same old rhetoric by shouting, "Term limits!" But having thought this through, I believe instituting term limits would most likely cause more chaos, dysfunction, and lack of progress than we already have now. My feeling is if we were to move all elected positions to shorter, or limited terms, the effect would most likely produce similar results as a business that has a high turnover rate of employees. What I believe to be much more dangerous to our constitutional republic, is that corporations can employ full-time lobbying groups that spend billions of dollars to influence favorable laws that ultimately game the system for their economic gain.

This is not partisan. Both parties are littered with long-term elected bureaucrats who enriched themselves at the taxpayers' expense. That is why I believe we must reform campaign law, putting a stop to donations from corporate lobbyists to individual politicians. We must close K Street so we can apply rules to Wall Street that will ensure Main Street that our representative government works for us, not those with the most money.

One way to eliminate lobbying would be to pay our elected government higher salaries. No, I have not lost my mind! The idea is to attract career management people with better character and to reduce the need for elected government to go elsewhere in order to earn additional income. Many of these people are highly educated, so paying them more while demanding they focus their attention on us rather than themselves would be a far better way to achieve effective government. My view is pay now for effective leadership committed to us or pay later for ineffective leadership that gets paid off by them.

If the idea of paying higher salaries to elected officials didn't get you, this one might, but remember, my goal is to produce career-driven, long-term management by competent people who are no longer influenced by Wall Street financial power. Here are a few measures to get this done:

• Use US tax dollars to pay for and mandate television networks to provide equal airtime to all candidates running for elected positions. This would give candidates with fewer resources equal time to make their case before the American people.

• Donations to individual candidates would not be allowed. All donations would be made to the candidates' representative party and would then be divided equally among the candidates.

• All corporate donations would be disallowed. This would ensure corporations with unlimited financial resources cannot use their wealth as a power to influence. Donations would be capped at 10 percent of a person's annual income (personal income, not corporate). The maximum annual income level to make a 10 percent donation would be capped at $200,000, capping the largest donation to any one candidate at $20,000. Doing it this way would stop those who make the most money to have more power than you do at the ballot box.

Some of you might think morality, law and order, education, or climate change is what's needed to maintain civility. All those things matter, but what is also critically important is an economy that produces jobs, as well as a stable monetary system. The truth is that if the majority of our citizens are not doing something productive or our monetary system becomes fragile and faces collapse, the results could produce chaos in our streets.

The problem is that as our population increases and technology advances, the task of creating jobs for the masses will be much harder. If we analyze how jobs are created, we see many jobs are built around large industries that became successful. The problem is some of the jobs in these industries can be destructive. This is where the balance of too much or too little regulation matters. The greater the regulation, the greater the chance of creating courtroom cases that must be settled by judges and lawyers. Additionally, the greater the regulation, the more need for businesses to buy insurance as protection should they make a mistake.

I have nothing against lawyers, insurance companies, or any other industry that provides a measure of fairness and security. Having said that, allowing them to strangle the life out of productive businesses is when we need to reanalyze their value. There is no question we are a better country because we have worker's compensation laws and malpractice lawsuits that provide patients the assurance that doctors are not doing things they shouldn't. What becomes a problem and a cost to businesses, and ultimately a cost to the consumer, is when claims are settled not due to what is right or wrong but what is most economical.

I will provide an example. My brother and I own a construction company in the city of Chicago, and because we do a lot of work downtown, we are signatory to several different construction unions. What this means is that although our employees do work for us, the union is there to make sure employers treat employees fairly. The union and business owners are in essence partners through what is called a collective bargaining agreement. The agreement establishes an hourly wage, daily work hours, the rules of regular pay versus overtime, etcetera.

One day, our office received a call from one of our employees stating he did not receive his check in the mail. Our office manager apologized and proceeded to find out what happened. Her research found that the check was received and that it had already cleared our bank. The manager called the employee back and said, "You must have made an error because we see through our bank statement the check has been cashed."

The employee denied he had received the check and called his union representative, saying we did not pay him for the work he had done. The representative called our office and said, "You have twenty-four hours to issue a new check. Otherwise, he will take the matter to arbitration."

At this point, I decided to call the representative to discuss this rationally because it didn't make sense for us to write another check when we knew the original one had already been cashed. I called and politely suggested he let our employee know we had provided proof that the check had been cashed.

The representative responded, "I don't care if you have a cashed check or not. The member says he didn't get it, so write another one!" He then proceeded to tell me that if I didn't write another check immediately, I would be paying for a lawyer as well as the cost of arbitration and that it would be far less expensive if I just wrote another check.

After ending that conversation with a few pleasantries, I decided to go after whoever had cashed the check to see if they had a photo of the person's license or something that we could use to prove this employee did in fact cash it. We learned the check was cashed at a local currency exchange place, so I called the owner of the exchange to see if they could offer some assistance. I politely asked him if he had a record showing who had cashed the check. He quickly replied that no, he did not. I explained in further detail what had happened, hoping for a better response, and he replied, "It's not my problem, pal."

I will admit that by this time, I began to get a little heated. I said, "You have responsibility in this matter because he cashed a check without identification," and I added that I would be contacting my lawyer regarding his negligence. He replied, "Go ahead, pal. I have no legal obligation to check a person's identification, so good luck."

This happened back in the 1990s, and by now, hopefully, laws have changed, but the bottom line of this story was I had to make a decision: Do we write another $1,000 check to an employee who without question had cashed the first one, or do we go through arbitration with the union? If arbitration favored the employee, the potential cost would be $10,000, and if we won, the best-case scenario would be a cost of approximately $5,000. So, just like every other company out there, we chose the least costly scenario to settle this issue. We sacrificed establishing a principled outcome because it was $4,000 less expensive if we won, and $9,000 less should we lose.

This process of settling unfair or false claims happens with automobile accidents, doctors, restaurants, construction companies, manufacturing companies; the list goes on and on. The system of regulation employs millions of lawyers, judges, and insurance companies. There are many cases like mine in which people elect to settle whether it's right or wrong because it is more cost effective to do so. What transpires is not only a loss to the business; eventually, these legal costs get passed on to you, the consumer, in the prices you pay for goods and services.

It is critical to understand that it is always the people at the end of the line who pay for these added costs. If we raise taxes on the wealthy because they own the stores where you buy your goods and services, they simply pass the tax on to you through higher prices. If an insurance company pays a claim of any kind on behalf of their client, they immediately raise the price of the client's insurance or drop them when their annual policy ends. We must understand that when the cost of insurance rises, the business or service that receives the increased insurance premium simply passes the increase on to you through the price of their product or service. The moral of this story is that you pay for it.

This adds to the list of reasons we must fight against monopolization or consolidation of our industries. If our legal and insurance systems remain as is and the competition within our industries continues to shrink, we are essentially assuring ourselves that we will pay more for what we buy. If the people selling us products or services are 100 percent certain we cannot buy what they have to offer anywhere else, they become confident and even reckless regarding the selling price of their product or service. In the world of economics, this is referred to as supply and demand. If sellers know they have a product that has more buyers than the available supply, they raise their prices. If corporations are able to dominate and remove all competition, becoming the only supplier available, the result is higher prices and poorer service.

The solutions to these problems are not easy. Our way of dealing with these issues has been to call on the government for help. The government, in turn, begins increasing regulations on price control, employee safety, racial discrimination, etcetera. Government begins to create agencies that hire people to intervene regarding how businesses operate on a daily basis. They create charts and quotas that businesses must adhere to or face penalties. The problem is this increased regulation and growth of government are also costs that you pay for.

If we visualize the processes of taxing, regulating, etcetera, and view them in a pyramid, we see any effort to change or penalize those at the top of the economical food chain (corporate monopolies, commercial banking) ultimately works its way down to us. If we logically analyze this, the solutions become clear. We should reduce the size of regulatory government and incentivize competition by engaging innovation within small business.

These changes could help, but we must restructure our legal system to end frivolous lawsuits that allow lawyers to ravage our businesses. This type of lawyering has the same effect as a shoplifter: they both add enormous cost to the products we buy. The law should punish those who attempt to use the legal system to extract money from businesses for frivolous claims. Even though we might blame the lawyers for being unethical, if our legal system allows this type of lawyering without consequences, then it is the system at fault, not the lawyer. To change the system, we must first recognize and agree there's a problem that needs fixing. In the case of reducing frivolous lawsuits, this is a daunting task because there are layers upon layers of protections built into the legal system. The nucleus of the problem is the no-fault claim process that lets lawyers represent clients in cases they know they do not have a chance of winning.

As in my situation, because businesses are subject to just about any kind of a claim, they've been forced to provide layers of protection, and as part of that protection, they buy insurance that deals with frivolous lawsuits. When businesses buy insurance, if a claim is filed, instead of the business dealing with the claim personally, it gets redirected to the business's insurer. The problem is, like my writing a second paycheck to the union employee because it was the least costly way to solve the problem, the insurer handles the frivolous claims in the same manner and also tries to settle the case with as little legal cost as possible.

Let's break down the process that transpires when a claim is filed. In most cases, a lawyer files the initial claim or charge against a business for their clients in the appropriate court of law small claims, local, state, or federal). The court schedules a date to hear the complaint and notifies the attorney representing the business. The business then notifies their insurance company that a claim has been made. The insurance company analyzes the claim to see if the business owner has coverage for that particular claim, and if it does, the process of representation begins.

If the claim is viewed as legitimate or something that could be expensive to defend at trial, discussions ensue regarding settling the case before trial begins. Yet this settlement of the case when, many times, the business did nothing wrong is the problem. You see, the insurance company doesn't view the claim as being fought over what is right or wrong. Even if they know a claim is most likely bogus, they analyze what the potential cost would be to defend against it and then offer a settlement to make it go away. Once the claim is settled, the cost is recorded, then added to the business's insurance premium the following year. Once that happens, the cost is then added to the price you pay as a consumer.

The sad part is most people believe it is the insurance company that pays for the claim, so the attitude that develops is "What difference does it make? It's not the business that pays. It's their insurance." The truth is, no matter how much the business owner paid to be insured, the business will pay the cost of settling a claim when they renew their policy. Of course, the business can shop insurance providers to see if another carrier will offer the same coverage at less cost, but because the settlement of the claim is public knowledge to all insurance companies, any company providing a quote will include the cost of the settled claim.

Throughout our discussion, I've tried to provide examples of these things that whittle away at prosperity. It is these unproductive systems that attach themselves to something productive that ultimately destroy it. The balance between protecting someone from a negligent business and allowing people to be compensated for claims they shouldn't have filed is one that must be addressed. Our politicians should be working on fixing issues like these instead of spending countless hours stumping for campaign donations.

This next subject is somewhat controversial, but it needs to be discussed. I come from a day and age when people receiving any kind of government assistance were considered weak, and others thought they should be ashamed of themselves. This messaging came through our educational curriculum, our parents, and the overall psyche of the general public at the time. There is a vast difference between the attitude and expectations of the country I grew up in and the one we live in today. I do tread the topic of entitlements or governmental assistance carefully when trying to compare the past with the problems we face today. Having said that, as we continue, please try to remove political prejudice or preprogrammed talking points when considering what I say.

My concern is that politics, along with social media, have devoured our ability to be open minded and are attempting to guide our citizenry through subliminal messaging to reach predetermined conclusions that fit into their ideological agendas. I believe many readers might unknowingly view my thoughts from the perspective of their ideology, meaning they might analyze what I've said and then rationalize it against the talking points they adhere to in their political ideology, rather than considering them with an open mind.

This psychological process is what transpires when people go to work every day and leave the management of their country to those they are supposed to trust. We count on our newspapers, journalists, and television networks to provide truthful information in short segments to keep us informed while we go to work and raise our families. Information outlets always have been subject to ideological persuasion, but their impact on the citizens was much less in the past. In the 1970s, our television channels were 2, 5, 7, and 9, and later on, channel 32 was added. There were essentially two major newspapers in Chicago, the *Chicago Tribune* and the *Chicago Sun-Times*. They were partisan, the *Tribune* politically leaning right and the *Sun-Times* leaning left, but the truth is there were only a handful of people who actually had time to read the newspaper, so there really wasn't a daily confrontation of people battling one another over political ideology. There were plenty of battles such as the growth and power of unions, protesting the Vietnam War, civil rights, women's rights, etcetera. Yet because the coverage only came from our newspapers and local television, much of the country continued their lives somewhat carefree or even oblivious to what was happening around the world.

Are we better or worse off as a country with the plethora of information we receive? There's no question we are better informed. Our lives have become easier in many ways because of things like MapQuest, Amazon shopping, or search engines that entertain us or provide answers to our questions. The question is whether this inundation of information delivered through technological devices is so great that it will remove our ability to think independently. There are plenty of examples around the country proving the answer to my question is most likely yes. We see them through the plethora of debates being waged about a slew of issues. What should concern all of us is the trend of our twenty-four-hour news coverage that seems to be focusing more on the outrageous, thus delivering a message of chaos.

Why do I mention the impact of this technological onslaught on our solving problems? Because I want you to reflect on whether your thoughts are really your own or if you have become a puppet driven by network propaganda. Take a moment and ask yourself, "Do I reach conclusions based on logic and a balanced source of information, or do I formulate my conclusions to fit within preprogrammed guidelines of an ideological viewpoint that fits the standards of a political agenda?"

You see, if we become a nation of people guided by partisan politics designed to find disagreement and separation, then our ability to analyze issues using logic rather than political agendas will take away our ability to change the things we don't like.

The question now is how do we reverse the propaganda machine that has divided Americans into segments of people at war with one another? Could I be completely wrong that the divisive propaganda we are fed is not intentional but accidental? Yes, I could be wrong, but the results remain the same: a divided citizenry that cannot stop a runaway governmental freight train comprising bad policy that is paid for by the creation of more debt. So as we continue, please remove the shackles of political talking points and open your mind to solutions.

Regarding the discussion of welfare, food stamps, disability, and all other state or federal programs that deliver aid to people in need, the first stigma that should be cleared up is this idea that African Americans are the people collecting the greatest amount from welfare programs. I will not post percentages of who gets what because that approach only adds to the divisional rhetoric pertaining to the subject. My problem is not that people get help when they're in need. My problem is the bureaucracy that is supposed to manage and lift these communities out of hopeless environments actually creates conditions for them to stay there.

You might think my next suggestion contradicts my thesis of smaller government, but stay with me because the concept is not more government, but finding better qualified management to be involved in governing. If we analyze what plagues our disadvantaged communities, the first things that enter my mind are illegal drugs, poor education, broken-down neighborhoods, and single mothers left to raise their children. None of these should be a surprise or controversial to discuss openly. Additionally, we need not blame one political party more than the other because they have equally created poor policy and mismanaged taxpayer dollars intended to help those in need.

We did not fail to fix impoverished communities because we didn't spend enough tax dollars. We failed because of poor strategy and a lack of qualified management to properly maintain the changes once they'd been implemented. Anything that does not have a result-driven plan that is managed daily to ensure success always will fail. The most successful people in the world did not become successful because they had a good idea. They became successful because they created well-managed, cost-effective systems to deliver their ideas on a massive scale.

Good management starts by identifying the problems, then creates solutions that begin to reduce and ultimately fix the problems entirely. We've already identified jobs, drugs, education, and single parenting as the nucleus of the destruction, so let's start there. My thought is to create community-building trade centers that are specific to individual impoverished communities. I will explain later how we will pay for this. I don't think Wall Street is going to like it.

Each state would receive federal dollars based on their proportion of impoverished areas. The process would begin by erecting an educational trade center that would be used as the main hub for new construction in the communities in need of rebuilding. Qualified building tradespeople would be hired to teach and train workers living in the community. My definition of "qualified teachers" would be people who have ground-up construction skills and knowledge of each trade, as well as the management skills required to teach students what it takes to run or work on a construction project. The education would focus on construction knowledge, but it also would prepare the students regarding the expectations of an employer.

Building a well-managed, disciplined structure from the start will be critically important to the program's success. For a student to be eligible to attend the educational trade class, they must be drug free and able to attend the program on a full-time basis. Because marijuana is legal in many states, drug testing would be applicable to illicit drugs such as heroin and cocaine. Anyone thought to be high on legal or illegal drugs at work would be excluded from the program.

Once a management staff was hired, the first construction project for the students would be to build childcare centers for single moms. The second construction project would be drug rehabilitation centers for the community. Once the rehabilitation centers were built, like the management/training done at the construction trade center, a qualified person from the community would begin hiring and educating staff to work there. Using people from the community will deliver hope, team building, and an overall sensation of caring for one another.

Using more tax dollars to hire more police and more teachers without an effective management plan can no longer be a strategy. When addressing these communities, we must understand they are in despair and feel there is no path for them to succeed, so without effective management that provides consistent procedures that measure progress every week, nothing will change. We cannot expect something to be fixed by simply throwing money at it. Success comes from the will to succeed and the discipline of remaining consistent on a daily basis.

As part of the management strategy for a community to continue receiving federal dollars, the local governments would be required to do bimonthly neighborhood inspections, making sure their streets are clean, store windows are washed, and the trade/rehab centers are being run properly. Additionally, there would be specific funding for kids fourteen and older to earn money for community cleanup jobs. I understand that there are child labor laws, but we must do all we can to inspire a sense of pride and love for community within the children who grow up in these neighborhoods. Allowing them to make a couple of bucks while keeping the sidewalks and local parks clean will give them a sense of pride.

Trust me, I know there are people reading this who are thinking, "Have you lost your mind? How the hell can we pay for this? Do you realize you are creating more government oversight and more regulation?" I absolutely do, but my feeling is with the amount of money we are already haphazardly spending, I am certain if we formulate effective management teams that are accountable and purpose driven, the money we already spend on waste, as well as fraud, will more than pay for the changes I propose.

We must remember these communities are our fellow citizens, and we want them to be a part of our nation's success. The more we can provide a sense of hope and inclusion, the less chance we have to suffer tragedies. Like it or not, agree or disagree, our nation is in a fight for its life. What makes us great is the idea that everyone in America has a chance to achieve great things. If we allow a sizable percentage of our population to live in despair, we are essentially suppressing their free spirit and input to create. We must promote, persuade, push, and manage all segments of people throughout America to help them achieve.

Conclusion

As the chapter title implies, we can no longer accept the status quo to solve our nation's problems. Our leaders really have reached the end of the road, and the results of decades of their corruption, collusion, deception, and inability to formulate an effective strategy are now upon us.

I stated clearly, if you don't like my ideas, then present your own. Our leadership is littered with armchair quarterbacks that simply wait for someone bold to present an idea, and if it tests well in the polls, they support it; if it doesn't, they ridicule the idea. We cannot expect that a governmental system influenced or coerced by the power of money will ever work out well for the common citizen.

Now more than ever we need the bold to step forward and challenge those who attempt to silence their input. We see that Washington, DC, is paralyzed with dysfunction and an inability to get things done. Yet they will fight to the death to thwart any attempt to change in the system that allows them to thrive. It is our duty to preserve for our children what was preserved for us, so we must challenge those who have become roadblocks to a brighter future for generations to come.

Social Security: What Defines Fairness?

What defines fairness is essentially the argument that divides our political parties and, ultimately the American people. The questions are who should decide what is fair, and are those who presently do deceiving those who seek it? This is not a trick question or a judgment; it is simply the ongoing political debate that is happening in Washington, DC, to determine the fate of America's citizens. The truth is the more we turn to government to be the judge of what is fair, the more we must demand that the governmental structure be free from corruption and not influenced by powerful groups through lobbying.

Although there are a multitude of governmental programs that should be addressed in reference to fairness, I chose Social Security as our topic because it has many different elements that put fairness into question regarding how and when people are eligible to receive benefits, as well as deciding whether it is appropriate for Congress to have access to the surplus dollars held in the Social Security Trust Funds. We will discuss Congress's authority to use the surplus from our tax-funded entitlements in greater detail throughout the remainder of this book.

The Beginning

To provide a brief history, on August 14, 1935, the Franklin Roosevelt administration signed into law the Social Security Act, which at the time was a 1 percent tax on citizens' annual earnings. To avoid a lengthy explanation of Social Security's taxing history and the promises politicians have made throughout its existence, I will advance the conversation to 1983, when the Reagan administration made significant changes that drastically altered the use and abuse of the program under the Social Security Amendments of 1983.

Some younger readers may not realize that during that year, the Reagan administration revamped a faltering Social Security program by raising the age of eligibility for early- and full-retirement recipients. Although raising the age of eligibility from sixty-five to sixty-seven doesn't seem like much, we must remember, there are ten thousand people retiring per day for the next twenty years, so the change directly affected 7.3 million people in that two-year period.

The Reagan administration also imposed a graduated tax increase on a person's income. When Reagan was elected in 1980, the original 1 percent tax was raised to 5 percent. This was done by raising the cutoff point of one's annual salary, meaning the amount of money made in a given year before the tax would stop being deducted. The cap was placed at $27,000, so a person now had to pay a 5 percent tax on up to $27,000 of their annual income. Once their yearly wages exceeded that threshold, the tax was no longer deducted.

After the Social Security Amendments of 1983, the tax increased from 5 percent to 6.2 percent. The reform bill also was designed as a graduated tax on a person's *total* annual income. After the change the tax would no longer stop being deducted once a person's yearly wages reached $27,000—the government could continue taxing that income up to a higher cap level each year.

In addition to the graduated tax on income, the government creation of Medicare/Medicaid added another 1.45 percent tax on annual income, but this did not have an income cap. In other words, it did not matter how much you made annually: you would pay the 1.45 percent Medicare/Medicaid tax.

Our first question regarding fairness should pertain to whether or not it was fair that Congress took the $2.9 trillion surplus from the Social Security Trust Funds to pay for budget overruns, war, and Wall Street bailouts. The next question is should we continue letting them use treasury bonds as a replacement for our surpluses without our permission? Congress has granted themselves the authority to use annual surpluses from our entitlements to pay for other government expenditures. To justify this, when Congress uses the cash from our entitlements, they issue treasury bonds to our account (a government

IOU) and then pay marginal interest. The politician's pitch is that treasury bonds are the safest investment in the world and should be considered the same as cash, so we shouldn't worry about their using our money because they are paying us interest.

To ensure that you understand the significance of this, let's examine what this meant to Social Security. After the 1983 reform, what transpired was a massive overflow of tax dollars in comparison with what was actually being paid to Social Security recipients. In other words, Reagan's reform was designed to build large surpluses to cover the massive increase in retirees once the boomers hit the golden age of sixty-seven. It was a "save for a rainy day" approach to a problem they knew was heading our way. The problem is Congress saw this extra money in our entitlement accounts as something they should be able to spend. That's how the "kick the can down the road" style of government began. In their eyes, surpluses are for them to use, no questions asked, and as long as you, the US taxpayer, continue to believe the government IOU sitting in your account is as good as cash, everything will be all right!

Understanding the power Congress has granted themselves regarding discretionary usage of commingled surpluses is critically important, especially if they are able to get the Affordable Care Act to become another taxpayer funded entitlement. We will discuss the significance of that controversial legislation later, but for now, the political debate in Washington, DC, regarding who pays their fair share in taxes should also include the question of whether we continue allowing Congress to use entitlement surpluses on discretionary spending. We must never lose sight of the fact that it's not the federal government that pays the benefits we receive from programs such as Social Security and Medicare/Medicaid. The US Treasury Department is merely the bookkeeper and redistribution arm of the tax dollars they collect from us.

Politicians Want Tax-Funded Entitlements

As we continue the conversation on fairness, the significance of Congress's authority and their ability to use commingled trust dollars also becomes part of the debate on whether or not the United States should become a socialist country. Before you consider this option, let's first examine how government has performed thus far. You see, the discussion regarding capitalism versus socialism is really a false argument. In many ways, we are already a socialist country. What's not being explained is that the vast number of entitlements or subsidies we receive have been funded by the success of capitalism. The breakdown our nation faces is not due to the ineffectiveness of capitalism. It stems from ineffective government not managing our money properly and allowing Wall Street greed, corruption, and monopolization of our industries. Why? Because they are being rewarded handsomely for doing so.

We are witnessing a political war that will ultimately decide our fate as a nation. The politicians depict this battle as one between the haves and the have-nots. The truth of what's transpiring is a quest for power between two political ideologies. Yet both these ideologies seek to grow the size and power of a centralized government that will become the arbitrator of tax redistribution. But they have been the arbitrators all along, and they sold our souls to their wealthy political donors long ago. They pursue tax-funded programs because it gives them the ability to disguise the use of our tax dollars.

That's why converting the funding structure of the Affordable Care Act to be paid for similar to how we pay for Medicaid or Social Security is important. What that achieves is it becomes a tax on all Americans, and the government will determine the amount. In other words, once they can establish an entitlement to be a single-payer system, this gives the government complete control to decide the amount needed to fund the program. It also gives them an enormous amount of power to determine what kind of care or benefits an individual will receive. Yet what is most significant is these programs provide Congress with more tax-funded entitlements that have the potential of producing surplus dollars that can be used for discretionary spending.

I hope those in favor of socialism are starting to get this. Every program, whether it's Social Security, health care, or the recent promise of free education, is nothing more than an attempt to gain another tax upon our citizenry that can—and most likely will—be used to produce a surplus for discretionary use. This is not by accident. History provides that many countries that were once prosperous have been destroyed by governments that overwhelmed their citizenship with the burden of debt that grew from the expansion of single-payer entitlements. This is presently happening to Greece and Venezuela, and their fate will ultimately be the same as Cuba's.

Are Social Security Benefits Fair?

Moving on, I would like to address the fairness of benefits and the age of eligibility. Statistics show most people in lower-income areas begin working at a much younger age than those coming from the more affluent ones. There are many kids coming from poorer communities that, at best, hope to finish high school, and many are forced to begin work as early as the age of sixteen. Comparing this with people from more affluent communities, although they might have a part-time job flipping burgers while attending college, the majority of these kids really don't start working until after they graduate from college.

The second thing that differentiates the poorer kids from the more affluent ones is the type of jobs they do for their careers. In general, they have limited options and make far less money. Additionally, the jobs available to them most likely will be more hazardous than the ones available to those who get a college degree. The poorer person who starts working at a younger age generally works in an environment that is more hazardous to their health and is less likely to live as long as the college graduates in the higher-paying jobs that, in most cases, are less hazardous.

My intention in presenting this information is not to cause more division or to further promote the idea that some people are brought up in privileged environments while others are not. My intention is to analyze the fairness of a program that pays benefits to a person based on the reality of that person's working career and the life expectancy of those who receive benefits, as well as to review and possibly reward the people who do low-paying jobs that provide our society with many benefits, such as police, first responders, and teachers.

We as citizens should be thankful for those who teach our children or put their lives at stake to keep our communities safe. In many cases, most of these jobs pay little, yet they require highly effective people to perform them properly. It is my feeling that we should reward their sacrifice and show our gratitude by recognizing them through the Social Security program. I suggest this not just because it's the right thing to do. I believe my proposed change will provide incentives for those who are considering this type of career.

So as a way to create a balance for those who began working at an earlier age, as well as for those in careers that bring value to our communities yet pay little in annual salary, I suggest we lower their Social Security eligibility age to sixty-three, while possibly raising the eligibility age to those who earned significantly more income to sixty-eight. This is a simple measure that does not require government expansion, and it would not stifle our economy because it doesn't require ridiculous oversight.

It shouldn't be hard for us to find agreement that our citizenry comprises people who are wealthy and people who are poor. The change I propose would not penalize those who are prosperous, and it would help inspire a sense of fairness in our poorer communities that we recognize them in a significant way for the work they do to help maintain a civil society. By adjusting the age of Social Security to honestly reflect the life of the recipient would help inspire a better attitude, assuring our citizens that our governing policies are not designed to benefit one person by shortchanging another. This is not an idea that should be contested by left or right political talking points It is a change that delivers fairness, and it sends a message that all citizens are recognized for their contributions.

Conclusion

Many of our problems can be easily solved without spending enormous numbers of tax dollars on government think tanks that require months or even years to create solutions. Most of the answers to our problems are simple. The prosperity we've achieved as a nation has produced an ineffective government that attempts to justify their salaries by overcomplicating our issues. I won't apologize for that statement because each of us knows in our hearts it's true. These folks have made a mess of the only country we have, and we've reached a point at which serious changes must be made. My greatest concern is whether or not our collective citizenry has lost the ability to see the forest for the trees. We must understand the solutions to our problems will not be fixed by the people who created them. It is time for us to join hands and change the stagnation that has become standard operating procedure in Washington, DC.

Expose the Root

The title of this book is without question provocative. To suggest the solution to our nation's problems must be a political revolution is a bold statement, yet it is my belief that there is no other option to save our nation. If we don't change the power residing in Washington, DC, and put an end to their partnership built on deception with Wall Street and private-equity lobbyists, then our future as an independent citizenry will have reached its end. We must decide: Will we continue to allow our nation's leaders to divide us into political tribes at war with one another, or will we rise as our founders did and change the rules of an imperial government?

I would like to refresh what it is I'm trying to do. You see, like you, I am just an ordinary citizen who is fed up with the nonsense and corruption that has infested the leadership of not just our nation but others around the world. The phrase "For the love of money is the root of all evil" is often misquoted as "Money is the root of all evil." The way I see it, that misquote is a scapegoat for those who do evil things for money. Money is simply a method of payment for a service or product. The problem is that what people are willing to do for it ultimately gives it a bad name.

From the beginning, I've attempted to expose the elements within our society that have become greedy and corrupted and have ultimately colluded in order to gain supreme power over our citizenry. The barons of Wall Street and private-equity firms seek to control the supply of goods and services, as well as the payment of interest from the indebted, while our government seeks power over its citizenry and the merchants in their quest to create endless taxation paid to the Treasury Department.

To be sure, Wall Street and the federal government are two extremely powerful forces, and the fact that they have joined hands to gain control of our citizenry is extremely dangerous to the future of our independence. Yet throughout this book, I've presented two recurring thoughts that provide proof that it is our citizenry who hold the royal flush in this house of cards.

I hope by now you understand the power we have. But for those who don't, our citizenry comprises 326 million people. If we were to assemble those guilty of bad behavior within our federal government and throughout Wall Street, at best they might total 5 million. Even if we included the others working directly under their leadership, there couldn't be more than 8 million people. If we could find a way to unite as a citizenry to stop corruption, we would outnumber them 318 million to 8 million.

The second power we hold is that the integrity of our fiat monetary system is derived from the power of our tax dollars. We must never forget that *we* are the gold that backs our monetary system, so the true power that makes our nation great is not Wall Street or an imperial government. It is and always has been the American people.

Time for Real Change

What I propose will most likely be ridiculed as delusional, with the experts saying I have no idea how the system works. I say to those attackers, "Prove me wrong and explain in full detail how and why you believe that what I'm proposing won't work." You see, the difference with my approach is that, instead of waiting for the government and the wealthy to come to us in search of another bailout or allowing them to create another tactic to further devalue our assets, I say we become proactive to ensure that it is they, not us, who pay for the next special assessment.

Before I suggest these changes, it is important to understand how the system that we are proposing to change works. We must start with a better understanding of the fiat monetary system and fractional lending. What we've learned thus far is that the validity of the dollar being accepted as the international currency is mainly due to it being backed by the strength of the America taxpayer. Additionally, the world's top investors here and abroad understand that our nation's laws give Congress the authority to increase taxes should there be a need for a monetary bailout to protect the dollar and our economy from collapse. There is no better example than the 2008 mortgage crisis to highlight how America's government will use tax dollars to pay for the sins of corruption in order to ensure the illusion of integrity pertaining to the dollar so it can remain the leading choice as the international currency.

The statement that the American people are the power and strength of the fiat monetary system cannot be argued or discredited as conspiracy. Because the entire financial structure rests on the backs of the taxpayers, it is critically important for you to understand how the fiat monetary system, as well as the fractional banking system, works.

Let's review 90/10 fractional loaning. Simply stated, it means for every $1,000 deposited by a bank's client, regulations require the bank to hold $100 (a 10 percent reserve), while allowing the bank to loan the remaining $900 (90 percent) to other clients.

After analyzing how the banks use fractional loaning to generate profit, one begins to recognize that 90/10 fractional banking is essentially a pyramid that can only be sustained by the perpetuation of new loans. It does not take a math scholar to understand that should a lack of confidence cause the majority of a bank's clients to withdraw their money, the 10 percent reserve would not go very far in returning their funds before the bank became insolvent.

The banks need a constant circulation of deposits in order to generate new loans, thus generating more interest income. The interest a bank collects from these loans is what generates their profit, as well as reimbursing a small portion of their clients should they want to withdraw their money.

The difference between fractional lending and the Federal Reserve's management of our fiat monetary system is the bank is using money already in circulation to create new loans while the Federal Reserve uses the fiat monetary system to create new currency to pay for deficit spending by the government. Our citizenry pays the interest on the debts to both entities, either through a personal loan with the bank or our tax dollars used to pay interest on rising debt. The interest a bank receives for their lending is more individualized on a per-client bases, while the Federal Reserve's creation of money becomes a loan to the US government, thus increasing our national debt, which in turn becomes a higher interest payment for us, paid for by our taxes.

This entire process has been complicated with untruths because the Washington, DC, politicians do not want us to understand the truth. I mentioned this earlier, but the big lie is that the Federal Reserve is not under the control of the government. The government and Wall Street created the Federal Reserve in 1913 to be a scapegoat to separate our nation's political leaders from the consequences of their bad policies. Additionally, the Federal Reserve allows politicians to distance themselves from responsibility for bailing out Wall Street. Yet what is not discussed, and what you will learn from this chapter, is that the Federal Reserve allows the government to make a profit on our citizenry by increasing our payment of interest on rising national debt.

The fact is the Federal Reserve is bound to follow the laws that Congress created. It was Congress that created the law that limits them from examining the Federal Reserve's balance sheet. This restriction was created to perpetuate the illusion that they are independent from political influence, but if the government wanted to see the Federal Reserve's balance sheet, all they would have to do is change the law. The reality is the Federal Reserve's job of independently policing the banking industry is based on the laws that the government set. If they want to do something outside the scope of their authority, they require permission from the government to do so.

The deal cut between the banking elite and the government was the creation of an entity that would provide cover for both to profit off the backs of the working class. The Federal Reserve is not a secret cabal. It is simply a bunch of economic geeks who sit around analyzing incoming and outgoing digits to determine how our economy is performing. The cabal that really does exist is the US government and commercial banking, which both use the Federal Reserve as cover for their deception.

Exposing How the Government Uses the Federal Reserve

Although the Federal Reserve's official job is to analyze economic data to determine how our economy is functioning, it seems their real job is to create fake money in order to increase our national debt, which in turn increases the amount of interest we pay annually.

The following information may provide answers as to why. In 2018, the (Congressional Budget Office posted on their public website) that the Treasury Department took in $3.3 trillion in tax revenue and spent $4.1 trillion, leaving an $800 billion deficit. It is not Wall Street's or the Federal Reserve's fault that the government overspent what they received in taxes. Yet to prove it is the government that controls the Federal Reserve and not the other way around, let's review how the government pays for their budget overruns.

The Treasury Department is responsible for paying our nation's bill. Once they realize they do not have enough money to pay expenditures, their job is to notify Congress that they will need additional revenue above and beyond what they are projected to receive. Congress directs the Treasury Department to sell treasury bonds to make up the shortfall. The bonds are sold to the commercial banks, which then send the treasury bonds to the Federal Reserve. The Federal Reserve directs the Treasury Department to print new money and deposit it into the commercial banks. Once the banks receive the cash deposit, they then pay the government's bills with this newly printed money.

So how did I reach the conclusion that the US government runs the Federal Reserve? Because the Federal Reserve does not have the option to deny the government the money it needs to pay for its budget overruns! It doesn't matter whether their chairman thinks it's a bad idea to keep printing money for budget overruns, the Federal Reserve must do as they are told and create more money to supplement the budget shortfall.

More Government Deception

I believe a better way to think of the Federal Reserve is as a pass-through entity used by the government, the Treasury Department, and commercial banking. The reason I say this has to do with the perception that the Federal Reserve in itself is not supposed to be profitable. By Congress's design, the Federal Reserve is a zero-loss/zero-gain institution, so once they pay the cost of their operation (employees, rent, supplies, etcetera), any excess income is then deposited in the US Treasury.

Since the Federal Reserve is really just a pass-through agency, what I have to say next calls into question what I believe to be another deception by the government. It was widely reported that after the Great Recession, the Federal Reserve (through a process referred to as quantitative easing) purchased $4 trillion in treasury bonds and mortgage-backed securities. Let's not forget that their accounting ledger is kept at a zero balance, so the $4 trillion asset purchase was done by the Federal Reserve creating fake money, and printing the fake money added debt, thus increasing interest payments for you, the taxpayer.

The Federal Reserve is not supposed to make money beyond expenses, and when they do profit, they deposit that money into the Treasury Department. What this means is the increased interest you are paying on the Fed Reserve's $4 trillion holdings actually becomes interest income to the Federal Reserve! The question I have, has our government found another way to bilk its citizenry by using the Federal Reserve to create money out of thin air and then getting paid interest on it?

The following was posted on the website of the Federal Reserve Bank of San Francisco:

> The Federal Reserve's income is derived primarily from the interest on US Government securities that it has acquired through open market operations. Other sources of income are the interest on foreign currency investments held by the System; fees received for services provided to depository institutions, such as check clearing, funds transfers, and automated clearinghouse operations; and interest on loans to depository institutions (the rate on which is the so-called discount rate). After paying its expenses, the Federal Reserve turns the rest of its earnings over to the U.S. Treasury. (For more information on how the Fed works "the balance, and Investopedia" is a good resource for information).

A bank makes its profit through the collection of interest from clients who borrow money from the bank. The Federal Reserve makes its profit by receiving interest on the treasury bonds they buy on the open market, as well as the revenue they collect from the banking industry for their administration fees.

Here's what happened during and after the crisis: Wall Street received bailouts from the government paid for by our taxes. Then Wall Street used the bailout money to buy our foreclosed homes at a discounted price, as well as buying back stock options in order to inflate the value of their businesses. What our government did is even worse because they helped Wall Street and then perpetrated their own theft. Here's what transpired.

In 2006, the Federal Reserve held $600 billion worth of treasury bonds. In 2019, they held $2.5 trillion in treasury bonds and an additional $1.5 trillion in mortgage-backed securities: $4 trillion in total. Prior to the 2008 mortgage crisis, the Federal Reserve on average annually contributed $23 billion to the Treasury Department. Since the crisis, they have contributed on average $90 billion annually. Information can be found on the (Board of Governors of the Federal Reserve System's website...recently updated on January 10th 2019).

In earlier chapters, I proved that Wall Street and private equity, with the help of our federal government, clearly capitalized on the 2008 mortgage crisis. What this chapter proves is that so have Washington, DC, and the Treasury Department!

Understanding this process begins to bring clarity as to why the government, year after year, has budget deficits and continues to raise our national debt. The question that enters my mind—as it should yours—is has the US government figured out a way to create a hidden tax by increasing the Federal Reserve's balance sheet by buying treasury bonds with fake money, thus increasing their collection of interest from the taxpayer?

Let's consider what happened one more time. The Federal Reserve instructed the Treasury Department to print $4 trillion of new cash. The Treasury Department printed the cash and gave it to the Federal Reserve. The Federal Reserve used the cash to purchase $2.5 trillion in treasury bonds and $1.5 trillion in mortgage-backed securities. The Treasury Department now was obligated to pay interest to the Federal Reserve for these bonds and securities. The Treasury Department used the tax dollars they received from the American people to pay interest on the treasury bonds and mortgage-backed securities. The Federal Reserve used those interest payments to pay their expenses and then sent the $90 billion in profit back to the Treasury Department.

Our Money Is Not Their Money

Earlier, I asked that you make a mental note for later discussion regarding the surplus dollars. I now turn your attention back to the authority Congress has to use the surplus held in our taxpayer entitlements and the government's ongoing need for money beyond what they collect in taxes to pay for their annual budget deficits.

What has developed from the government's excess spending and borrowing is a "robbing Peter to pay Paul" method of money management. As our debt began to accumulate, the government began to use everything at their disposal to pay the interest on the rising debt. What the commingled surplus dollars provided was a way for Washington, DC, to silently pay for their overspending by using money they already had access to within the Treasury Department. The commingled surpluses allowed them to borrow money without drawing attention to themselves, and because this money was borrowed internally, it helped alleviate future bond-buyer concerns regarding our nation's rising debt.

To better explain my thesis, I believe the creation of single-payer entitlements such as Social Security and Medicare/Medicaid, coupled with Congress's authority to use surplus cash held within these entitlements, was significant in allowing a reckless government to use a "kick the can down the road" style of money management. Congress's authority to use $6.2 trillion of surplus cash from our commingled Treasury Department accounts, rather than having to sell $6.2 trillion of treasury bonds on the street, provided shelter from the consequences to the politicians who had created unaccountable budget deficits.

To better understand why access to surplus cash from our entitlements is an advantage, it's because there are only two ways for the US government to obtain extra income beyond what they already collect from us in taxes. The first method is to sell treasury bonds, which means borrowing money and raising our national debt. The second method is to increase the taxes collected from the American people. Yet open the door to deceit and illusion, and you can be sure a politician always will find a way to use it to their advantage. In this case, each time the government needed money, they pulled cash from our entitlements to pay for their budget overruns, and all they had to do was place a treasury bond in our entitlement accounts as a replacement for the cash they took.

If we recall what we learned about the fiat monetary system collapsing if the perpetuation of borrowing stops and that it is far easier and less conspicuous for a government to use cash surpluses already held in the treasury to buy treasury bonds, then it should be easy to understand why politicians are trying to create more single-payer entitlements that get funded through tax collection. This is not complicated. If the US government can generate and have access to internal surpluses, it is far easier and less noticeable to use the internal surpluses to buy treasury bonds rather than externally sell them to countries like China and Japan.

The bottom line is our politicians attempt to act like they operate with integrity while they are deceptively using and abusing our money. For those of you who have no idea what Congress did, the accounts listed below all had the cash surpluses I've listed. What was once cash in these accounts is now a government IOU, also known as a treasury bond.

America's Debt

Social Security	$2.9 trillion
Office of Personnel Management retirement fund	$998 billion
Military retirement fund	$828 billion
Medicare/Medicaid	$308 billion
Other retirement funds	$287 billion

To Whom the US Government Owes Money

The following represents our national debt and what percentage of the debt is owed to whom:

Foreign governments	30 percent
Banks and insurance companies	15 percent
The Federal Reserve	12 percent
Mutual funds	9 percent
State and local governments	5 percent
Union pension funds, 401(k)s, private investments	29 percent

I hope you have the same reaction as I did when looking at this information. Congress removed our surpluses as a method to pay for their overspending. Look at the accounts they took money from. They have raped and pillaged our retirement funds on every conceivable level! The first question should be "Why?" and the simple answer is because we allowed them the power to do so. The second question should be "Why would we consider creating more entitlements that they would control?" In my view, our trusting the US government to protect our money is akin to hiring a fox as the nighttime watchman at a henhouse.

How the Government Pays for the Budget Deficit

This process of generating money beyond what our economy can produce is where corruption and conspiracy begin. There have been a plethora of books written about the wealthy families controlling the world's banking who have supposedly conspired with our government to create what is now known as the Federal Reserve/central banking system.

The question is "Who has more power: the government or Wall Street, commercial banking, and private equity?" The answer is neither. My primary focus throughout this book has been to help you realize that our citizenry has tremendous power over those entities if we choose to unite and use it.

I cannot stress enough that the intentional division of our citizens is done to distract and hide the accumulation of unsustainable debt. Additionally, this division will make it much easier for the government to formulate and enact what they plan to do next in order to pay for it.

Let's start with understanding that the government must prove to the people they borrow from or they sell bonds to that they can afford to make the interest payments to the bondholders, as well as pay in full once the bond matures. The buyers of treasury bonds do analyze the government's gross domestic product income-to-debt ratio to ensure the government is a safe investment.

This is why it is so critical to understand: it is not the government that pays for the things that make America function. You, the taxpayer, pay for the function of our government and all their extended programs. When government is spending too much, they are borrowing money from your entitlements, your Wall Street retirements, and other countries. When they borrow money, it is you who repays what they borrow.

The Real Reason for the Affordable Care Act

Every day, we see the drama continue between the two rival political parties arguing over the Affordable Care Act. The Democratic Party rails about how the rich do not pay their fair share, while the Republican Party says we must reduce the size and regulation of government. The fact is both of what the respective parties advocate for need to happen. We do need less government and less regulation, and we should see to it that the tax system is designed that an equal share is paid in taxes based on total income. But the reality is neither party actually does what they propose. They dramatize their arguments not for the purpose of fixing things, but to use them as a method to distract while they incorporate the things they wanted all along.

What follows may come off as a tad conspiratorial, but let me be clear: I do not blame one political party more than the other regarding the Affordable Care Act. In my view, its creation was actually a collusion between both parties seeking to achieve a long-term goal. I believe the Republicans and Democrats are simply playing good cop/bad cop, and at the end of this illusion, they will somehow find common ground mandating the ACA, or something similar to ultimately become a tax funded entitlement program.

Let's begin with a logical question. If we had a $2.9 trillion surplus in our Social Security Trust Funds and a $308 billion surplus in Medicare/Medicaid, why did the government need to create the Affordable Care Act? Why not simply cash in the treasury bonds to replenish our entitlement accounts, and if we still needed additional revenue to provide free health care, then why not keep it simple and increase the payroll tax on Medicare/Medicaid to cover the difference?

It's because the surplus dollars they took from Social Security and the other accounts are gone, and they don't have the money to repay them. It is because the politicians keep lying as though they have our money that I want the American people to make them prove it. They don't have the money to pay us back, and they didn't use the option of increasing the payroll tax on Medicare/Medicaid because that would have been too transparent. They needed a new entitlement program with complex taxing tentacles, one that would not be easy to follow in terms of how much tax revenue is received and how much is paid in expenses. A simple Medicare/Medicaid tax would have made it way too easy to see how much money goes in versus how much goes out.

To prove my theory, the following information describes a few of the ways the Affordable Care Act will provide additional tax revenue to the government. This is also where my good cop/bad cop theory applies. The proof of this happened when the Republicans controlled all three branches of government and they did not repeal the Affordable Care Act. Every Republican ran their campaign on repealing it, yet once they were in full power to do so, they did not do it. Instead, they cut some of the taxing elements that had funded the act, yet many of the taxes still remain. The Republicans will say, "We tried, but the remaining taxes cannot be removed." In the end, I believe many of those taxes will remain, and the good cop/bad cop hoax will find agreement on using a higher payroll tax on Medicare/Medicaid to fund health care for all.

I think the best way to depict the Affordable Care Act is to envision America as a ship filled with gold being consumed one bite at a time by a giant kraken.

A Quick Blurb from Website Debt.org

In 2010 the Obama administration stated to the American people that the10-year projected cost for Obamacare would increase our debt by $940 billion dollars. In 2012, the Congressional Budget Office updated the estimated cost to $1.8 trillion for the period from 2012 to 2022, with $510 billion of it to be partially offset with receipts and cost savings. By 2018, when the law was fully implemented, (the Congressional Budget Office) again recalculated and announced that total expenses would be closer to $2.5 trillion. Obamacare's provisions are intended to be covered over the next ten years by a variety of new taxes on individuals and certain health-care industries, changes in the IRS's tax code, and offsets to some Medicare/Medicaid expenditures.

Taxes Built into the Affordable Care Act

- A 3.8 percent surtax on investment income from capital gains and dividends that applies to single filers earning more than $200,000 and married couples filing jointly earning more than $250,000

- A $50,000 excise tax on charitable hospitals that fail to meet new "community assessment needs," "financial assistance," and other rules set by the Health and Human Services Department

- A $24 billion tax on the paper industry to control a pollutant known as black liquor

- A $2.3 billion-a-year tax on drug companies

- A 10 percent excise tax on indoor tanning salons

- An $87 billion hike on Medicare payroll taxes for employees, as well as the self-employed

- A hike in the threshold for writing off medical expenses to 10 percent of adjusted gross income from 7.5 percent

- A new cap on flexible spending accounts of $2,500 a year

- Elimination of the tax deduction for employer-provided prescription drug coverage for Medicare recipients

- An income surtax of 1 percent of adjusted gross income, rising to 2.5 percent by 2016 on individuals who refuse to go along with Obamacare by buying a policy not okayed by the government

- A $2,000 tax charged to employers with fifty or more workers for every full-time worker not offered health coverage

- A $60 billion tax on health insurers

- A 40 percent tax on so-called Cadillac, or higher cost, health insurance plans

Instead of approaching the American people with a simple plan to increase the payroll tax on Medicare/Medicaid, what they did was rile our citizenry into a frenzy, labeling one group of Americans as oppressors while painting those in need of health care as victims of the oppressors. The truth is the uproar had nothing to do with one group of citizens attempting to oppress another. The uproar happened because our government delivered a catastrophic tax increase at a time when businesses already were struggling to survive. A wise government would have notified businesses in advance that the Medicare/Medicaid payroll tax would be increasing. Approaching it this way would have given businesses enough time to incorporate the additional cost of health care into the cost of doing business, which means higher prices to the consumer.

We Are the Strength of Our Nation

I've stressed several times that we, not the government or the financial pyramid, are the power of America. In 2018, taxpayers paid $3.33 trillion in taxes. In 2019, the projected total is $3.44 trillion, and in the year 2020, our tax revenue is estimated to be $3.64 trillion. Our share of the world's GDP is listed on (Worldometer's website) as 24.3 percent with a total population of 325 million people. Our closest rival is China, which has a population of 1.4 billion people compared with our 325 million, and the same website lists China as contributing 15 percent of the world's GDP.

The proportional breakdown of who pays the $3.643 trillion tax bill in 2020 varies depending on which website you pull information from. The breakdown I've provided comes from various sites such as (the balance and Investopedia's website) the proportional breakdown is as follows: $1.822 trillion comes from individual taxpayers (you and me). Then a combination of employees (us) and our employers, (each paying half, pays an additional $1.295 trillion to entitlement programs. Then:

Corporate Income = $256 billion

Excise Tax = $157 billion

Estate Tax and Misc. = $64 billion

Federal Reserve = $49 billion

So, the American people will pay approximately 50 percent of the total $3.64 trillion tax revenue individually, and we contribute half the $1.295 trillion of tax paid to the government as entitlement taxes. In a nutshell, we pay individually $2.46 trillion of the total $3.643 trillion of tax revenue paid to the Treasury Department. That, my fellow citizens, is why I say, "We are the power!" Without us, their game is over.

Now that I have revealed our nation's true power, let's reflect back on what caused the American Revolution. What was the final straw that broke the camel's back, causing the New Englanders to revolt against Great Britain? Although there were a multitude of reasons, the primary reason for throwing the tea into Boston Harbor was the king's taxation without representation. In other words, the people felt they were doing all the work while getting little support from the ruling class, yet the ruling class was profiting immensely off the backs of the people.

Is the history that plagued our forefathers still plaguing us today? Did they make a mistake when they formed our nation's governing foundation as a representative democracy rather than a real democracy? Is it time for us to change from a representative government that decides for the people to the people deciding for themselves through a voting referendum?

Our representative government has allowed greed and corruption to put us in a vulnerable position. My feeling is, before we allow them to steal our future entirely, we should propose a plan that allows us to take our future back. Let me be clear: I am not proposing another American Revolution or an antigovernment revolt. My goal is to spur a movement of unity, one in which we come together as one people demanding integrity and accountability from our government. A movement that puts an end to a corrupt government deciding the fate of a nation's people and creates one that delivers a real democracy that allows the voice of the people to decide their destiny as a collective citizenry.

Conclusion

I've presented the stepping-stones of what is and has been causing the destruction of our country. Attempting to decide who is most responsible no longer matters. The truth is we are responsible because we let this happen.

When trying to find solutions to our financial problems, we must find the root of the issues. In our personal lives, the fix to our financial problems is simple; if we don't have enough income to pay for something, we make cuts. Of course, some use the option of credit, but if there's still not enough income, the consequences are dire. This can be difficult when it comes to our government's financial problems because many times, they create a multitude of financial taxing mechanisms used to pay for the programs they create. What I mean is they use far reaching multi-layered taxing mechanisms to pay for programs such as the ACA. By using this multi-layered taxing, even if a government program should end in insolvency many of the taxes used to pay for it still remain. You see, the rule of the game of politics and Wall Street greed is to get as much of our money as possible to flow through them and give as little as possible back if something goes awry. The following are the various tools used to accomplish that goal:

- Wall Street greed
- The fiat monetary system
- The Federal Reserve
- Monopolization of industry
- Lobbying
- A representative democracy instead of a real democracy
- Overregulation

- Budget deficits and government overspending

I understand that what I present seems to many Americans as another David-and-Goliath moment in history. Yet we can agree the root of our problem began when Washington, DC, became corrupted. The good news is the methods used for this corruption and the leadership that allowed it to happen are easily defined. When David defeated Goliath, he had a small sling and a handful of rocks. What the government knows and the American people seem to have forgotten is that although we are David in this story, we have much more than a sling and a few rocks.

It is we, not them, who support the entire foundation of this nation. The corrupt politicians in Washington, DC, who do not want things to change understand the power of a united citizenry, and that's why they work so hard at dividing us. Once we collectively agree that we must change Washington, DC's systematic corruption, we can return to a sustainable future for generations to come.

How to Change the Future

Up till now, we've discussed the various political stepping-stones that have been destructive to America. In this chapter, we will begin the journey that leads us back to success.

In the last chapter, we concluded that the root of our problem has been poor leadership, as well as a government structure that allows our politicians to get themselves in trouble. To begin the rebuilding process, we must again discuss the root of what ails our nation. Earlier, I mentioned the various contributors that led us to financial destruction, but now we will figure out how to deal with the root of the problem, which is our $22 trillion debt.

We hear the battles waging among our politicians, as well as economists. Some say the rich should be taxed more, while others say lower taxes and less regulation are the solution to reducing our nation's debt. If we approach our debt with logic, beginning with the questions of whom the debt is owed to, how much it is really costing us, and why we continue to add more debt if we know it is destroying our country, we can begin to formulate a plan for how we can better control or eliminate our debt in the future.

It doesn't matter which website you go to. Liberal or conservative, they all list our nation's debt at somewhere around $22.5 trillion. Additionally, both sides agree that it is our citizenry to whom the US government owes most of their debt to: 73 percent. In other words, $16.5 trillion of the $22.5 trillion debt total was provided to the federal government through various financial investments we are involved with—$6.2 trillion of that $16.5 trillion figure was taken from our tax-funded entitlements. This Information is easily obtained on (US DEPARTMENT OF THE TREASURY) website.

It always has baffled me why other countries are willing to invest in treasury bonds when they hear politicians railing on our networks about the burden of our nation's paralyzing debt. I often wonder why anyone would invest their money in treasury bonds, knowing that our government is scheduled to overspend by $900 billion each year. What is it that other countries know that causes them to believe the Treasury Department is a safe place to store their money?

After applying good old-fashioned logic, I began to understand what it is they know about our debt and why they are not concerned about buying treasury bonds. First and foremost, they know America's government has the power to use taxpayer dollars for bailouts if severe economic conditions should occur. They also know if things go really bad, the only debt our government is obligated to pay is the interest on the $6 trillion that was borrowed externally. In other words, they understand Washington, DC, has the authority to control who, what, and when regarding the payment of debt, and given the fact that 73 percent of America's debt is internal, other countries know that if an economic calamity should arise, the federal government has the power to renegotiate the debt owed to its citizens.

What I mean is Washington, DC, has the power to create options. They could temporarily delay paying interest on the debt owed to us. They could lengthen the amount of time to the maturity of the bonds we hold in our portfolios. They could reduce the value of our bonds, as well as our currency, or they could simply pass a law that wiped out all our personal assets, deeming it our patriotic duty to bail out the sinking ship.

After dissecting what caused our nation's unsustainable debt, we realize it happened because poor leadership created policies that spent more than what the Treasury Department took in. Yet rather than cut back on spending in order to balance the federal budget, Washington, DC, wants more tax dollars so they can keep up with the rising interest payments on their debt to us.

It is important to understand the debt owed to us has tentacles that reach everywhere. It's the treasury bonds sitting in the Social Security Trust Funds and Medicare/Medicaid. It's the bonds in our Wall Street retirement accounts and our IRAs. If we analyze with logic, we begin to see how and why our government and Wall Street have carefully engineered a system that leaves us with no other option but to place our savings in their shark-infested waters.

The truth they've been hiding, and why it is important to divide and confuse our citizenry, is the US government has no conceivable way to repay what they borrowed from our entitlements other than to borrow more money. Yet the irony of the debt discussion is if Washington, DC, were to borrow more money to pay back what they took from us, it would require us to pay higher taxes in order to keep up with the rising cost of interest on the total debt. It's time to reflect, people—are they that smart, or are we that dumb?

How Did Debt Get So High?

The following charts demonstrate how our debt has accumulated. The first chart displays the taxpayer dollars used to bail out Wall Street. The information I provide is available on many public websites. I found (ProPublica BAILOUT/TRACKER) to be beneficial because it provides updated information regarding payback status. What it doesn't depict is the cost to us each time our economy collapses, delivering financial disasters that devalue our homes, freeze our wage growth, and diminish our personal savings.

In almost every case, the bailouts were necessary because of mismanagement, deceptive practices, and/or corruption. Yet what should be viewed as most significant is the size of the bailouts once President Nixon changed our nation's monetary system from the gold standard to a fiat monetary system.

Government Bailout Debt

1970	Penn Central Transportation Company	$3.2 billion
1971	Lockheed Aircraft Corporation	$1.4 billion
1974	Franklin National Bank	$7.8 billion
1975	New York City, New York	$9.4 billion
1980	Chrysler Corporation	$4 billion
1984	Continental Illinois National Bank and Trust Company	$9.5 billion
1989	The savings and loan industry	$293 billion
2001	The airline industry	$18.6 billion
2008	Bear Stearns	$30 billion
2008	Fannie Mae and Freddie Mac	$400 billion
2008	AIG	$180 billion
2008	The auto industry	$25 billion
2008	The Troubled Asset Relief Program	$700 billion
2008	Citigroup	$280 billion
2009	Bank of America	$142 billion

US Government Budget Deficit Per Year

GOVERNMENT BUDGET DEFICIT					
1970	$2.8 Billion	1987	$149.7 Billion	2004	$412.7 Billion
1971	$23 Billion	1988	$155.2 Billion	2005	$319 Billion
1972	$23.4 Billion	1989	$152.6 Billion	2006	$248.2 Billion
1973	$14.9 Billion	1990	$221 Billion	2007	$162 Billion
1974	$6.1 Billion	1991	$269.2 Billion	2008	$455 Billion
1975	$53.2 Billion	1992	$290.3 Billion	2009	$1.4 Trillion
1976	$73.7 Billion	1993	$255.1 Billion	2010	$1.3 Trillion
1977	$53.7 Billion	1994	$203.2 Billion	2011	$1.3 Trillion
1978	$59.2 Billion	1995	$164 Billion	2012	$1.1 Trillion
1979	$40.7 Billion	1996	$107.4 Billion	2013	$719 Billion
1980	$73.8 Billion	1997	$21.9 Billion	2014	$514 Billion
1981	$79 Billion	1998	$69.3 Billion	2015	$439 Billion
1982	$128 Billion	1999	$125.6 Billion	2016	$585 Billion
1983	$207.8. Billion	2000	$236.2. Billion	2017	$665 Billion
1984	$185.4 Billion	2001	$128.2 Billion	2018	$779 Billion
1985	$212.3 Billion	2002	$157.8 Billion	2019	$960 Billion
1986	$221.2 Billion	2003	$377.6 Billion		

The following chart shows an accumulation of debt composed of a multitude of expenses attached to the various elements of war. The important thing to learn from this information is that war is not paid for by money we have; it is paid for by using the fiat monetary system to print money in advance of collecting money through taxation. The reality is war is not just the loss of people we love fighting for our country; it is also debt that the citizens are expected to pay for through eventual taxation.

Cost of War

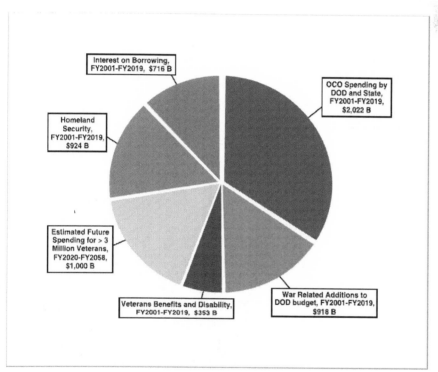

Source: The Watson Institute for International & Public Affairs, Brown University

The following chart shows what happened to Social Security after Ronald Reagan's reform. Total income is what was collected through taxation in a given year. Total cost is what the government paid out during that specific year. Annual surplus is the amount remaining for the year listed on the chart. Total reserve surplus at year-end is a running total of the surplus held in our entitlement account in the US Treasury. As the chart shows, from 1986 through 2018, the Social Security surplus was just under $2.9 trillion.

Social Security After the Social Security Amendments of 1983

Year	Total Income	Total Cost	Annual Surplus	Total Reserve Surplus
1986	216,833	201,522	4,698	46,861
1987	231,039	209,093	21,946	68,807
1988	263,469	222,514	40,955	109,762
1989	289,448	236,242	53,206	162,968
1990	315,443	253,135	62,309	225,277
1991	329,676	274,205	55,471	280,747
1992	342,591	291,865	50,726	331,473
1993	355,578	308,766	46,812	378,285
1994	381,111	323,011	58,100	436,385
1995	399,497	339,815	59,683	496,068
1996	424,451	353,569	70,883	566,950
1997	457,668	369,108	88,560	655,510
1998	489,204	382,255	106,950	762,460
1999	526,582	392,908	133,673	896,133
2000	568,433	415,121	153,312	1,049,445
2001	602,003	438,916	163,088	1,212,533
2002	627,085	461,653	165,432	1,377,965
2003	631,886	479,086	152,799	1,530,764
2004	657,718	501,643	156,075	1,686,839
2005	701,758	529,938	171,821	1,858,660
2006	744,873	555,421	189,452	2,048,112
2007	784,889	594,501	190,388	2,238,500
2008	805,302	625,143	180,159	2,418,658
2009	807,490	685,801	121,689	2,540,348
2010	781,128	712,526	68,602	2,608,950
2011	805,057	736,083	68,975	2,677,925
2012	840,190	785,781	54,409	2,732,334
2013	855,021	822,925	32,096	2,764,431
2014	844,276	859,230	25,046	2,789,476
2015	920,157	897,123	23,034	2,812,510
2016	957,453	922,276	35,177	2,847,687
2017	996,581	952,478	44,103	2,891,789
2018	1,003,373	1,000,233	3,140	2,894,929

Source: Social Security website

It's important to recognize how much surplus was held by Social Security after the Reagan administration's reform. We will never really know how our $2.9 trillion surplus was spent, but we can assume a large portion was on budget deficits, war, and Wall Street bailouts. The important thing to understand is the only way our government can pay us back is to collect a higher amount of tax revenue than the Treasury Department pays out in expenditures. The only way for that to happen is to increase our taxes or create new tax-funded single-payer entitlement programs that produce cash surpluses, but that merely allows the government to continue using excess dollars from commingled treasury accounts in order to pay higher interest on debt, which creates more debt.

Unfortunately, poor leadership and government corruption always leave the citizens in a quandary of who should pay more taxes. As I've stated before—but it bears repeating—if we tax the rich because they supply the majority of our goods and services, the tax increase is simply passed on to you through the price you pay. Additionally, if government overregulates or demands too high a tax burden, corporations simply move to places more willing to agree to their terms. There is no question that our government's lack of smarts and their corrupt actions, coupled with the cunning deceptions of Wall Street's financial pyramid, has put our citizenry in a vulnerable position.

What follows are my suggestions for how to begin fixing the damage that has been done. Again, I say that if you don't like my ideas, it's okay to criticize. But while you are criticizing, be sure to include why the idea won't work and explain how the suggestion that you provide will. In other words, don't just criticize; take part in the process of creating solutions.

Start by Relinquishing Internal Debt

I've expressed throughout this book that I believe divisional politics are being used to distract our people from learning the truth, which is our government has reached the end of having excess internal cash surpluses to pay for their runaway debt, and they know the time is near when they will be required to notify our citizenry that a massive tax will be necessary to bail them out. My thought is, instead of letting them deliver the final blow to our future, I suggest we deliver a blow to them first, and there's no place they're more vulnerable than the $6.2 trillion they took from our entitlements.

I am not willing to have my taxes increased because our government needs more money so they can repay the money they pilfered from us. So instead of engaging in political banter, I suggest we use the debt the US government owes our entitlements as a bargaining chip to start negotiations with Congress. This might sound a tad crazy, but what I propose to do is to wipe out the entire $6.2 trillion debt the government owes our entitlements.

I understand some of you might react to this suggestion with anger, while others might say this would create worldwide fear that our financial system is on the brink of collapse. The truth is Congress does not have the money to pay us back, and the only way they can do it is to increase our taxes or sell more treasury bonds, thus creating more debt and a higher interest payment.

Our cable networks provide a plethora of economists who say not to worry about the money owed to our entitlements because the government is paying us loads of interest on the treasury bonds held in them. The (Center on Budget and Policy Priorities website) provides information that shows the annual interest payment from the US treasury to Social Security as follows:

2018: $83.1 billion

2019: $82.2 billion

2020: $81.8 billion

2021: $80.9 billion

Similar payments are projected to continue through 2027.

The bottom line is the economists' stating that this is a good deal for us is a ruse, and our accepting this ruse as truth lets Washington, DC, continue their pursuit of higher taxes. The $83.1 billion of annual interest the Treasury Department pays to Social Security is paid with the tax dollars they collect from us. If we do the math, understanding we're presently paying on average $82 billion of interest to Social Security alone, that means if we use the entire $6.2 trillion owed to our entitlements, we're annually paying ourselves $166 billion of interest! The way I see it, wiping out the entire $6.2 trillion debt would reduce our annual interest payment by $166 billion, which would have a direct impact on decreasing the government's annual budget deficit.

The question is how do the citizens go about setting up a negotiation with the government for debt cancellation? My goal is to get this book into the hands of both left- and right-leaning freedom watch organizations, as well as people like Oprah Winfrey who have large audiences who possess the power to start a movement. Many of these groups already have powerful organizations in which their voices are heard on a regular basis, so if they agree that cancelling an unpayable debt and saving $166 billion annually is a good idea worth pursuing, I believe that should be enough to get the party rolling.

All this debt creation already has put our nation's integrity at stake. We want people to feel secure when investing their money in treasury bonds, and it is critically important that the US government proves to the world they are prudent with our money, as well as with the funds from others who invest in treasury bonds. It is important to the health of our financial system that the dollar remains the favored currency because it provides many advantages to our nation and our citizenry as a whole. Make no mistake: China, Russia, and others are doing all they can to lessen the confidence in the dollar remaining the leading global currency.

Did They Really Pay Us Back?

It's time to discuss reparations to the American people for the damages that the US government and Wall Street created. In the subhead, I asked, "Did they really pay us back?" To clarify who I mean by "they," I am referring to the same people I have been discussing throughout this book: the Federal Reserve, the government, commercial banking, lobbyists, and Wall Street, along with their affiliated groups. My contention is that they did not even come close to paying us back, and the mere suggestion of it is insulting.

Yet before getting into my ideas about how Wall Street can pay us back, I thought we should review one more time why they should. There are a vast number of books and articles describing how much tarp money the Big Six Banks received from the Federal Reserve. There are also several publications that list the financial losses to the American people ranging anywhere from $5 trillion to $13 trillion as a direct result of the 2008 mortgage crisis. Yet what we've heard over and over from former Federal Reserve chairman Ben Bernanke and the Washington, DC, politicians is that retribution was paid because they handed out $80 billion worth of fines to the institutions responsible for the deception. We then hear statements from the (Treasury) that as of January 2018, US bailout funds had been fully recovered by the government when interest on loans was taken into consideration. A total of $626 billion was invested, loaned, or granted in the various bailout measures. The US government reports $390 billion was returned to the Treasury Department and that the department earned another $323 billion in interest on the bailout loans, thus resulting in an $87 billion profit.

Statements such as this demonstrate how little respect these folks have for our intelligence. Meaning it is proof Washington, DC, was not considering the citizens when referencing who was repaid for the hardship brought on by the Great Recession. It may be true that the money the US government recouped for the gifts they gave to the Wall Street banks, but what the Federal Reserve and Washington, DC, politicians proved by saying we (the people) were paid back was the only thing they were really concerned about was returning the money to the Treasury Department. Why? Because that money directly affects their world, not ours. In other words, they made certain the Treasury Department was replenished because that money directly impacts their operating budget. Had they been concerned with how the crisis impacted us, they would have made sure the masses of foreclosed homes that were sold at bargain-basement prices could not be used as comparable pricing to our homes, for allowing these foreclosed homes sold at a discount price, to be used as a comparable to others in the neighborhood caused catastrophic real estate devaluation all across America. Additionally, if Washington DC was concerned about the American people, they also would have made sure the Troubled Asset Relief Program money the banks received would be loaned to our businesses instead of letting the CEOs use it as cash to buy back stock options in their own companies.

There is no real way to calculate our total loss, but the following list depicts why I believe they still owe the American people for their crime:

- Froze wage growth for a decade
- Devalued our homes
- Caused a delay of a minimum of six years for eligible retirees while they attempted to recoup the losses in their 401(k)s
- Reduced wealth transfer with the increase of reverse mortgages due to the market crash
- Caused loss of capital in small business
- Reduced small-business startups
- Caused the loss of millions of jobs
- Foreclosed on ten million homes
- Caused the closure of many small and medium-size businesses

I apologize if I missed listing something that may have affected you. But I get so angry each time I go through these hardships that I am forced to stop. What a joke for anyone in Washington, DC, or the

Federal Reserve to suggest they did a good job and that we have been paid back! The government and the Federal Reserve have used our tax dollars time after time to bail out corrupt/reckless behavior, and if we do not unite to stop them, they will do it again. This is why I highlight the importance of stopping corporate monopolization, breaking up the too-big-to-fail banks, and changing from a representative democracy to a real one that decides big issues by voter referendum.

The good news in all that we've discussed so far is we know for certain the federal government does have the authority to change the governing relationship between them and the Federal Reserve. Yes, it would require both the Republican Party and the Democratic Party to agree on the changes, but the fact is it can be done.

Reparations

What has transpired over time is that instead of our politicians representing our citizenry, using our power in numbers, they instead sold their souls and ours to a system of lobbying that provides them wealth for their own gain. That's right. I said it: our government has become a partner to those with the most money, and they have chosen to divide our citizenry into as many groups as possible because they know our division empowers their strength.

It does not matter whether we identify left or right politically. There is a massive loss of trust in government and an overall disdain for Wall Street. I believe the only way we can restore trust in government is to ensure those we elect cannot be influenced any longer by lobbying. Additionally, we need to penalize Wall Street, as well as pay back the citizens for the damage that was done. So as we negotiate the $6.2 trillion debt forgiveness, we would include a plan that would monetarily penalize the financial institutions that benefited off the backs of the American people in order for them to pay restitution. What follows is an attempt to penalize those organizations.

On October 13, 2006, President George W. Bush signed into law the Financial Services Regulatory Relief Act (FSRRA). The signing was the culmination of more than four years of work done by Congress, the Federal Reserve, and others. The two points I would like to highlight regarding this law are, first and foremost, the passing of the FSRRA is once again proof that the federal government sets the guidelines for the Federal Reserve. The second point, and one that is extremely important, is the new law required that the Federal Reserve begin paying interest to the commercial banks on their reserves. Prior to FSRRA, the banks were required to hold 10 percent in reserve without collecting interest. Afterward, the Federal Reserve began paying interest for bank reserves, including the Troubled Asset Relief Program money given to them during the bailout.

My thought is instead of the Federal Reserve Bank using our tax dollars to pay interest on the reserves held in commercial banks and the $4 trillion on the Feds' balance sheet ($2.5 trillion in bonds and $1.5 trillion in mortgage-backed securities), we freeze the interest payment to both. Then for five years consecutively write a check to the American people (payable to every citizen divided equally) in the amount the Federal Reserve and commercial banking was supposed to receive. To make certain the penalty is fair, this stoppage of interest payments would only apply to the banks and their affiliates that received Troubled Asset Relief Program money, or anyone guilty of selling fraudulent mortgage securities.

My thought regarding every citizen getting a refund, even those guilty of walking away from their homes because they owed more on the mortgage than their home's value, is to avoid creating more division among us. Even though many people were wrong for ditching their debt obligations, if we want to achieve unity, we cannot single out anyone from receiving a payback for the hardship of the Great Recession. This horrific ten-year period of stagnation affected every one of our lives. Therefore, all citizens must be satisfied that the perpetrators of this crime have paid their debt.

The bankers might say, "This is a crazy idea. It will have a bad effect on the overall economy." Blah, blah, blah. The only effect this payback will have on them is severe damage to their overinflated egos, and it will minimally reduce their profits. To better explain what I meant by my last statement (money under 30's website) does a great job explaining how most of a banks profit come from the fees they charge for ATMs, overdrafts, penalty, commission, and application, etcetera. The interest the banks collect from the Federal Reserve for their reserves is minimal to their overall profitability. If the banks squawk too much, the Federal Reserve could temporarily lessen the pain by lowering the mandatory 10 **percent** reserve to a 5 percent reserve/95 percent fractional lending ratio. This would help bankers generate more income by allowing them to use an additional 5 **percent** of their reserves as potential loans. What this plan of action achieves is delivering the message to the American people that the government is once again working for them, and it also sends a message to the bankers that they will be penalized for risky or illegal behavior.

Bring Profit Home

This next suggestion has been widely discussed, and quite frankly, I am confused as to why our government is having difficulty finding agreement. We heard the political discourse during the 2016 presidential election that because of a high repatriation tax, there is an estimated $2.6 trillion of idle cash sitting outside our nation's border. The Trump administration recently lowered the repatriation tax from 35 percent to 15.5 percent, and, as a consequence, on September 19th, 2018 (marketwatch.com) reported $485 billion has reentered the United States. If we were to visualize that $485 billion being used specifically for the banks' fractional lending purposes, it has pumped a boatload of money into the American economy.

If it is true, $2.115 trillion still remains outside our borders. I would suggest lowering the repatriation tax to a flat rate of 10 percent. This would be an incentive to bring the money home, and it would deliver

$211.5 billion of usable revenue. Not to worry—I'm not suggesting we give $211.5 billion to Washington, DC. My suggestion is to deposit the money into Fannie Mae and Freddie Mac, then designate $105.75 billion for the community reinvestment program we discussed earlier. The remaining $105.75 billion would also go to Fannie Mae and Freddie Mac, but this money would be used to generate mortgage loans for first-time home buyers who have a good job and a decent credit rating.

In order to gain the most value from our repatriated tax deposit in Fannie Mae and Freddie Mac, we could help the Federal Reserve rid themselves of the $1.5 trillion of mortgage-backed securities (of which many are considered toxic assets) buy selling them to the American people. My reasoning is that rather than allowing the Federal Reserve to sell these mortgage-backed securities to private-equity groups at a discounted price, why not make them available to first- and second-time buyers, allowing them a chance at a good home? This could be done by placing the mortgage securities on Fannie Mae's and Freddie Mac's balance sheets, using them as the Federal Reserve's resale distribution arm. But I'm not expanding government by doing so. Financial engineers and regulatory tax attorneys would need to determine the exact details, but I chose Fannie Mae and Freddie Mac as the resale arm because they were my choice to deposit the $105.75 billion repatriated tax dollars to be used for first- and second-time home buyers.

The plan would include a public website and the multiple listings displaying the properties available for purchase. To handle the sales, a well-known commission-based realty company that would be responsible to show the homes, condos, or buildings to prospective buyers would need to be hired. By handling it this way, we would get the benefit of private-sector efficiency and, most importantly, help fight against expanding government.

As an incentive to move the properties, first-time homebuyers could receive a 50 percent property tax reduction for the first year, then a 10 percent graduated increase each year until the buyer is making the same tax payment as the other homeowners in the neighborhood. Additionally, to protect against devaluation of other houses in the community, the discounted purchase price would not be entered as a comparable sale. In other words, because these homes were sold at a discounted price, the price would not be listed in order to assure that the surrounding homes did not lose their market value.

Using my method or a similar one would generate property tax, spur economic growth by increasing construction/home repair, and create additional interest income for Fannie Mae and Freddie Mac, which would ultimately generate profit and tax revenue paid to the Treasury Department. It would be a tremendous shot in the arm to the American people, proving the government once again represents the citizenry. Last, but not least, it states the American dream is still alive!

Conclusion

We hear on the news about how wonderful our economy is yet the people in America know the truth. Yes, the economy is somewhat better, but we know something has gone terribly wrong for the nation's working class. Even though the economy has improved, each of us feels in our gut that a valley as deep as the Grand Canyon has been carved between those who have and those who don't.

Our representative government is no longer concerned about keeping the illusion that they are a government that works for the people. It has become abundantly clear that many of our leaders in Washington, DC, believe the citizens are boxed in and have no way out other than a government redistribution plan that they control. They believe as long as the media remains their partner in dividing our citizenry, and they can continue using us as taxpayer pawns to bail out their campaign donors, we essentially have no chance at stopping them from obtaining ultimate power. The folks at the top have crowned themselves kings and queens, and they see the fate of the American people returning to the fate of being governed by an empire.

The difference between present America and America long ago is that if we come together as one people, we vastly outnumber those who attempt to steal our freedom. I believe our government, just as Great Britain did before them, have overestimated their ability to control the people. The question of how much control the government has rests in our hands. Will we continue to be led like brainless puppets, allowing them to divide us into political tribes, or will we unite as one people and demand respect for our contribution to our country? Will we become sheeple satisfied by what a central government takes from one and redistributes to another, or will we fight to remain an innovative, independent citizenry working together as one nation?

I don't know whether my ideas will work. My only hope in presenting them is to spur on creative thinking and to challenge the status quo. We must recognize that the wealth gap in our nation has severely broadened, and if we accept the solution to reducing this gap as one to be directed by bureaucrats governing tax redistribution programs, we will have accepted a one-way ticket to hell. What is ailing this nation has been our willingness to accept the idea that someone else can do a better job at providing our families a prosperous future. It is time for us to decide!

Government Reset

I believe America may be on the verge of another revolution. Just as the boomers had a significant impact during the 1960s, I believe the millennials will have a similar impact in the 2020s and beyond. The question we face is whether our nation's future economic structure will become one that is governed through centralized government redistribution or our citizenry will reject central planning and redistribution as dangerous to the idea of an independent people.

To me, the answer to the question of how America's future should be governed must begin by analyzing how our present governmental system functions and deciding whether or not we stay with a system in which a few decide for many or we advance to a more progressive style of governing. Let me explain what I mean by that because the one I propose is nothing like the progressive ideology being presented today. That ideology is one that empowers government by giving them more authority. The progressive changes I propose will empower the people to have more authority over the government.

Before we discuss this, I ask that you please answer the following questions honestly: Are you satisfied with how our government presently functions? Do you feel *you* are being represented, or do you feel Washington, DC, is representing someone or something else? If you are among the few who feel government is doing a good job, then the following suggestions will likely not be of interest to you. But if you are like me and feel government no longer represents our citizenry because they are serving an agenda that is based on self-gain, then I believe you will like what I have to say.

Please allow me to present my case by detailing what has already happened within our political/monetary system that will prove that our present form of governing has been tainted beyond redemption. It is my opinion that our nation's fiat monetary system has reached the end of its ability to create perpetual loaning, and if left as is, we shall soon see its demise. Additionally, I believe that the reckless internal borrowing from our entitlements can no longer be sustained and that the significance of this will cause runaway inflation on interest rates paid on treasury bonds. Both our political and financial structures will no longer be able to hide the truth, and it is for this reason the divisionary tactics used by Washington, DC, have been deployed against our citizenry. The reality is that this is a fight for their life over yours!

I believe I've kept my word about remaining bipartisan while addressing the issues regarding our political and financial institutions. The way I see it, there's really no difference between what both political parties are trying to achieve because it's about ultimate power. Republicans and Democrats are simply playing good cop/bad cop roles in regard to their party's platforms, but in general, it is a collective effort to maintain a divided citizenry. Do I believe this to be a carefully crafted Republican or Democrat conspiracy? No, I see this as a natural reaction that occurred because our nation's governing framework allowed our political leaders to be influenced by the power of money. The result is we have two dysfunctional parties that are damaging the spirit and comradery of our nation's people.

I've explained this already, but it's worth repeating: the survival of our nation's fiat monetary system can only be sustained if it can continue to create perpetual debt. Many times, countries that are in trouble convert to a fiat monetary system to bail themselves out of hard times. They do so because the system gives governments the power to create money out of thin air. The problem is most governments and their citizenry do not understand that the money they print to bail themselves out now must be paid for with prosperity that is created later. What I mean is printing fiat money—or fake money—is essentially borrowing from future prosperity. If future prosperity never comes to actually repay the fiat debt, the debt continues to rise so high that it finally eliminates the chance for prosperity to prevail.

When governments convert to fiat monetary systems, what follows can be compared to the fate of a heroin addict. The analogy of the drug addict chasing heroin and a government hooked on fiat is that both started their addictions when their problems seemed insurmountable. Heroin calms the nerves of the addict, and fiat calms the nerves of a government that needs money during turbulent times. In the end, this fix ultimately produces the same results. Once the short-lived sensation of calm ends and the pain of their addictions begins to set in, both addicts are left with two options: rehabilitation or eventual death from overdose—or, in the case of a fiat system, a collapse from the overburden of debt.

What transpires after the calm ends is the heroin addict ends up in places they never thought imaginable prior to the addiction. Similarly, governments that at one time had good intentions find themselves deceiving their citizens as they attempt to mask their addiction to fiat and the rise of insurmountable debt. This is where the comparison ends because the effects of a heroin addict's death are limited to themselves and those who love them. But the government's addiction to fiat and the rise of insurmountable debt will deliver a death sentence to an entire nation.

It's the System, Not the People We Elect

I do not believe all politicians are evil, and I do not believe all politicians are seeking self-gain. But I do believe that reality changes once a newly elected official sees what's behind the curtain in Washington, DC. What becomes abundantly clear to the political apprentice is they have entered an impenetrable system that requires a lot of money to remain in. The apprentice quickly learns that if they hope to be reelected, the promises that were made on the campaign trail are secondary to reelection, so if they want to keep their jobs, they learn they must put aside the promises made to their constituents and join the cause of their higher-ranking members. What is the cause of these high-ranking members remaining in Washington, DC, for generations? First and foremost, it is power for themselves. Secondly, it is a collaborative effort to create perpetual tax revenue in order to sustain their own prosperity.

If we analyze what is transpiring in the upcoming 2020 presidential election, we should try to see past the political propaganda of the candidates and think about why it is they're saying it. If we listen to what they say while keeping in mind the government is in constant need of tax revenue to pay for rising debt, we begin to understand what they're selling is largely based on creating more tax income for the Treasury Department. When these 2020 candidates make promises, we should keep in mind that if our nation's debt is unsustainable now, how can any Republican or Democrat propose programs that offer more of something that is free?

Could it be they know something we don't? That maybe I'm right about the fiat system and that the reality is that in order for fiat to survive, the politician's job is to sell ideas to the public that will sustain perpetual debt? I ask you to put aside conspiracy theories and political jargon and think logically. If our fiat monetary system is built from the creation of perpetual debt and our banking system is built from a 10 percent reserve/90 percent loan ratio, can we agree that our entire economy is surviving off the back of purposely designed pyramids? To be certain we agree on the idea of a pyramid, let me ask the question differently: If the majority of a bank's clients were to withdraw their money at the same time, could the bank reimburse more than 10 percent of their clients' money?

It is this maddening pyramid process that causes good politicians to go bad because once they enter Washington, DC, they are forced to jump on the economic merry-go-round, searching for new ways to keep the fiat system alive while avoiding the concerns of insurmountable debt. At the same time, they are exposed to a lobbying system that delivers pure evil, a system that devours good souls by finding the weaknesses that exist within. If the newly elected official is well connected or shows promise, they will be presented with a golden key that will deliver whatever their soul desires. If the politician can be coerced to expose their weakness, that is when the lobbyist can use their power to manipulate. Even if the apprentice politician is careful not to expose their weaknesses, they still need campaign donations in order to be reelected.

What is lost in all this scrambling to find more tax revenue or campaign donors is the concept that prosperity is the only way the system can be sustained. The corrupt system thriving in Washington, DC, no longer comprehends that they are employed because prosperity provided enough money to employ them. The proof that they have lost the understanding of basic economics is shown by how they manage our nation's budget. If I said to you that the earth is four billion years old, your response would probably be similar to mine, which is "That's incredible!" Yet applying the same thinking to our annual budget and realizing our government is missing the mark by an average of $600 billion seems to go unnoticed.

There's only one way that this ends, and that's why I chose to write this book. Our government is nothing more than a junkie attempting to find new ways to pay for their fiat addiction. They are lost, and they are concerned about being exposed for their sinful acts of betrayal. They've lost all concept of how to negotiate on our behalf, and many of them are held captive by the lobbyists who threaten to expose their sins to their constituents if they don't play ball. Make no mistake: those at the top of the financial pyramid understand that Washington, DC, is maxed out on what it can afford to pay on debt. They have fully engaged their network of lobbyists to prompt the Washington, DC, sellouts, on what the government must do next in order to generate more tax income.

Network Messaging

The folks ruling the financial pyramid already know their next move, and they are confident that regardless of what happens next, they will remain at the top no matter what monetary system is deployed. Yet they also know there is one looming danger that could alter their fate. That danger is a citizenry finding common cause to reduce the power of Washington, DC. Once we know their fear, we begin to understand why some of these folks become significant shareholders in news organization and/or social networks.

I think we can safely agree that network advertisers use subliminal messaging in their commercials in order to sell products. If we can agree that this messaging is used to persuade buyers, then I think we can go a step further and apply the concept of subliminal messaging to our cable news, which we already know has been split into left and right political networks/supporters. Once we understand the truth, it's not a stretch to say the partisanship within these networks has an agenda, which is to promote political talking points to aid politicians in accentuating our differences.

Let's remember that unity is the one true adversary that can thwart the next course of action by our government and those at the top of the financial pyramid. Once we understand the greatest fear of those atop the pyramid, we begin to realize why the puppet masters use the media and our politicians to divide our nation. The question is how long will we remain the United States if Washington, DC, and our media networks continue to highlight our differences rather than to promote what we have in common? Will their division backfire and cause our citizens to divide into political tribes, ultimately causing them to flee to states that have like-minded people? Will these states of like-minded citizens eventually secede from the union?

Why would all these organizations work so hard at separating our citizenry into these political tribes? Why would they promote hate and resentment under the guise of equality? Because the stakes are huge! You see, if the citizens still have a high spirit of independence among them, their solution to ridding themselves of a corrupt representative government will be to demand a change to a real democracy, one that votes by referendum. Those at the top of the financial pyramid, as well as the government afraid of losing power, understand their next move must silence the voices of unity, and they must fast-forward an economic/governing system that is built on redistribution and government dependency.

There are a multitude of books written by investigative journalists providing conclusive evidence of the corruption in Washington, DC. Instead of complaining on Twitter or other various social anger outlets, I chose to write a book in an effort to convince my fellow Americans that it is time we reject their division and unite as one people. That we come together with the idea of maintaining our independence, assuring ourselves that the government is an aid to, not a dictator of, our future as a nation.

Identifying What We Must Reject

I've done my best thus far to avoid discussing the 2020 presidential candidates, but there are two whom I must mention. I'll start by giving Senators Bernie Sanders and Elizabeth Warren credit for being the only two candidates who really have gone after Wall Street's savagery and abuse at the expense of our citizens. They collectively stand against the injustice Wall Street has perpetrated upon the American people, and as I've proven throughout my writing, I agree with them on that point. But I will explain why I am in complete and total disagreement with their misguided solutions.

You see, both Sanders and Warren believe the solution to our problems is more social programs delivered through taxation of the rich and redistributed by Washington, DC. This shared belief in taxing the rich to give to the poor completely misses the understanding that any taxes applied to the rich are simply redistributed to the citizenry through increased prices on the goods and services we buy. Additionally, their idea is to give more power to an already corrupt government by elevating the government to the arbitrator of fairness between the haves and the have-nots.

Although they do seem passionate about their quest to take a stand against the wealthy, neither of these long-term Washington, DC, inhabitants admit that it was not the wealthy who mismanaged the government's annual budget deficit or ran the Treasury Department's coffers dry. Our nation's debt has risen because our federal government has too much power and too much access to the tax dollars held in our treasury reserves. It is this lack of truthfulness and their continued effort to deceive that caused me to speak out while I still could. It is an insult to our intelligence when bureaucrats such as Warren and Sanders suggest that more government regulation or intervention is what's needed to solve our nation's problems. It is also an insult to our intelligence when conservatives bloviate that any form of regulation stifles prosperity. We know through experience without some regulation, the greedy will rape and pillage this nation until there is nothing left.

If we do not change the authority and power given to our representative government, then we will continually achieve the same results we have in the past. If we do not change the unlimited discretionary monetary power granted to Congress, that gives them the authority to continue increasing our nation's debt. Our nation's monetary sovereignty will eventually be sentenced to death.

Empowering Our Citizenry

The word *revolution* is defined as creating a change through the use of force. What follows is not a promotion of violence, but a call to my fellow citizens to revolutionize the power of their collective voice demanding change and accountability from those who serve. The only way we can stop the destruction of the United States is to change the rules for those who are causing its destruction.

Washington, DC, meets every day to create new laws that restrict our lives. If they see a problem happening in our society, they immediately create a new law so it won't happen again. Yet the destruction of our future through their bad policies, coupled with their unlimited authority to use our money to fix the results of their bad policies, goes on and on without change. We know that when a problem needs solving in our civilian world, they immediately create new laws to stop it, yet the internal corruption and abuse of our money happens again and again. What this government hypocrisy clearly displays is that Washington, DC, has become an empire whose mantra is "Do as I say, not as I do."

In my view, being governed by a representative democracy that has been tainted by the power and influence of private-equity money is no longer a viable system that will change its internal corruption. We must recognize that electing a few good men and women hoping they will be the people we need to combat corruption is simply not enough. The change promised from generation after generation of elected leadership has had no effect at slowing down the destruction. What I am about to propose will be considered radical to some and a potential lightening rod to others, but I see no other way of fixing how we are governed.

I believe we should continue electing representatives, but only for the purpose of presenting proposals of new laws to our citizens so we can vote through referendum—thus, a real democracy! Instead of allowing our government to make backroom deals that ultimately decide our fate, I propose each party, Republican and Democrat, present its case, for or against, regarding changes to existing laws or creating new ones to the American people on national television. Let the lawyers be lawyers, allowing them to present their case to the judge, who is you, the people. Once the topic is presented and the political parties debate why or why not a new law should be considered, a vote by referendum would decide the final outcome.

The idea of democracy through referendum might have been difficult in the past, but with the advancement in technology, there is no reason the American people cannot be more involved in important decisions that will ultimately impact their lives. Here are a few ideas on how we could use modern technology to vote by referendum as well as suggestions to govern our future. I did mention a few of these ideas in earlier chapters but thought it wise to include them here so you can better understand them in full context. I ask that you review my suggestions with an open mind for if we are to create real change, we must disregard the engrained political talking points that cause all of us to reach predetermined conclusions. These ideas are conceptual and should be thought of as a starting point. My goal is to inspire ideas that can be built on by engaged citizens willing to think outside the box.

1. Issue mandatory US identification cards to all occupants. Include mandatory fingerprinting at the time the card is issued and enter the prints into a national database. Hire a qualified technology manufacturer to build referendum-voting stations and install the voting stations in all public centers, assuring easy access to citizens. Additionally, create a phone app that also could be used as a method to vote. Once a referendum is ready for a yes or no vote, it would be presented on the voting stations, allowing citizens several weeks to research before they vote. Once the citizen feels they are ready to vote, they simply put their finger into the protected scanner, check to be sure the proper information shows up on the screen, and apply their vote on the referendum.

I am certain mandating fingerprints on the identification cards would bring much controversy, and it is definitely something I would have opposed in the past. But having fingerprints in a national database could greatly assist law enforcement in solving crime. I understand this is a scary thought, but to me, the advantages outweigh the loss of our privacy. The truth is Facebook, Instagram, Google, and a multitude of other social media expose our personal lives far worse than a fingerprint in a secure database. Most importantly, this sends a message to criminals: get sloppy with a crime scene by leaving a fingerprint behind, and you will be caught.

2. Reform the law that gives Congress the authority to use surplus dollars held in taxpayer entitlements. In case of an emergency, we would allow Congress to use up to a maximum of 25 percent. Anything beyond that would have to be presented to the citizens and voted on through referendum. Additionally, the money Congress uses must be paid back with excess dollars created from a budget surplus. *It cannot be repaid by selling treasury bonds, thus increasing debt!*

3. Current law on lobbying only prohibits an elected official's spouse from becoming a lobbyist, while allowing other family members such as children, siblings, or cousins to become one. Lobbying reform should ban all relatives, as well as retired politicians, from becoming lobbyists.

4. Increase pay substantially to elected officials in the judicial and executive branches of government. At the same time, ban gifts and singular campaign contributions from wealthy donors, family members, and special interest groups and corporations. The idea of increasing government salaries is to eliminate the need for elected officials to find other sources of income. Increasing their pay might entice better people to consider government as a career choice.

5. Put an end to individual candidates receiving campaign donations. All donations would go to a general fund that is controlled by the respective party (Republican or Democrat). The donations would be evenly distributed among the candidates running for an elected position. Candidates could use their own money to finance their campaigns but would be subjected to audit to assure the public they haven't received money from special interests or wealthy donors.

6. End private lobbying altogether. Lobbyists and special interest groups would be required to present their desires, complaints, and ideas at a public forum on national television. Handling it in this way would allow the citizens to see what the lobbyists are up to. The goal is to eliminate backroom deals between

elected officials and corporations, private equity, and commercial banks.

7. Add two members to the Federal Reserve board. The members would be paid and elected by the American people and would serve a maximum of four years. The candidates must have extensive credentials in economics, making certain they comprehend the dialogue at the Federal Reserve board meetings. The goal is to remove any shred of doubt or conspiracy surrounding the Federal Reserve/central banking. This also would help promote transparency regarding potential dangers surrounding our nation's finances.

8. Require Congress to break up the Big Six Banks, as well as monopolies within Big Tech, Big Oil, and Big Pharma. Make low-interest federal loans available to small businesses in order to promote competition within industries controlled by monopolies.

9. Put an immediate stop to the Federal Reserve paying interest on our banks' cash reserves.

10. Any future economic bailouts must be voted on through referendum. Create laws that end the use of taxpayer bailout money (such as the Troubled Asset Relief Program) to buy back stock options.

It is bold for one person to suggest changes of this magnitude. Our imperial government does not want change, and they know the importance of keeping our voices singular. They also understand the danger a voice of reason can present if accepted by the masses. Stated differently, they know that a movement can quickly elevate to the status of a political revolution if it is presented properly. They also know the danger if a citizenry finds themselves in collective agreement that they're being cheated. The question is have we reached the point that we can put aside our differences so we can unite to root out the greed and corruption?

As we move on, we must collectively realize it's now or never for the people of this nation to unite. Throughout this book, I've presented the evidence that proves our elected government has abandoned their constituents. The only chance we have to preserve a future based on freedom is to reduce the authority given to those who cannot be trusted. There's an old saying that is used when trying to figure out if someone has gone bad: "Give them enough rope to hang themselves." We most assuredly gave our government enough rope, and the results have proven that we must take their overabundance of power and let them swing from the gallows.

Conclusion

We do need those with enormous wealth to invest in America, but we cannot allow it to be at the cost of our freedom. The corruption within our government connected to the power of central banking, along with a slew of massive private wealth, worked overtime to get governments all over the world hooked on fiat debt. The collective goal of the Federal Reserve and those at the top of the financial pyramid has been to increase worldwide government borrowing. Their plan was to target a country's maximum borrowing capacity based on its annual gross domestic product, then maximize the debt while being careful not to collapse the economic structure.

The problem is that all these countries—including ours—have reached their maximum capacity. The politicians can no longer keep kicking the can down the road. Yet we should recognize that along this journey, many politicians, along with private wealth groups, have filled their bellies with our money. These people have expensive habits, and they are ravenous sharks always in pursuit of more chum for their consumption. Because we've reached the end, this is where the real concern begins. You see, they want to keep what they have, and they understand how angry we will become once we figure out the only future we have is one that will be decided by them.

It's time we face the truth because our final judgment day is upon us. Our government cannot be fixed if we do not come together and demand a change to how we govern ourselves in the future. The present governing structure will consume the balance of our wealth and will devour our independence. The only way forward is a democracy in which the people decide changes and new laws. We must rid our governing system of the attachments that consume our personal wealth; we must end the power the financial pyramid has over our government. The question is simple: Can we come together as one people to build a better future, or will our future be decided by what greed and corruption decides to redistribute to the masses? This is our first referendum. What will we decide?

Nationalism versus Globalism

Never before has the identity of our nation been in such turmoil. Somehow, after World War II, America became the financial nanny state, as well as the military police for many countries around the globe. Did this happen because our nation's political leaders felt compelled to help others, or was it because they, along with the financial sharks, realized there was chum in the water for easy feasting? Based on what we've seen happen in our own lives, it is doubtful our government's intentions were driven by compassion and were more likely centered on building an empire.

President Trump has fueled the debate on whether or not America should remain the peacemaker, as well as the military might, for the rest of the world. He has outwardly questioned our nation's political leadership, as well as others from around the globe, challenging them to explain why it is America should continue to pledge the same percentage of our GDP spent on national defense as other nations, especially when their GDP pales in comparison to the size of America's. He has stated to the American people, as well as our NATO partners, that his agenda will be to put America first in every negotiation. This concept is glorified by some and vilified by others. Those who oppose it portray it as a nationalistic charge by a dictator wannabe, while those who do like the idea of America first see it as nothing more than patriotism.

Make no mistake, this debate about nationalism versus globalism and how we will interact with other nations will become the pivotal point in our nation's history. Our ancestors had to decide whether or not they would be governed by Great Britain. We must decide whether America will remain a sovereign nation governed by the Constitution of the United States or become part of a world organization governed by a United Nations agreement. It is for these reasons that I believe we can no longer trust a representative government that is beholden to the lobbyists to decide our future.

The Truth Behind the Debate

Why is it that everything Washington, DC, touches is such a mess? The thought that a nationalistic view of putting one's own country first when negotiating deals is being construed as a bad idea is simply baffling, especially when Washington, DC, is going to have such an enormous budget deficit for the unforeseeable future. This depiction of nationalism becoming Hitlerism is yet another deception of subliminal messaging because the idea of our citizenry having nationalistic pride does not fit into the global governing agenda. You see, globalism has been the financial pyramid's agenda from the start. The problem is because the Federal Reserve and the central banking system have sold the idea of the fiat monetary system worldwide, now our government has joined the global party.

Let's start by highlighting the hypocrisy from our politicians regarding the debate of nationalism versus globalism by analyzing their position on nationalism when it comes to our military. We hear the politicians chant, "Rah, rah, rah," as they boast how America's military is number one. Yet when the discussion of national pride in civilian America happens, it is degraded and called dangerous, white supremacy, Hitlerism, anti-immigrant; the list of adjectives goes on. The question is "Why?" Is their concern about nationalism that they know they are using identity politics to divide our nation's people and that nationalism within a majority demographic could cause a Hitler-type movement? If this is their concern, then why not stop using divisional politics and work on bringing people together by using nationalistic pride as our greatest resource for unity?

So why promote nationalism and unity as unquestionable assets when they pertain to our military yet display utter disdain for them in civilian America? The answer is simple: *they do not want unity of any kind!* You see, in civilian America, the politicians define unity as loyalty to a political party or ideology. In other words, unify citizens independently where they are loyal specifically to segregated groups, not to one nation. Why? Because they want Americans opposing Americans to ensure there is no chance of a unified majority that has the potential to demand change.

As I try to reason my way through the strife in our political environment, I cannot help but revert back Rahm Emanuel's comment: "You never want a serious crisis to go to waste . . . The crisis provides the opportunity, for us . . . to do things that you could not do before." If we begin to analyze American politics from Emanuel's perspective, we begin to shed light on why our political leaders approach everything as though it is a crisis. Yet this does not answer the question as to why this constant crisis mode is necessary and what it is they are trying so hard to hide or change. After pondering this for a while, the answer becomes clear. Nationalism—or, phrased differently, unity of citizenship—poses the threat of becoming an uncooperative participant in a global agenda.

We really should pause for just a moment so we can collectively applaud these people for just how cunning and deceptive they are. When we begin to peel back the layers, realizing that every move they make is a premeditated attack to dictate our future, what becomes abundantly clear is the danger that a representative democracy brings to our future, as opposed to a real one that the people decide. If my hypothesis is correct, the question becomes "Is the agenda to demonize nationalism done to minimize the importance of remaining a sovereign nation, all while they condition our citizenry to be more receptive to a United Nations constitution?"

If the goal is to follow a United Nations constitution, the question is "Why?" I believe it's because the world, not just America, has become a victim of fiat system addiction, and I believe the negotiations of global contracts has everything to do with the expanse of money and the next stage of dealing with the world's debt. In other words, I believe this to be the final move by the Federal Reserve/central banking system to become the singular dominating force that controls and supplies the world's governments with money.

I am aware that any mention of a United Nations constitution will trigger the word *conspiracy* among United Nations advocates and that they use this label to discredit dissenters of the global agenda. If you're wondering why, it's because labeling something as a conspiracy is a tactical use of subliminal messaging to ultimately seek and destroy logic from becoming a known truth.

My point is this: it is not conspiracy to say there are people at the top of the political and financial world who know things far in advance of anyone else, and it would be ridiculous to think that the folks atop the financial pyramid are not planning outcomes to ensure they do not lose their wealth should bad things happen. I'm not sure about you, but I would be concerned if they weren't planning ahead to ensure the systems we have in place can sustain themselves on a long-term basis. (In fact, our government is supposed to be doing that with our tax dollars.) As I have proven with the examples I've provided, when these folks create concepts, they do it in such a way that change will transpire from one generation to another as a natural occurrence over time. They use the educational system, the media, political discourse, and catastrophic events to achieve the results most advantageous to obtaining their objective.

So why the political debate of nationalism versus globalism or capitalism versus socialism? It's an easy question to answer. Our government's reckless spending and debt creation have caused their chickens to come home to roost, and their ongoing policies of kicking the can down the road have finally reached their end. In other words, they are slowly easing America into a national framework that will conform to the International Monetary Fund (IMF)/United Nations once our nation's debt is unsustainable and will suffer collapse.

The following is a short explanation of what the IMF is, when it was created, and its role in the financial world. It should be noted that its main headquarters, which are located at 1900 Pennsylvania Avenue in Washington, DC, are a stone's throw away from the Federal Reserve. My purpose for providing this information is because I believe if we allow our present fiat monetary system to fail, our government already has a plan of action to use the IMF as the mediator for bailout, and once this transpires, it will ultimately attach our nation's monetary system to a global currency.

What Is the International Monetary Fund?

The International Monetary Fund is an organization that consists of 189 countries. It was created in an effort to secure financial stability, facilitate international trade, promote high employment and economic growth, and reduce poverty around the world. Harry Dexter White and John Maynard Keynes devised the concept for the IMF, and their idea was presented in 1944 at the Bretton Woods Conference. The IMF came into formal existence in 1945 with 29 member countries and the goal of reconstructing the international payment system. It now plays a central role in managing and balancing payments from countries having difficulty due to international financial crises. Member countries contribute funds to a pool through a quota system, and countries that are experiencing problems can borrow money from the pool.

Through the fund and other activities such as gathering statistics and analysis, surveillance of its members' economies, and the demand for particular policies, the IMF works to improve the economies of its member countries. The organization's objectives stated in their Articles of Agreement are to promote international monetary cooperation, international trade, high employment, exchange-rate stability, and sustainable economic growth and to make resources available to member countries in financial difficulty. The IMF's funds come from two major sources: quotas from member country and loans. The size of a member's quota depends on its economic and financial importance in the world. Nations with larger economic importance have larger quotas. The quotas are increased periodically as a means of boosting the IMF's resources.

After World War II, war-torn countries were a mess and in need of rebuilding. To the countries that had suffered the destruction, the war was catastrophic. To the world's financiers—J. P. Morgan, John D. Rockefeller, Amschel Rothschild, and a slew of others—the rebuilding process would deliver endless prosperity. They knew that using the gold-backed monetary system to fund rebuilding would not suffice due to the built-in self-correcting mechanisms that shut down the availability of currency once economic conditions become inflationary. The war's massive destruction needed a monetary system that would allow trustworthy governments to create an endless supply of currency on an as-needed basis. The financial engineers knew the fiat monetary system would provide the flexibility these governments needed, but they also knew from history that the system would eventually collapse from the overburden of debt.

What we learn from these events is the people atop the financial pyramid always have a plan. They created the IMF long ago, and just as Emanuel said that crises create an opportunity to do something you think you could not have done before, the IMF was born due to the tragic carnage left behind after World War II. Proof that these folks are patient is provided by analyzing the IMF's membership growth. There is a grand total of 195 countries in the world. In 1945, the IMF had 29 member countries, and in 2019, that number has increased to a staggering 189.

When people are quick to suggest conspiracy when logic has been presented, it is either because they are shallow in the brain department and simply can't think outside their spoon-fed talking points, or they have an agenda. Of course, none of us can know exactly what the ultimate goal is, but the facts that the IMF's main headquarters are in Washington, DC and that 96 percent of the countries around the globe are IMF members give off the aroma of empire-building and a one-world currency.

Why a Sovereign Monetary System Matters

As Americans, we should be thankful for what we have. Yet we also must acknowledge we are not exempt from the possibility of an enemy attack or a potential collapse of our economic stability. Most importantly, we must realize if our debt becomes unsustainable, America will be subjected to receiving a bailout from the IMF. Why does this matter? After a monetary system reaches debt default, the benefits the citizens receive from their tax-funded entitlements are no longer managed or reviewed by their government as a sovereign nation. The benefits become subject to review and most likely denied by the IMF's contributing members. In other words, the loss of sovereignty and opening our fiscal budget to global review means what we get or how much we can achieve will be subject to input from other governments in the global network.

It's worth taking a moment to explain what this means, and there's no better example to use than Greece.

Greece's Debt Crisis

The Greek debt crisis was the dangerous amount of sovereign debt Greece owed the European Union between 2008 and 2018. In 2010, Greece said it might default on its debt, thus threatening the viability of the euro zone. To avoid default, the European Union loaned Greece enough money to continue making payments. Since the debt crisis began, various European authorities and private investors have loaned Greece approximately 320 billion euros. This was the largest financial rescue of a bankrupt country in documented history. As of January 2019, Greece has repaid 41.6 billion euros and has scheduled debt payments that extend beyond the year 2060.

In return for the loan, the European Union along with the IMF affiliates required Greece to adopt austerity measures. The reforms that the supporting European Union members created were intended to strengthen the Greek government and their financial structure. Yet the impact of these austerity measures caused Greece to enter a long-term recession lasting from 2010 until the end of 2017.

The important part of Greece's deal with the (Eurozone and the IMF's 1.8 billion contribution) is that their incoming revenue and outgoing expenses were subjected to review, meaning their expenditures were approved or denied by other European, American, and private investors' authorities. Additionally, what is extremely critical to understand is the final decision levied by the named authorities and private investors was that Greece was required to adopt austerity measures for the entitlements their citizens received based on the demands of non-Greek authorities.

My point is, should America go into debt default and need money from other countries such as Greece did, every benefit we receive as citizens would be reviewed and subjected to elimination if these outside authorities deemed it necessary. This means Social Security, Medicare/Medicaid, pension benefits, welfare, subsidized housing programs, school lunches, and drug rehabilitation programs. I could fill up twenty pages if I were to list all the programs and subsidies that would be under someone else's review, and more than likely, every one of them would be significantly reduced or completely eliminated if the IMF felt it had to be done in order to satisfy the interest payment on the debt.

In 2011 Jeff Cox listed on CNBC's website ten of the most significant austerity measures required for Greece to receive IMF bailout money.

- Taxes will increase by 2.32 billion euros this year and 3.38 billion, 152 million, and 699 million in the three subsequent years. There will be higher property taxes and an increase in the value-added tax (VAT) from 19 percent to 23 percent.
- Luxury levies will be introduced on yachts, pools, and cars, and there will be special levies on profitable firms, high-value properties, and people with high incomes.

- Excise taxes on fuel, cigarettes, and alcohol will rise by one third.
- Public sector wages will be cut by 15 percent.
- Defense spending will be cut by 200 million euros in 2012 and 333 million each year from 2013 to 2015.
- Education spending will be cut by closing or merging 1,976 schools.
- Social Security will be cut by 1.09 billion euros this year, 1.28 billion in 2012, 1.03 billion in 2013, 1.01 billion in 2014, and 700 million in 2015. There also will be means testing, and the statutory retirement age will be raised to 65 from 61.
- The government will privatize a number of its enterprises, including the OPAP gambling monopoly, the Hellenic Postbank, several port operations, and Hellenic Telecom and will sell its stake in Athens Water, Hellenic Petroleum, PPC electric utility, and lender ATE bank, as well as ports, airports, motorway concessions, state land, and mining rights.
- Only one in ten civil servants retiring this year will be replaced and one in five in coming years.
- Health spending will be cut by 310 million euros this year and 1.81 billion euros from 2012 to 2015.

Get Angry, People!

Our sovereignty as a nation should not be reduced to a political talking point in an attempt to label someone a racist, bigot, or xenophobe or to comparing the idea of national patriotism to a madman like Adolf Hitler. We are without question a nation of immigrants, but every immigrant must become a proud American, accepting the stepping-stones of our past that helped lead us to a better future. America remaining a sovereign nation with our own currency and a budget determined by our government is of great importance to our remaining free citizens. The people toying with our sovereignty as folly for political gain should be jailed for such a treasonous act. They are playing Russian roulette with our future, and I don't know about you, but this makes me angry. How dare they put in jeopardy something that is so important to the people who pay them?

The folks at the top of the financial pyramid couldn't care less about our nation's sovereignty. They already have a multitude of residences throughout the world, so if America should collapse, causing disarray in our streets, they will already be in their Swiss chalet somewhere at the top of a mountain. In their eyes, if another American civil war breaks out or our entire monetary system collapses, they are the main controllers of the IMF, so once the dust settles and the rebuilding process begins, this means pure profit to them.

I hope you are getting the severity of what's at stake. This process of dividing our citizens is to ensure Washington, DC, and the people they do deals with that the majority of our citizenry remains a limp, lifeless people who are powerless to stop what they deem to be your future. If we are dumb enough to allow this division to continue, then we deserve the same fate as Greece. It is a fallacy that we did this to ourselves; we've worked countless hours and have paid an enormous amount of taxes to a feckless government that enriched themselves while they sold our future to the highest bidder.

We can save this country, but it cannot and will not happen if we continue to let the political scientists put up walls of division in our society. We can have differences, and it is important to openly debate those differences, but we must never let our differences separate us so greatly that we lose our overall freedom. The politicians aren't putting us into these identity groups because they plan to strengthen our rights as people. They're doing it to weaken our overall strength as a unified citizenry.

It is time to wake up, people. Nationalism in America should not be thought of as a derogatory term. It should be viewed as having diversified industries that have an allegiance to the country that gave them an opportunity to succeed. Nationalism should be a diversified citizenry brought together by effective leadership, one that promotes commonality, not hatred and division. It should be a common pride in our country that, regardless of our differences, we remain a sovereign self-sustaining nation built from a collective people who believe in the American dream.

Conclusion

We must understand that the idea of globalism and the concept of creating a worldwide level playing field for global trade are how they are delivering their sales pitch, but that's not the real plan. The reality is they are funding the growth of other nations, creating central banking systems around the globe, and using our financial infrastructure to pay for it. They profit from the low labor cost and less restrictive governments, and when their financial speculation fails, they use our Federal Reserve system to bail their asses out.

Yes, we want the rest of the world to grow, and we do want their wages to rise as ours once did here in America, but we cannot continue to give our government and the Federal Reserve the authority to use our money to subsidize it. Globalism is a worldwide fistfight, and our government has cut off our arms in this battle. Make no mistake: the idea of globalism to every country competing in it is to kick our American ass.

This movement to tear down and degrade our nation's past by portraying it as one we should be ashamed of has everything to do with building a new America that will have far less opportunity and much more dependency on a centralized government. In other words, the process of growth has been stalled, and the expectations of what our citizenry should expect to achieve have been greatly reduced. To create this so-called level playing field, they needed to create stagnation and lower expectations here in America while the slow process of wage increases and massive profiting happens for them while they do business in other countries.

My fellow Americans, if we allow them to continue, we will be nothing more than a division on a United Nations economic map. Because we've been high achievers, the rest of the world will view us as someone who should not be given more. In fact, they will look at our elevated status and demand that we be equalized with the rest of the world. Is this what you want? You see, this process of political correctness and identity politics is the beginning stage of the future plan. Instead of promoting an innovating spirit, they see your future as one that has reached its limit. The idea of central government is to use the tax system to drastically tear down one economic group while elevating another. Is this what we want?

Please don't misconstrue my message. In order for America to grow, we must expand and compete in the global market. My point is if we continue to allow a them to run up debt from overspending and they continue to allow monopolies to form, the global market will never be available for the common citizens to compete in. Having a national spirit of being a proud, productive, innovative American people is our only chance to avoid an imprisoned future!

Conspiracy, Deception, Truth

I cannot say everything I've presented thus far is exactly how or why America has reached the point at which I believe we must choose to remain a representative democracy or establish a real democracy. In my view, the choice is simple. Either we continue to be run by an effectively rudderless government overburdening us with debt, or we unite and demand a change to a real democracy so we can preserve what remains and start rebuilding a better future.

How do we as a citizenry get past the divisions and hatred that have been engineered as a destructive force to our unity, and how can we identify the truth? We know for sure we cannot trust our government to deliver the truth, and we know they have decided to dance with the devil. We cannot trust the media because for every opinion purporting to be telling the truth, there is an opposing opinion exposing that so-called truth as a lie. The only thing we have to help us see through this fog of deception are the outcomes of past events, but even this can prove to be difficult because the deceivers have had a hand in writing history.

The truth is our division helps keep coercion, deception, and the hiding of it alive. Because they have manipulated us to place blame on one another, this has provided cover for the Federal Reserve, the financiers, the treasury department, and a two-party political system. The reality is that conspiracy, deception, and division are merely tools designed to reduce our ability to see the forest for the trees. These tactics keep alive the idea that we are free, when in reality the financiers and our government have deceptively built an imperial structure similar to that of Great Britain.

Conspiracy or Deception?

If I said to you that Washington, DC; the Federal Reserve; and the world financiers plan to slowly shift the governing power of the Constitution of the United States into a state of connectedness with a United Nations constitution by using legal language within climate and global trade agreements, many of you might say, "Conspiracy!" If I said the move to the fiat monetary system in 1971 was designed so the financiers and the Federal Reserve could profit from the creation of massive debt and taxpayer bailouts and their endgame was to collapse the monetary system in order to create a one-world currency, many of you might again say, "Conspiracy!"

The truth is none of us really know whether or not the wealthy financiers such as the Rockefellers and the Rothschilds really want a one-world monetary system or a one-world government or, for that matter, how much wealth they really have. What we know is worldwide connectedness of global trade of goods and services has dramatically increased. We also know that the US dollar is the leading international currency used to pay for the exchange of such products throughout the world. In fact, we should be extremely proud that because of our tax dollars being the integrity of our nation's fiat monetary system, we've provided the Federal Reserve, central banking, and the Big Six Banks the strength to convince other governments around the world to use central banking as monetary policy and to use the US dollar as their leading currency. So if we apply this truth to the question of whether there is a movement toward a one-world-currency, understanding that 90 percent of the world is already using central banking to govern their monetary systems and according to the IMF's official website 61 percent of those central banks hold US dollars as their reserves, I would say the idea of a one-world-currency is right around the corner!

The War for Power

This still leaves us with the question of whether or not there is a movement toward a one-world government. I believe a fight looms in the darkness, one that should be considered the most dangerous of all, because this fight will determine who will be the ultimate power of the world. I believe this fight unknowingly exists between the powerful financiers and the governments that seek to control the masses. When I say a fight unknowingly exists, my point is the folks at the top of the (financial pyramid) may be getting lulled into a sense of comfort, believing they say jump and the bureaucrats will do precisely what they want. These financiers seek power to manipulate governments by getting them hooked on debt, but governments get their power from creating taxing mechanisms that can reach every living, breathing entity that produces economic prosperity.

It's easy to understand how a one-world currency could benefit the financiers living atop the monetary pyramid, especially if they control the banking as well as the majority of the goods and services provided to people around the globe. It's also not hard to understand the value to governments having control over a singular currency, as well as data-tracking methods that give them the ability to have information on every financial transaction that happens throughout the world. Applying logic, it's really not a stretch to consider both the governments and financiers could favor a one-world currency.

The difference between these two power-hungry demagogues is the financiers could care less about people in general. What matters to them is collecting their interest on massive debt and assuring profit is gained on their investments, as well as maintaining personal protection to keep their dynasties safe. Governments, on the other hand, have to deal with citizens, so their power is derived from their ability to tax their people and industries as much as possible without creating a unified movement of dissatisfaction—in other words, avoiding civil unrest. Governments also need scapegoats such as the Federal Reserve to facilitate confusion, diversion, and deception to keep the citizens off balance and to provide political cover from the tragedies that befall the citizens due to bad policy and corruption.

Yet for a one-world government to win the war of total power, they must somehow find a way to entrap Wall Street, private equity, and commercial banking. This is why I believe a war between the government and the financiers will begin someday soon. Although the monopolists and the Big Six Banks might be happy the government has turned their head by allowing them to consolidate, I believe the dirty little secret of why the government is letting this happen is so they can use this corporate consolidation to simplify finding hidden profits in their offshore accounts.

You see, a centralized government must have access to a constant stream of tax revenue. Corporate profits have found tax shelters in places such as the Cayman Islands and Swiss banks. These shelters are the government's giant pot of gold at the end of the rainbow. As long as they allow these financiers to consolidate while maintaining a connectedness by supplying them with taxpayer bailouts, I believe the government is moving in on the illusive target of where the financiers store their wealth.

The Truth

How do all these battlefronts play into our lives? Most economists predict our nation's growing debt will eventually collapse our economy. China and Japan have made significant advances in becoming alternative currencies to the dollar, gaining confidence from other countries as well as outside investors looking for a safe haven to invest surplus cash. Because of the mortgage crisis, China has been able to create concerns on a world stage, instilling fear that treasury bonds are no longer safe for investment, pointing out the danger of the US government's ongoing budget deficit.

Many economists also have expressed their belief that the Federal Reserve is rendered powerless to help in the next economic crisis because of the $4 trillion they hold on their balance sheet. The economists believe the bloated balance sheet will limit the Federal Reserve's ability to buy more treasury bonds should another crisis occur. The consensus among the economists is the Federal Reserve no longer has the necessary tools in their tool belt to effectively change the momentum of a downward economic spiral.

That's why it's important for us to understand the danger that looms in our not-too-distant future. The next dilemma to hit the too-big-to-fail banks will most likely be triggered by the $4 trillion in consumer debt and the $1.47 trillion in combined student loan debt. Although there are other debt bubbles to be concerned with, I highlight consumer debt and student debt because any significant downturn in the economy whatsoever will likely cause an immediate increase in loan defaults.

In addition to these potential loan defaults looms a dangerously overvalued stock market. Many economists we see on the Saturday morning business channels feel the stock market is presently overvalued by as much as 40 percent. If they are right that the Federal Reserve has lost its ability to help, this means our economy and taxpayers will absorb the full impact of the loan defaults, and the result will most likely cause the stock market to self-correct by producing a major sell-off.

What does this mean to us? If the economy begins to crash, the Federal Reserve will signal to the Treasury Department to print more money. But in order for them to print more money, the Federal Reserve will be required to sell treasury bonds on the open market. They must use the open market to sell treasury bonds because, as the economists point out, the Federal Reserve already has a bloated balance sheet that will prevent them from buying more bonds.

We also know the US government will be of no help because they already are overspending their annual budget significantly, and they already used up the surplus cash from our commingled entitlements.

The reality for us is our feckless leadership has put us in a vulnerable position to pay higher interest rates to those willing to buy treasury bonds.

Where does all this crappy governing leave us? In my view, it leaves us exactly where the government and the financiers wanted all along, which is one step closer to a one-world currency and the sovereignty of our monetary system being compromised, thus in need of assistance from the United Nations and the IMF.

I can hear the confusion in the questions: "Aren't these people Americans? Why the hell would they do that?" The truth is that the financiers don't give a rat's ass about this country or your American dream. You are sheep grazing in their field and nothing more. They view our citizenry as a poor return on investment because of our lawsuits, our unions, and our bloated government regulations that make it next to impossible for them to make a profit.

But why would the government want such a horrific outcome for our people? If we recall Emanuel's comment about taking advantage of a crisis, we realize that allowing America to fail due to massive debt would deliver a crisis of mammoth proportions. With the Federal Reserve and the Treasury Department's commingled cash surpluses having been exhausted and the country in a state of panic, Washington, DC, would call on the IMF for a partial bailout. This would expose our nation's sovereign rights as an independent country to the governing monetary rules that apply to those who borrow from the IMF and/or the United Nations.

The financiers, the US government, and the Federal Reserve already know the default process well because they are the main figureheads involved in the IMF banking operation. This commingled partnership are the people who largely control the reins of the IMF. Their long-term pursuit of establishing a worldwide central banking system and a global economy that has a one-world currency has been put on hold because of the pesky US citizens' belief that we should maintain our sovereignty as an independent nation. In their view, an economic crisis of this magnitude is precisely what the doctor ordered.

Conclusion

What will happen to us? The economic crisis will destroy every last shred of our independent spirit while providing opportunity for Washington, DC, to establish new procedures of redistribution, taxation, and measures of austerity for Social Security, Medicare/Medicaid, and all other entitlements. Most significantly, it creates a new scapegoat to provide political cover, allowing our government to use the monetary contract established with the IMF and the United Nations as the new blame agent for forcing rules upon our citizenry that must comply with a UN constitution.

I hope I've earned your trust that I am not a person driven by a left or right political agenda. The only agenda I have is to be the warning shot to the American people that doom is sitting just outside our door. The only way we can stop the devouring of our independence is to unite as one people, demanding change to the amount of authority given to the deceivers.

It is up to you to decide: will our future be one that is governed by restrictive laws, security cameras, controlled speech, and controlled measures of tax redistribution? Or will we filter through the fog of financial conspiracy, government deceptions, and the division of our citizenry by delivering the truth to the deceivers—America is our home, and our sovereignty is not for sale?

Gen Y: It's Up to You

The fate of our nation's sovereignty is going to be decided during your leadership. I admit that is a terrible way to start a chapter, but I believe it is a true statement. Some of my generation (I'm a boomer) may not agree, but I believe the boomers and the early Gen Xers owe an apology to Gen Ys for the mess we've left behind. But Gen Ys will have to decide whether they want to lead or to be led? Do they want an America built from an independent spirit, or do they want to be a people dependent on government?

I was fortunate enough to have the opportunity to coach all three of my children in several sports, so I feel like I have an understanding of how the Gen Ys think and respond in a competitive environment. In one sense, I believe they are, without question, the most educated and unbiased of any generation in our nation's history. I believe racism, bigotry, and any other racial tension will be considerably less with this generation than any in America's past. Additionally, the issues surrounding inequality and gender identity will most likely be eliminated once the Gen Ys become more involved in leadership.

The concern I have for Gen Ys is that once they ascend into leadership roles in Washington, DC, will the naivety of an educational system that promoted that the world is a fair place be so deeply ingrained in their DNA that it sets them up to fail? By now, most of them have learned after entering the competitive job market that the concept of everyone getting a chance to win is a load of crap. America is and always has been a dog-eat-dog world that only provides opportunity to those who are willing to work for it.

The apology I mentioned that should come from the boomers is for our soft parenting and our accepting an educational curriculum that we knew was delivering a false promise to our children. We also took our eye off the ball by allowing ineffective governing, wasteful spending of our tax dollars, corruption without consequences, and accumulation of massive debt. And to further compound our negligence, we allowed our government to use the surplus cash from our reserves, knowing full well they already had a massive budget deficit and that there would be no chance of them paying it back.

Okay, now that my apology is over, I wouldn't hold your breath waiting for other boomers to do the same because apologizing and admitting fault are not among our attributes. In an earlier chapter, I brought to your attention the fact that the horrific economy and job market the Gen Ys entered after college was similar to the one experienced by younger members of the boomer generation. Additionally, I mentioned how things got a whole lot better once a couple of college dropouts ignited the technological revolution, each creating an idea in their garage, that would revolutionize how the world functioned. These innovations eventually became Apple, Microsoft, along with a plethora of others companies created by brilliant innovators that ultimately changed the way we communicate, how we manage our businesses, and how we buy products and services. But what the technological revolution did most was lift our spirits in what was an extremely difficult time in American history.

What's important to take away from the technological revolution is what seems to be a future without hope can quickly change to one of tremendous prosperity. Unfortunately, the other lesson we learned is that prosperity most often becomes a victim of greed, and once greed has ravaged everything that produced prosperity, it seeks to consume whatever prosperity still exists within the masses.

The information that follows is negative, but it is the proof that greed has no conscience. I ask that as we continue, you turn off your preconditioned political ideas and consider the logic I present. The following are just a few things the Gen Ys will need to be concerned with in the future. These are the results once greed begins to consume prosperity.

Stealing Family Inheritances

The boomers are listed in several publications such as (Forbes, business insider, money-usnews) as the wealthiest generation in the history of mankind. After the 2008 mortgage crisis and the stock market crash, their wealth has been drastically reduced. What transpired after the Great Recession was that a large portion of the boomer's wealth (through foreclosure, reverse mortgages, etcetera) fell victim to those at the top of the monetary pyramid.

What remains of a once-prosperous group is now an aging population with an insecure future. What does this mean to you, and how will this affect you in the long term? The two subheads listed below are what you and your parents should be concerned about in the not-too-distant future.

Medical Expenses

If a deceased parent did not have Medicare/Medicaid and dies with unpaid hospital or doctor bills, their estate (if it has the money) is responsible for paying the bills at the time of death. State laws do vary. Some actually require adult children to pay for a deceased parent's medical debts, such as hospital bills and nursing homes, when the estate cannot cover the entire cost. If you live in one of the following states, it's worth checking into current inheritance law; currently these states are listed as having various punitive measures.

Alaska	Louisiana	Ohio
Arkansas	Maryland	Oregon
California	Massachusetts	Pennsylvania
Connecticut	Mississippi	Rhode Island
Delaware	Montana	South Dakota
Georgia	Nevada	Tennessee
Idaho	New Hampshire	Utah
Indiana	New Jersey	Vermont
Iowa	North Carolina	Virginia
Kentucky	North Dakota	West Virginia

Reverse Mortgages

In many cases, reverse mortgages are the direct result of the mortgage and stock market collapse. The tragedy for the boomers was the stock market crash caused many to lose their entire retirement savings. Even though the market significantly rebounded, there are many people who have missed out because they no longer trusted their life savings in the hands of Wall Street, so many who needed to rebuild their savings actually lost out because they sat on the sidelines due to their mistrust in Wall. Unfortunately, because of the loss in savings, they have been forced to use the equity in their homes to subsidize their living expenses.

What is important for you to know is that heirs to an estate get six months to deal with a reverse mortgage loan payoff. Otherwise, the bank takes title to the home. It is to the heirs' advantage to move quickly because until the loan is settled, the interest on the balance and monthly insurance premiums will continue to eat away at the remaining equity in the heirs' inheritance.

Not to bore or overwhelm you with data, but the following chart displays a state-by-state account of reverse mortgages issued in a single year. Let's remember that I pointed out earlier that the fiat system must have perpetual debt. What the reverse mortgage chart shows is that the people who caused the Great Recession are now converting what would have been your inheritance into debt. The end result is the perpetrators of the greatest heist in history will finish their theft by foreclosing on your parents' home if you are unable to pay the loan balance. Please don't be naive and think this was by accident!

State-by-State Reverse Mortgages

State	HECM Traditional	HECM For Refinance	HECM For Purchase	Total	AVG. Interest Rate	AVG. Principal Limit	AVG. Home Value
ALABAMA	594	9	19	622	4.659%	$102,027.00	$174,743.00
ALASKA	38	1	0	39	4.631%	$186,082.00	$315,346.00
ARIZONA	1,633	239	191	2,063	4.609%	$161,144.00	$272,218.00
ARKANSAS	294	5	6	305	4.567%	$95,337.00	$162,280.00
CALIFORNIA	9,325	3,269	531	13,125	4.553%	$285,406.00	$469,914.00
COLORADO	2,188	681	133	3,002	4.583%	$206,962.00	$349,939.00
CONNECTICUT	419	7	8	434	4.446%	$177,839.00	$284,524.00
DELAWARE	185	6	13	204	4.562%	$149,622.00	$250,878.00
FLORIDA	3,712	763	327	4,802	4.639%	$158,840.00	$267,271.00
GEORGIA	361	104	62	1,127	4.627%	$131,873.00	$223,624.00
HAWAII	162	8	15	185	4.481%	$324,478.00	$550,046.00
IDAHO	342	29	54	425	4.580%	$137,948.00	$235,866.00
ILLINOIS	919	56	14	989	4.616%	$140,154.00	$229,816.00
INDIANA	522	14	21	557	4.608%	$93,697.00	$159,983.00
IOWA	221	2	10	233	4.669%	$97,829.00	$166,385.00
KANSAS	215	1	8	224	4.613%	$96,164.00	$160,132.00
KENTUCKY	291	4	3	298	4.628%	$99,507.00	$168,654.00
LOUISIANA	582	46	10	638	4.592%	$122,171.00	$206,751.00
MAINE	194	3	3	200	4.519%	$155,976.00	$260,172.00
MARYLAND	720	67	23	810	4.545%	$177,336.00	$297,015.00
MASSACHUSET	767	54	13	834	4.436%	$232,443.00	$386,885.00
MICHIGAN	699	49	14	762	4.600%	$116,162.00	$196,645.00
MINNESOTA	419	25	14	458	4.526%	$151,296.00	$260,382.00
MISSISSIPPI	283	4	3	290	4.639%	$93,819.00	$160,453.00
MISSOURI	489	16	15	520	4.539%	$113,730.00	$191,649.00
MONTANA	216	8	6	230	4.540%	$160,486.00	$277,260.00
NEBRASKA	140	3	2	145	4.584%	$102,370.00	$174,651.00
NEVADA	456	102	42	600	4.650%	$128,830.00	$221,416.00
NEW HAMPSHIRE	161	6	8	175	4.687%	$162,059.00	$277,250.00
NEW JERSEY	1,093	73	28	1,194	4.565%	$197,593.00	$322,076.00
NEW MEXICO	316	4	16	336	4.565%	$146,321.00	$247,238.00
NEW YORK	1,965	309	33	2,307	4.563%	$257,790.00	$424,370.00
NORTH CAROLIN	1,131	62	99	1,292	4.575%	$133,791.00	$227,623.00
NORTH DAKOTA	46	1	2	49	4.540%	$112,562.00	$197,888.00
OHIO	724	40	149	913	4.627%	$111,222.00	$189,065.00
OKLAHOMA	431	6	13	450	4.621%	$98,792.00	$167,652.00
OREGON	993	287	44	1,324	4.583%	$200,569.00	$338,416.00
PENNSYLVANIA	1,253	76	64	1,393	4.556%	$124,545.00	$208,706.00
RHODE ISLAND	109	5	2	116	4.372%	$178,454.00	$298,331.00
SOUTH CAROLIN	683	34	96	813	4.643%	$143,036.00	$242,679.00
SOUTH DAKOTA	49	1	3	53	4.718%	$122,740.00	$209,839.00
TENNESSEE	807	71	22	900	4.522%	$122,107.00	$207,703.00
TEXAS	3,385	712	129	4,226	4.635%	$135,556.00	$228,137.00
UTAH	769	69	223	1,061	4.535%	$182,931.00	$315,010.00
VERMONT	85	1	1	87	4.647%	$150,850.00	$256,363.00
VIRGINIA	1,030	47	37	1,114	4.611%	$161,751.00	$270,940.00
WASHINGTON	1,333	398	63	1,794	4.616%	$228,562.00	$382,635.00
WEST VIRGINIA	165	0	3	168	4.639%	$91,067.00	$155,728.00
WISCONSIN	369	10	2	381	4.628%	$112,871.00	$191,838.00
WYOMING	102	2	8	112	4.566%	$146,374.00	$255,169.00

Source: Reverse mortgage website, accessed November 15th 2019

It cannot be disputed that the mortgage crisis was the result of corruption and collusion. It happened because our leaders in Washington, DC, were more focused on building an empire than protecting their constituents at home. Yet we must consider whether the outcome of this catastrophe will be what the kingpins of the financial pyramid and Washington, DC, wanted all along. Is it possible that Washington, DC's decision to build an empire and a global economy needed to diminish the wealth of the boomers to ensure there would not be a transfer of wealth to the Gen Ys? Is it possible this happened because they want worldwide socialism, and stopping the transfer of wealth is part of creating what they refer to as a worldwide level playing field? The result of the crisis was ten years of stunted wages, 40 percent home devaluation, and, last but not least, a loss of wealth being passed from one generation to another. If these results are not part of their plan, then we must conclude that they suck at their jobs and need to be replaced.

When Prosperity Begins

It is hard to see light when you are smothered in darkness. Yet when a small speck of light peeks through, it is as bright as the sun! If you hope to have a life of independence and prosperity, you must identify the darkness that is smothering the light of your future. It's time to regain prosperity, but before we do, we must understand what it is that the financiers already know.

As America was growing, the world's financiers could invest in a vast number of things, such as bridges, homes and buildings, rail systems, electrical grids, power stations, industrialization, streets, and neighborhoods. From their viewpoint, investing in America was low risk because they could pretty much dictate the payment rules as well as the interest rates on their loans. Also, extremely attractive when it comes to building a nation are vast resources, low labor costs, no labor unions, and virtually zero legal liability added to the cost of doing business. In a word, *huge* profits for the financiers.

Yet we should understand that prior to investing in America's growth, these same people already had experienced this process decades earlier in Europe. They made huge profits from financing Europe's infrastructure, and once the infrastructure began to be prosperous, the next stage of their financing was geared toward government, municipal, and corporate bond buying. This process of funding government through the sale of bonds happens because governments are prone to spend beyond their means and have the power of taxation, so the financiers consider the bonds to be low-risk investments. Additionally, because most of the financiers still operate businesses within these countries, buying bonds in the government's time of need helps maintain goodwill between the government and the financiers, which serves as a useful tool for the financiers when it comes to deal making.

The financiers understand the multiple stages of investing in nation building. It begins with the formation of a small government; establishing a monetary system, farming, and industry; and building small communities. Once the infrastructure and monetary system are up and running, the potential to achieve a profitable return is great because wages start out low, and there is minimal government regulation and, in many cases, an inspired workforce that is grateful for the prospect of long-term employment. This blend quickly produces prosperity. Once prosperity emerges, so, too, does the system of taxation and the growth of the nation's government. How long nations can sustain prosperity depends on the vastness of the country's resources, the size and effectiveness of its government, and the rule of law assuring that society and governing structures are free from corruption and greed.

When Prosperity Declines

What transpires after years of development and massive profitability for the financiers is that the working class begins to feel they've been taken advantage of. In almost every case, nations that have sustained prosperity will eventually have a workforce that begins to protest for higher wages. As a method of squelching civilian unrest, governments create tax-and-spend programs to help ease what could become massive protests or labor strikes. The problem of too much or too little taxation begins to develop because as these welfare systems grow, in most cases, the government does not have enough tax revenue to pay for them. Because it is risky politics to demand more taxes from both the financiers and the working class, the process of selling government bonds and the creation of debt begins.

The problem is that once the borrowing starts, it becomes necessary to continually increase taxes on the citizenship to pay for the added expense of social programs, as well as the rising cost of interest on the growing debt. This presents the quandary of whether the cost of government and its regulatory policies is too big, as well as the debate over whether some citizens are paying too much tax and the wealthy not paying enough. It is intricacies such as these that begin to whittle away at prosperity. Yet all the things I've mentioned are no surprise to the financiers because they understand what happens as a result of a nation's growth, and they know that when growth reaches its peak, what follows will be a stage of decline.

The Before and After

Once a nation begins to decline, many of its citizens, as well as its industries, become dependent on government subsidies for many years, so the expectation of getting help must be slowly reduced over time to avoid civil unrest. The problem is the government and their vast array of financiers realize the system is seriously capped out, and this process of lowering expectations must be expedited. America's decline and the lowering of our expectations is the main element of the drama being played out in Washington, DC, right now.

There's no greater proof of lowering expectations than what the mortgage crisis achieved. Prior to the crisis, in general, Americans had much higher expectations pertaining to our nation's future. Afterward, with the ten-year stagnation and 40 percent home devaluation, the optimism of a bright future dissipated. What was to be the beginning of the boomers' retirement and the largest transfer of wealth from one generation to another became an insecure aging population forced to work longer, uncertain as to whether they will have the financial resources to survive.

Yet during this decline, we see our nation's borders are open to a vast flow of new immigration. What is notable is these new immigrants are coming from extremely oppressed regions throughout the world. In other words, it's an immigrant base that comes with low expectations of high wages or benefits. In fact, the only expectation they have is to find a job. Applying logic, I believe it's safe to assume what's happening regarding immigration is not by happenstance. Our government and their commingled financiers favor immigration from impoverished regions. They understand these people are willing to work for low wages, have little expectation regarding benefits, and are grateful for whatever they get.

What's important to understand is that by creating ten years of wage stagnation and a 40 percent devaluation of assets and opening the floodgates to poor immigrants, they have effectively turned back the clock on wages, as well as the expectations of a nation's people. What is most significant to the perpetrators who stole our wealth is that the newcomers likely have no awareness of what happened during the mortgage crisis or the $6.2 trillion theft of our entitlements.

The reality is, for America to compete in the global market, our benefits and wages (basically the cost of doing business) was too high, by creating deflation and stagnation, while at the same time regenerating a citizenship with lower expectations, is most certainly not by accident. Understanding this process and what it is they're trying to achieve explains the sudden push of socialism as the solution to our problems. Our imperial government and their commingled financiers know that socialism and immigration from impoverished regions are the natural transformation when prosperity becomes too weighted down. If you are among those of you who believe socialism is somehow a progressive idea, that is precisely what our government and the financiers have been persuading you to believe.

You see, this idea of converting to socialism is progressive, but not in the way you've been led to believe. Socialism is the default stage when prosperity can no longer produce enough revenue to cover the inefficient, oversize government. It exists because prosperity provided the revenue for it to exist. Socialism should not be thought of as progressive; it is, in fact, regressive. It is the shift between a citizenry that once was prosperous to one that has little expectations of becoming prosperous. Real progressivism would be a constructive governing plan that eliminates the policies and procedures that caused the destruction of prosperity.

I believe Gen Ys have the energy and the smarts to reverse the downward slide, but they must first recognize that converting to socialism actually empowers those who are responsible for destroying prosperity. It will not be an easy task to remove the destructive people and policies that are responsible for our nation's decline. It will require an organized political movement, one that demands change to the authority given to our government and removes the burden of ineffective governing, corruption, and waste.

We must collectively understand that the quickest way to return to prosperity is with innovations that provide a plethora of good-paying jobs to our citizens. Let us not forget that before the technological revolution, America was in significant decline. What the technological revolution proved was that free people inspired to innovate provide the best strategy to achieve prosperity.

The following are true progressive ideas that could help reverse our nation's decline. I will reiterate one more time that my only hope in presenting these ideas is to spur on young leaders all across America. The lie that bureaucrats are looking out for you by attempting to sell you the concept of socialism is a trap. The truth is they know the deals they cut with the monopolists and the financiers exclude new innovations that can provide a better future.

Real Progressive Ideas

- Change from a representative democracy to a democracy by referendum.
- Create a new political party called the Logician Party. The platform would be to promote unity among all citizens, pass a balanced budget amendment, protect individual state laws, annual review and means testing of all government subsidies, remove wasteful spending, and elect candidates who have superior management credentials.
- Reduce our nation's debt. Immediately eliminate the $6.2 trillion payable to Social Security, Medicare/Medicaid, and military retirement and use the savings from the reduced interest payment to pay the annual shortfall. This would eliminate the need for a tax increase.
- Completely eliminate the Affordable Care Act. This must include all present and future taxing mechanisms. Increase the payroll tax on Medicare/Medicaid to provide universal health care through the use of the already established Medicare/Medicaid system.
- Limit Congress's access to the surplus dollars held in entitlements to a maximum of 25 percent. Before using the funds, Congress must notify the citizens and request approval through a voting referendum. Money they borrow must be repaid in full before any more can be borrowed. Additionally, Congress must repay the money they borrow with real revenue, *not* through the sale of treasury bonds. This will ensure no increase to our nation's debt.
- Prohibit all family members of elected government officials (not just spouses) from lobbying or participating in special interest groups that can coerce government.
- Direct all campaign contributions directly to a representative political party, not individual candidates. The donations would be distributed equally among all candidates running for political positions. Ban campaign donations from wealthy donors that are paid directly to candidates running for office.

- Increase government pay. The idea is to promote higher-caliber citizens willing to consider government as a career choice. Additionally, the higher pay would end the need for elected officials to consider unethical ways of obtaining more income.
- Use tax dollars to fund innovative ideas. Include all states in a nationwide innovation competition, and let the citizens vote on the best idea. This would put an end to cronyism and inside deals known to waste millions of taxpayer dollars. This also would inspire an innovative citizenship, ultimately helping create new jobs and new technologies.
- Review the list of recipients getting government subsidies: Big Oil, Big Pharma, and several other industries. Hire an independent private-sector accounting firm to analyze the data for each recipient to decide whether the government should continue its subsidies. The money saved by eliminating illegitimate recipients would be applied to balancing the budget.
- Assemble the G20 nations and NATO members to create a nationwide illegal drug task force. Members of the task force would agree that if a drug lord from any member's homeland should enter another member's homeland and sell drugs, the legal system would take action. In the case of armed drug cartels, the two countries involved would agree to consolidate their resources and use military force to eliminate them. Since we are the world's leading military power, we could offer assistance to members who lack resources. There would be fee for our services, which could be paid for in cash or a trade credit to the United States.
- Publicly account for all money that is ceased from white collar crime, the drug trade, organized crime, and the multitude of other and deposit all proceeds into the Treasury Department as another method to help balance our nation's budget. This solidifies the phrase "crime pays" to ring true!
- Create management teams for hire that could assist countries wanting a Westernized governing system and a central bank monetary structure. The services provided could be paid for with cash or a trade credit with the United States for incoming

supplies. The key is to promote Western ways without force and to ease the global exchange of goods and services.

Conclusion

Soon it will be Gen Y's time to lead. By now, you know the truth that the world is not a fair place, and only a select few get a chance to win. The ideologues pushed the "fairness" curriculum in our schools promising this approach would deliver utopia. The truth is that the promoters of the idea that everyone gets a chance to win never really planned on utopia. The real agenda was to significantly reduce the aspiration to achieve prosperity in our general population.

I implore you to understand that the need for socialism happens because stagnation and regulation have replaced innovation and prosperity. Stagnation is the direct result of the loss of inspiration and innovation. Innovation creates something that produces prosperity; stagnation means growth has stopped, and decay has begun to set in. Overregulating is a nonproductive attachment to innovation, thus a detriment to prosperity.

The messaging we hear from the brainiacs in the technology industry and the government think tanks is that technology will eventually replace the need for people. Have they forgotten it was the innovation of people that created technology? You must not buy their doom-and-gloom messaging that innovation is no longer something the average citizen can participate in or create. Their idealistic and arrogant suggestion of providing you with a government living wage creates a stagnant, restricted future for you, while at the same time allows them to monopolize their respective industries.

Never let anyone take away your chance to innovate and compete! The truth is that prosperity dies because those who gain the most from it seek to monopolize it. Our government has become a partner to those who pay them the most, and they have determined your future to be one of redistribution. You must decide whether you want a life of fighting a powerful government and begging them for more as your way of achieving prosperity or a chance to innovate and compete in order to create your own. True progressivism would not leave a corrupt government as is, and it would not succumb to redistribution as its only means of providing a better future. True progressivism would weed out stagnation, overregulation, monopolization, and corruption because anyone hoping for their life to progress knows those are the true destroyers of prosperity.

The Logician Party

In the last chapter, I suggested the creation of a new political party: the Logician Party. I realize this sounds like a daunting task, but is it really that big a deal compared to what's already been accomplished? The fact that America's inception began with a handful of people living on the East Coast in small towns with wooden sidewalks that have since developed into enormous cities with massive skyscrapers is proof of what we can do. We've built roads, bridges, stadiums, air transportation, mass transit, monetary systems, satellite technology, the internet, and military supremacy, so the idea of a new political party doesn't seem like much.

Like it or not, the deceptions I've compiled throughout this book are true. It is time to decide: Do we assemble as one people and demand change, or do we do nothing and be led like lambs to the slaughter? The reason I suggest a new party and a new way of governing is that corruption has completely consumed the old system. The only way to fix it is to eliminate every conceivable loophole that allows the power of money to influence elected government to do the wrong thing.

Our country has reached the end of prosperity for its citizenry, and it is not because of something we did. This happened because America's imperial government partnered with the world's financiers, and they collectively raped and pillaged our nation by using the fiat monetary system as a lethal weapon. I've provided enough evidence to prove that the government's kicking the can down the road has finally reached its end. Additionally, I've explained that once corruption and greed are done destroying every last drop of prosperity, the perpetrators responsible for the molestation simply move to the next phase, which is a progressive decline into socialism.

Make no mistake: the government believes they are in control and that they can weather any societal storm that comes their way. They control our monetary system, they control health care and Social Security for the aging boomers, and they have successfully converted our nation's people into political tribes at war with one another. Yet their greatest accomplishment was gaining control of the school curriculum and teaching our children that mediocracy will be the wave of the future. In other words, they are confident they have total control over our fate.

To help you understand how dire things can get, I've included an emergency order (from Federal Reserve's History's website, accessed on November 15th 2019) that President Franklin D. Roosevelt delivered to the American people in 1933. My goal has been to alert our citizens that we must formulate a plan and demand change while we still can. The following explains the dangers of what can happen if we don't.

Sec 95. Emergency limitations and restrictions on business of members of Federal Reserve System; designation of legal holiday.

(a) In order to provide for the safer and more effective operation of the National Banking System and the Federal Reserve System, to preserve for the people the full benefits of the currency provided for by the Congress through the National Banking System and the Federal Reserve System, and to relieve interstate commerce of the burdens and obstructions resulting from the receipt on an unsound or unsafe basis of deposits subject to withdrawal by check, during such emergency period as the President of the United States by proclamation may prescribe, no member bank of the Federal Reserve System shall transact any banking business except to such extent and subject to such regulations, limitations and restrictions as may be prescribed by the Secretary of the Treasury, with the approval of the President. Any individual, partnership, corporation, or association, or any director, officer or employee thereof, violating any of the provisions of this section shall be deemed guilty of a misdemeanor and, upon conviction thereof, shall be fined not more than $10,000 or, if a natural person, may, in addition to such fine, be imprisoned for a term not exceeding ten years. Each day that any such violation continues shall be deemed a separate offense.

(b)(1) In the event of natural calamity, riot, insurrection, war, or other emergency conditions occurring in any State whether caused by acts of nature or of man, the Comptroller of the Currency may designate by proclamation any day a legal holiday for the national banking associations located in that State. In the event that the emergency conditions affect only part of a State, the Comptroller of the Currency may designate the part so affected and may proclaim a legal holiday for the national banking associations located in that affected part. In the event that a State or a State official authorized by law designates any day as a legal holiday for ceremonial or emergency reasons, for the State or any part thereof, that same day shall be a legal holiday for all national banking associations or their offices located in that State or the part so affected. A national banking association or its affected offices may close or remain open on such a State-designated holiday unless the Comptroller of the Currency by written order directs otherwise.

If you are confused about what this means, Roosevelt demanded that every American citizen and business alike immediately surrender their gold to the Treasury Department, and if they disobeyed the order, the consequences would be a $10,000 fine or not more than ten years in prison! Although history muddies the waters as to the exact reason he seized the people's gold, some historians say it was to fund the war. Others say it was because the monetary system had collapsed due to corruption. The truth is Roosevelt issued the order because, like now, the Federal Reserve had printed too much money, ultimately causing inflation in the prices of goods and services and then advancing to unstoppable deflation once the economic bubble burst.

Because the truth would provide evidence that our government allowed the rich and powerful to destroy the lives of their citizens, we will never know exactly what happened. What we do know is the day gold was seized, its value was $20.67 per ounce, and one week after the seizure, Roosevelt reset the price to $35.00 per ounce. The reports vary as to exactly how much gold the government seized. Regardless of the total dollar amount, what they did by immediately inflating gold's value to $35.00 per ounce was net a 72 percent profit for the Federal Reserve at the expense of the American people.

Here's the point: governments with unchecked authority can do things you thought they couldn't, and if we allow this deception and division to go on, the changes they can and will make will most assuredly benefit the few at the cost of many. As I've mentioned several times throughout this book, it is the citizens, not government or the financiers, who are the strength of America. I say this because their entire Ponzi scheme is dependent on our tax dollars and our investment in the stock market. In other words, we have several tools in our tool belt to make them listen.

The Washington, DC, bureaucrats thought they were smart by cutting deals with Wall Street. They strengthened Wall Street by creating laws that allowed citizens to put tax-deferred investments into Wall Street–managed retirement accounts. This move essentially consolidated all our money into one place, and it provided Wall Street and the government an easy method to buy and sell treasury bonds. This tax-deferred savings let Wall Street make enormous profits by charging management fees on our retirement accounts while at the same time providing a powerful tool to the Federal Reserve regarding buying and selling treasury bonds.

Yet because the massive amounts of money residing in Wall Street are, in fact, our money, it gives us a unique power to collectively prevent them from buying treasury bonds or any other bond derivatives. A unified boycott of purchasing treasury bonds would have an immediate effect because the bonds held in our retirement accounts have been an easy source for the Federal Reserve to sell long- and short-term Treasury Department products to Wall Street. In other words, the money in our retirement accounts aids the Federal Reserve in easily selling bonds. This, in turn, allows the Federal Reserve to print more fake money, which they give to the Treasury Department so the government can pay for their overspending. A boycott would significantly affect the process, and it would most definitely express how much power we have as a unified citizenry. We could send a powerful message that until we are satisfied that our government is free of corruption and collusion, our money will be unavailable to aid their budget deficits.

Once we get their attention and bring them to the negotiating table, we can address the bald-faced lie that they intend to pay us back the $6.2 trillion taken from our commingled entitlements. Neither our government nor the Federal Reserve has $6.2 trillion of idle cash sitting around to repay us. That would require the Federal Reserve to sell more treasury bonds, and more treasury bonds result in increased debt to us. How do they pay for this increased debt? With our tax dollars.

My thought is a unified citizenry (or the newly formed Logician Party) could use the $6.2 trillion debt as a bargaining chip to negotiate the changes we want to our governing. By giving up the $6.2 trillion they owe us, we could drastically reduce the annual interest payment on the total debt, which we are essentially paying to ourselves anyway. Additionally, the forfeiture of the $6.2 trillion would reduce our nation's overall debt-to-gross-domestic-product ratio, bringing it down from 102 percent to 72 percent. The effect of reducing our debt and ridding the government of corruption sends a clear message to the world's investors that our nation's financial situation is under control.

If we do not act, the fiat system will collapse, and so will the inflated price of the stocks we own. Once we grasp that the Federal Reserve selling treasury products and our banking system's 90/10 fractional loaning are merely Ponzi schemes, this process of conjuring money out of nothing should cause all of us enormous concern.

It should cause all of us additional concern that when the Federal Reserve printed money to bail out the banks and Wall Street rather than making this money available to the public to help regain economic stability, the executives of those firms used the money to buy stock options in their own companies. Why did they do that? Because they wanted to inflate the value of their companies' stock. They created the illusion to potential buyers that something special was happening with their company that caused the stock's value to escalate, yet what they were really doing was tricking buyers into paying more for their stock. How did this affect them? It allowed the executives to reward themselves with huge bonuses.

The reality is they've designed a financial pyramid, giving us no other option but to put our money in their system. The deferred income being invested in IRAs and 401(k)s was designed by financial engineers to siphon our money into their system on a long-term basis. Understanding this brings up the concern I pointed out earlier: What happens if our government needs to seize gold or assets the way Roosevelt did? The massive amounts of money in our privately held retirement accounts are managed by Wall Street and the Federal Reserve. This means they are poised to seize or significantly devalue what we have, and there's not a damn thing we will be able to do about it if we do not act now!

It is time to stop venting on Twitter and wasting our time arguing that the Republicans are bad for this and the Democrats are bad for that. Both parties are influenced by the power of money and consumed with corruption. America became great because its citizens had the freedom and ability to be creative. Our being a free-wheeling, unrestricted people allowed us to become the innovators of the world. It is time to innovate a new political party! One that is free of corruption, one that is fiscally sound, and one that is built from prudence and solid management principles. There will never be another America if we let this one slip away without a fight. Then we will have let down every soldier who has died in the name of freedom. Who among us will be the leader of this Logician Party?

Conclusion

Many people suffer from what I refer to as "the day before syndrome." This syndrome applies to our daily lives in so many ways. It could apply to a person who thought they were completely healthy and went to their doctor for a minor chest cold, only to find out they have four months to live due to incurable lung cancer. It might apply to a person who ran out of time today and delayed a phone call expressing their love to Mom or Dad until tomorrow, only to find out that Mom or Dad died that night in their sleep.

My fear is that our nation is fast approaching the consequences of the day before syndrome. The day before Roosevelt's executive order, the citizens holding gold during the Great Depression felt as though they were secure. Yet the following day, their lives were changed immediately with the stroke of Roosevelt's pen. I urge all my fellow citizens to put their effort and their trust in their own ability to achieve, not the government's promise to give. We must act immediately to ensure our financial system and our leadership are built on a foundation of integrity and not deception.

The lady with the torch in New York Harbor is sinking, and we must act now to save her. This nation has faced far worse tragedies than ridding ourselves of a corrupt government. Yet we must understand that every battle America has won was won by a united citizenry. If we want our government to work for the people, we must collectively join hands and demand that they do!

United We Stand—Divided We Perish!

Each of us knows in our heart that something has gone terribly wrong, and we inherently sense that if we do not change our leadership's self-destructive path, it won't be long before our nation's demise. As I've stated throughout this book, it's okay if you disagree with some—or, for that matter, all—of the suggestions I've shared with you. It's also okay if you have better ideas than mine. All I ask is that you share them with the rest of us! The only goal I had when I began writing was to alert my fellow citizens of a danger that lurks in divisional politics and to draw their attention to a monetary system that is compromised by corruption.

The mortgage crisis was not just a warning shot. It was a cannonball blasting a giant hole in the side of the great ship known as the United States. Like the poor judgment of the *Titanic*'s captain, Edward J. Smith, speeding through the night while surrounded by dangerous icebergs, America's imperial government has navigated our country into deadly waters. What the world learned after the *Titanic* sank was that this legendary ship did not have a sufficient number of lifeboats to save all its passengers. Almost all the second-class passengers were left to plunge into the icy waters and suffer immediate death. The American people learned from our most recent mortgage crisis that, just as the *Titanic*'s top brass were only concerned about supplying lifeboats for a select few, as our nation plunged into the icy waters of deflation and economic stagnation, only a few were to be saved.

The difference here is the passengers on the *Titanic* had no chance to plug the giant hole in the ship, and they had no alternative but to die within minutes once hitting the frigid water. Although we do have water gushing over the side of our ship, if we band together and put aside our differences, we can patch the hole and get our ship back to the mainland so we can rebuild for a safer voyage.

There are a small percentage of left and right political radicals who are getting way too much attention. Our cable news networks are battling to see who can gain the highest viewership, and unfortunately, they've decided the best way to do this is to sensationalize and propagandize their reporting. This dangerous mix of left and right radicals and the media's sensationalizing of events has caused Washington, DC, to become nothing more than actors and actresses dramatizing current events as a method to divide their constituents.

Meanwhile, we've done what we always do. We begin our day preparing our kids for school, and then we faithfully head off to work. Once we get to our jobs, in most cases we work with people from different ethnicities, religions, and cultures. Yet no matter our differences, we work together as teams, getting the job done. But the media and politicians have collectively created the perception that America is moments away from requiring martial law in order to enforce civility on what they portray as a racist society. It is time we put a stop to the nonsense of a few agitators attempting to gain fame through sensationalism. It is also time to expose an imperial government that has turned on their people because they need to hide the truth of their deception.

The world we function in every day does not have an enemy around every corner. We do not go to our grocery stores and mistreat people because of their skin color or because of the way they look or dress. Americans are extremely tolerant people, and for the most part, we have accepted every culture that has come our way. That does not mean we are passive and allow people to shun who we are or let them demand we change our culture to be more to their liking. America is a place where everyone finds a way to fit in, and everyone pitches in for the greater good.

America is and always has been likened to a hockey game. We go about our day with passion, flying full speed on the ice, trying to score any time an opportunity should arise. If someone takes cheap shots on us or our teammates, we drop the gloves and fight until we achieve a resolution to our differences. Once a resolution is reached, we get back to the game, and when the winner and loser of the hard-fought battle are determined, we look one another in the eye with respect and shake hands, knowing every one of us put it all on the line. Even if we lose, we congratulate our opponent for winning on that given day, and each of us has that never-quit spirit that drives us to win the next game tomorrow.

The reason I chose to write this book is that there is an attack on our winning spirit. Our politicians, with the aid of media, are using every tool available to silence, control, and manipulate the outcome of our lives. They want a citizenry who conforms, not innovators who create. We must resist and squash anyone attempting to damage the independent, innovating spirit of the American people. We must be willing to fight and bloody our noses against this pack of financial hyenas seeking to feast on our bloody carcass.

The arrogance displayed by imperial Washington, DC, and their monopolist partners proves they feel as though they already have won the game. Yet unlike us, when we lose, they do not dare look us in the eye to acknowledge their victory over our independence. Why? Because the game they play is built on deception, and they know our team never really had a chance to win. If we got close to winning, they made sure they had the power to change the rules. In a nutshell, that is the problem. We are participating in a rigged pyramidal game in every aspect of our financial existence. The governing that is supposed to protect us has been hijacked by deception, corruption, and greed. If we want to preserve our independence, we must become a unified team to ensure they no longer have the ability to change the rules each time we begin to prosper.

It's time for straight talk. There's really no way to determine exactly how many people in America are actually racists, bigots, homophobes, xenophobes, or whatever other adjective is presently being used. I say to those of you who think you're perfect—you're not. For those of you trying to be perfect—it's impossible, so learn to laugh at your mistakes. For those of you arrogant enough to believe your opinion is superior to others—it's not. For those believing you have the golden ticket because you sin less than others—a sin is a sin, and the size of one's sin does not mean one is free from judgment.

None of us are perfect, and if we're trying to become perfect, we will never get anything accomplished. We are a nation comprising multiple cultures, colors, and religions, so we must understand that there always will be some numbskulls out there who say and do stupid things. If we become a society that tries to create rules that force people to conform to our sensitivities, we will become a society with restricted ability to achieve.

We need look no further than Washington, DC. Our governing structure has become an absolute joke and should be viewed as the best example of what we do not want to be. Our government is paralyzed by the restrictions of their own politically correct rules. It's time to ask ourselves the question "Have we really become so sensitive or so full of our own self-absorbed crap that we will limit our future to be governed by Washington, DC, deciding what we can or cannot say during our daily lives?"

How far will we let this go? Will our comedy clubs need government officials to judge the material of standup comedians, assuring their humor meets PC standards, and if not, will the comedian be fined or jailed? Allowing ourselves to continue on the path of becoming a thin-skinned people is a one-way ticket to hell. Again, we need look no further than Washington, DC, to see what hell looks like. These imperialists are so full of their own narcissism and attempts at displaying perfection that they can't even answer a question without assuring their answer has been poll tested.

If we don't like what someone has to say, it doesn't mean we have the right to make sure they never say it again. Attempting to silence the things we don't like said in this manner could eventually cause the same outcome for the things we might say in the future. We are a people from all regions of the world. We will never see things the same, and we should enjoy a good laugh at one another for the different things we do within our individual cultures. The problem is not that we have different cultures. The problem is we are trying to force different cultures to be the same. There are unquestionably real cases of hatred and racism that must be dealt with harshly, but if we are to remain a multicultural nation, we must all work at being more tolerant.

It is for this reason I decided to reach out and share my views. We should collectively agree it is not necessary to unite on religion, culture, or politically correct dialogue approved by Washington, DC. Where we must find unity is remaining committed to the preservation of our independence, being able to say or do what we choose, as long as it's within the constitutional rights afforded us. We also should agree that for us to remain independent, our dialogue with fellow citizens must be respectful. And we must collectively understand that allowing Washington, DC, to become the enforcer of civility is a surrender of our independence and an acceptance of an imperial government deciding for all.

Where Do We Go from Here?

I've tried to represent the truth by exposing the stepping-stones that are contributing to our nation's destruction. I've also shared suggestions that could help regain the path to a sustainable future. There are several economists and political scientists who believe our country's downfall is all but a foregone conclusion. In their view, the only way this will end is a complete collapse of the fiat monetary system and the return of a monetary system regulated by the gold standard.

There will most likely be naysayers regarding my idea of the $6.2 trillion debt forgiveness, saying it can't be done because of the legal complexities, or have concern that debt forgiveness will be viewed as default, thus damaging market confidence. Make no mistake—the system and the rules must be changed, and if we continue to go about it their way by running budget deficits until the system collapses, the big loser in that scenario is us. Their way ensures all the people involved in controlling the rules now will most likely have more authority once the system collapses.

The debt forgiveness I propose is between us and our government. Forgiving the $6.2 trillion gives us the ability to use the debt forgiveness as a bargaining chip, thus a chance to preserve our monetary system and personal wealth and to rein in Congress's authority to use commingled cash surpluses in the future. Additionally, it helps put an end to deception and collusion by the government, the Federal Reserve, Wall Street, private equity, and the commercial banks. In other words, instead of allowing them to reorganize the rules once again to assure their victory, it gives us a chance to negotiate the rules to ensure a sustained future for our children.

I mentioned this earlier, but it's worth repeating. At best, there are a maximum of 10 million people at the top of this financial pyramid, which means we outnumber them by 315 million! The entire structure exists on what we pay in taxes. Do not tell me there's nothing we can do or suggest that we do not have the power to negotiate. If we collectively decide to demand change, this argument won't last longer than a day. You must understand that they realize the danger our unity could present, and it is for this reason they're working so hard at dividing us into political tribes at war with one another.

If the collapse of the fiat monetary system happens on their terms, it's game over for us. If we use my debt forgiveness and reduction of their authority approach, it's game over for *them*! Stop allowing them to pit us against one another. Learn to laugh again, and don't view your fellow citizens as your enemy—view them as part of your strength! Trying to force everyone else to think the same will most assuredly create people of limited intelligence. Some of the best ideas were delivered by those we least expected. For us to be an innovative nation, we must understand that every idea has the potential of becoming a great idea.

There is only one thing required of us to take control of our future—reject division! From this day forward, let's not view others based on the color of their skin or the clothes they wear. See them for their ideas and congratulate them for their input in making our country a better place. Don't hate them because they're different. Learn what's different about them, and consider how their way of doing something might help our nation become a better place. Let us put aside our differences and come together as one people sending a message to Washington, DC: change is coming, and it won't be on your terms. It will be on ours!

Conclusion

Webster's definition of *greed*: a selfish and excessive desire for more of something (such as money) than is needed.

The definition of *deception*: the act of causing someone to accept as true or valid what is false or invalid.

In the end, what has been presented as a conspiracy or a cabal regarding our nation's financial system is nothing more than deception and greed. Our government participates in the illusion that the Federal Reserve is all powerful and that they can do as they please without any government authority to change it. That is a lie. They *do* have the power to change the rules, and the Federal Reserve is obligated to follow the rules our government gives them. The Federal Reserve is a convenient scapegoat our government and those at the top of the financial pyramid use as political cover for bailouts and the continuation of greed.

You see, continuing the conspiracy narrative that the Wizard of Oz controls the Federal Reserve sends the message that our government is kept from the truth, but more importantly, what this narrative provides is political cover that allows deception and greed to thrive. The mortgage crisis happened because the laws governing Wall Street and our banking institutions allowed it to happen. The Federal Reserve bailouts were given to the perpetrators that sold deceptive mortgage products under the direction of the US government, not the Federal Reserve.

The problem we face, and why we must unite, is our government has finally run out of options to sustain the financial pyramid. The government and the Treasury Department no longer have internal surpluses that can used to pay for budget overruns. Additionally, the long-awaited boomer generation ascending into retirement is now upon us. As I've explained, unless the government creates alternative methods to increase revenue to fund their annual budget shortfall, the truth that our monetary system will collapse will soon be exposed. This is not conspiracy; this is our reality.

In the chapter Private-Sector Jobs Creation, I disclosed that many of our jobs are created by some of the worst parts of our society. I don't believe it is a conspiracy to suggest illegal drugs in America could be a method of job creation or that using a complex tax code instead of a flat tax could be because the complexity of the tax system provides a plethora of high-paying jobs. Most importantly, our present tax code provides benefits only available to those atop the financial pyramid.

Last, and most importantly not least, we must understand that the social programs offered through tax redistribution can only be sustained if they are paid for by prosperity. If prosperity becomes limited, social programs will be reduced or eliminated. This is not complicated—if prosperity is diminished, austerity will occur. If austerity does not occur, our nation will fail. These politicians saying that if you vote for them they will give you more are lying. How could anyone promise more when Washington, DC, is already running a massive annual budget deficit?

I will close with the most important truth of all. It might be that the ideas I've presented won't work in the exact manner that I've presented them. Maybe all they need is your input to make them work. The truth is what I've presented is undeniable. If we continue to let them divide us, we never again will have the chance to set the path to our own future. If we choose to remain political tribes at war with one another, we will be depicted in the history books as proof that diversity in a singular nation has no chance of survival. Our failure to recognize and respect one another for whom we are as individuals will empower those who believe a society must comprise homogenized people in order to sustain itself. America has been an experiment from its inception, and right now, with the help of Washington, DC's political division, we are failing that experiment.

I ask that you share with others what you've learned from this book— that singularly we will perish, yet unified, we can thrive. Let's cheer the ideas of our fellow citizens and help inspire them to reach their goals as they will in turn help us achieve ours. No team or nation is great because of one person. Things become great when the forces of resistance are kept to a minimum. If America fails, it will not fail for some. It will fail for all. It's time to silence division and hate and promote what we have in common: the United States of America!

Acknowledgments

I would like to thank my beautiful wife, my amazing children, my wonderful mother-in-law, and the best grandchildren a papa could want for inspiring me to complete this writing. They understand what I've written will be viewed as controversial, yet because of their love and support for me and our country, they encouraged me to continue. My wife became my most trusted adviser on delivering the truth. Regardless of whether or not my writing is effective, I thank her for her patience.

I also would like to thank my business partner/brother for the support he has given. He also provided me with truth when my messaging became redundant and the support to continue. I also would like to thank our extended family of employees who have helped us be successful in good times and bad. My brother and I care deeply for them and their families, and we appreciate their dedication to professionalism.

In addition, I would like to extend a personal thank-you to a special person I met through social media who helped me with her intimate knowledge of how the Federal Reserve and banking system function. Her input helped me avoid creating more conspiracy theories and provide information based on truth.

Last, but not least, thank you to the readers for giving me a chance to express my views. Please tell everyone you know about this book. If the only message you take away from this is the importance of unity being our only chance of remaining an independent people, I will have accomplished my goal!

Made in the USA
Columbia, SC
30 January 2020